The 99th Monkey

Also by the Same Author

Minyan: Ten Jewish Men in a World That Is Heartbroken

Wild Heart Dancing

The 99th Monkey

A Spiritual Journalist's Misadventures
with Gurus, Messiahs, Sex,
Psychedelics, and Other
Consciousness-Raising Experiments

Eliezer Sobel

Published by: Santa Monica Press LLC
P.O. Box 1076
Santa Monica, CA 90406-1076
1-800-784-9553
www.santamonicapress.com
books@santamonicapress.com

Printed in the United States

Santa Monica Press books are available at special quantity discounts when purchased in bulk by corporations, organizations, or groups. Please call our Special Sales department at 1-800-784-9553.

ISBN-13 978-1-59580-028-2
ISBN-10 1-59580-028-X

Library of Congress Cataloging-in-Publication Data

Sobel, Eliezer, 1952-
   The 99th monkey : a spiritual journalist's misadventures with gurus, messiahs, sex, psychedelics, and other consciousness-raising experiments / Eliezer Sobel.
      p. cm.
   ISBN 978-1-59580-028-2
   1. Religions. 2. Religious leaders. 3. New Age movement. 4. Spiritual biography. 5. Religious biography. 6. Sobel, Eliezer, 1952- I. Title.

BL85.S63 2008
299'.93092--dc22
[B]
                    2007041436

Cover and interior design and production by Future Studio Los Angeles

Portions of this book were excerpted from articles that originally appeared in *Quest Magazine*, *Yoga Journal*, *The New Sun*, the *New Age Journal*, and Paul Krassner's book, *Magic Mushrooms and Other Highs: From Toad Slime to Ecstasy*.

For Shari

Contents

Jean Cocteau was once asked,

"If your house was on fire,
what would be the one thing
you would save?"

"The fire," he replied.

Prologue

There was once a famous population of Japanese monkeys—the irrepressible *Macaca fuscata*—living on the island of Koshima in 1952; incidentally, the year I was born. Scientists provided the monkeys with sweet potatoes dropped in the sand, and observed that they generally seemed to relish the new treat in spite of a certain unpleasant grittiness. One day an enterprising young primate named Imo discovered that if she took her potato down to the water's edge, she could rinse off all the dirt and enjoy a much tastier meal. Imo taught her mother and playmates the trick, and gradually, over the course of six years, one monkey after another adopted the practice.

Then in 1958, a remarkable event occurred: the number of potato-washing monkeys reached what is called a "critical mass"—99, say—and when the next potato was washed, it caused a tipping point, and suddenly, not only did the entire monkey population on Koshima Island start performing the new procedure, but all of the monkey populations on neighboring islands spontaneously began washing their potatoes as well.

"The 100th Monkey" became the name New Agers and futurists used for this unusual phenomenon, and they extrapolated from monkey experience to show that this is also the way the human community makes dramatic, collective paradigm shifts into new ways of thinking, being, and behaving. Once a critical mass of people have transformed their essentially materialist worldview to a spiritual one, for example, the entire population of the planet will spontaneously choose to come along for the ride. The dirty sweet potato of being a self-centered, acquisitive, power-hungry creature, blindly bent on the destruction of life as we know it, will be gently washed in the stream of loving-kindness, peacefulness, and the desire to serve God and humanity, ushering in a golden age of peace and prosperity for all people.

Fat chance. Not with the likes of me around. I am the 99th Monkey. If you don't get me, you don't get your critical mass, and it screws up the whole works. I seem to be single-handedly holding back the Great Paradigm Shift of the Golden Age simply through my continuing to be a resistant little putz.

(If it makes you feel any better, I recently learned that this whole story about the monkeys and the potatoes is not accurate, that it didn't really happen that way at all. That *really* annoyed me, considering that I'd just based a whole book on it.)

I met Ram Dass, my first spiritual teacher, in 1975 in New York when I was 23 years old, several weeks after completing the *est* training in Boston, which was several months after having spent one and a half years screaming my head off in Primal Therapy. I was desperately trying to cure myself of being me, a futile pursuit that would continue for three decades, and would take me all around the world to meet shamans, healers, and gurus; stay in ashrams and monasteries; sit for long hours on meditation cushions; chant in foreign tongues; and live up to 40 days in primitive huts on solo retreat.

I experimented extensively with psychedelic drugs, ancient spiritual techniques and outrageous new ones. I was massaged, shiatsu-ed, and rolfed; took hundreds of consciousness workshops, human potential seminars, and self-improvement courses; sat with psychics, channels, and tarot readers; experienced Primal, Gestalt,

Bioenergetics, Object Relations, generic talk therapies, and anti-depressants. And that's the short list. (The complete one gets embarrassing. Suffice it to say that it includes learning the Tush Push exercise in a Human Sexuality weekend—you don't want to know—as well as having an obese female therapist sit on my head at Esalen Institute, so I could re-experience being smothered by my mother.)

As editor in chief of *The New Sun* magazine in the '70s and the *Wild Heart Journal* more recently, and through being a freelance spiritual journalist, it has often been my *job* to do all these things. Like a scout sent ahead to report back, I often saved others a lot of time: "You don't have to go deep into Brazil to do all-night rituals involving the ingestion of ayahuasca, chanting in Portuguese to Oxum, the Mother of the Waters, and throwing up out of a church window at four in the morning—I already did that."

Most stories like this end with an epiphany: the seeker finds what he or she was looking for, writes a book about it to inspire others, and then, with any luck, appears on *Oprah* and becomes very wealthy. Unfortunately, in my story, I remain more or less the same guy—or as my friend Eddie Greenberg would say, the "same old schmuck"—at the end as I was at the beginning.

An earlier version of this book was turned down by one publisher, who said, "The main character's story just doesn't seem to hang together."

Buh-buh-buh-but, I thought: This is a *memoir*; this is auto-biographical . . . I *am* the main character!

But he was right. My story doesn't hang together. Whose does, really? Nothing bugs me more than those self-help authors who start out as a complete mess, find a magic solution, and then try to sell the rest of us on a new and improved way to live, while getting very rich in the process. At least this much I can promise you: apart from a few laughs and some good stories, this book will very definitely *not* change your life. Fortunately, every bona fide spiritual teacher worth their salt will remind you again and again that you don't *need* to change your life in order to get enlightened, find God, or be your true Self.

Again and again, we seekers of truth are told that our primordial, essential nature is *always already the case,* always and only available now, no matter what the circumstances of our inner or outer lives, and therefore all desire to change our inner or outer lives in order to somehow get closer to the ever-elusive spiritual prize is not only fruitless, but is actually the problem itself. Seeking truth, God, enlightenment, or Buddha-Nature is the equivalent, it has often been said, of a fish swimming endlessly in search of water. Once our great quest has commenced, we have already missed the point and are on the wrong track.

Had I only known.

I recently read Tolstoy's story, "The Death of Ivan Ilyich," because in dramatic contrast to *War and Peace,* it is very *short.* The story invites contemplation of perhaps the worst accusation of all: *a life lived wrong.* But Ivan doesn't get it until he's lying on his deathbed. You and I still have time, although not a whole lot, really. Which is why I generally never read memoirs or biographies. Who can afford to spend their time reading about someone *else's* life?

Nor do I presume that you should spend *your* time reading about *my* life. Unless, of course, it's funny. And ask anybody: I'm usually a pretty funny guy, apart from those times when I'm lamenting the fact that, like Ivan Ilyich, I may have lived my entire life completely incorrectly and now it's too late to make it right. It isn't too late, of course, given that another thing the sages often like to chuckle about is that enlightenment is "only a thought away," or that God is "closer to us than our own breath." Nevertheless, we all know time is short, and so it's good to always keep in mind what the famous Tibetan yogi Milarepa once said:

> *You people who gather here*
> *think that death will*
> *come sauntering over to you.*
> *NO!*
> *Whenever death comes,*
> *it strikes like lightning.*

I got caught in a riptide in the Outer Banks of North Carolina a few summers ago, and didn't know that the trick is to swim parallel to shore, as opposed to panicking and thrashing about wildly and coming extremely close to drowning. Close enough to get a glimpse of the shocking recognition, "Oh my God, I'm actually drowning, this is it. I can't believe I'm dying today." Milarepa was right: it *did* feel like lightning, coming out of nowhere when I least expected it. There are lots of stories about people who emerge from such experiences with a renewed sense of aliveness and appreciation, and begin living with more passion and making major lifestyle changes and so on. Leave it to me to be the one guy who manages to blow a near-death experience and just carry on as if nothing much had happened.

Be that as it may, if you're going to take the time to read a book, it ought to, at the very least, have an impact. Father William McNamara, a Carmelite monk, once said: "Never read good books. There's no time for that. Only read great ones."

Or funny ones.

❋ ❋ ❋

Books that impacted my life in my early 20s:

1) *The Fountainhead* by Ayn Rand. The day I finished *The Fountainhead*, I dropped out of the music department at Northwestern University, having decided to be an architect like Howard Roark, the hero of the book. However, I then discovered that Northwestern didn't *have* an architecture department, so I enrolled in the closest thing to it, Interior Art and Design. I went to the first day of classes where we were asked to make little couches out of construction paper, and I dropped out of college completely. And thus began the sequence of adventures recounted in this book.

2) Nearly everything by Jack Kerouac, particularly *The Town and the City* and *Desolation Angels*. He stirred the passionate, poignant prose-poet in me, the vagabond artist-seeker, albeit with a credit card, very generous parents, and a suburban, upper-middle-class Jewish sensibility. In other words, I was absolutely nothing like Kerouac.

3) *The Outsider* by Colin Wilson. Like a million other people, I thought the book was about me. Someone finally gave me a label I could get behind. And while I still romantically fancy myself an "outsider," it could also be argued that I simply do not like to work and, with one exception, have never had a real job in the world for longer than about nine months.

The true Outsider, Wilson explains, is someone who has somehow intuited or glimpsed the vast, empty, infinite possibility of eternal life and spirit, but is now somehow separate from that experience except as a nagging memory, and their life is fueled by the intense and obsessive desire to "get it back." Their art and their religious life become an expression of that quest for authenticity and essence.

The most difficult part for Outsiders, Wilson says, is the realization that although as humans they have been given the most extraordinary and abundant gifts and an infinitely mysterious and magical existence filled with beauty and love, they seem to be ironically lacking only one thing: *the simple ability to appreciate and enjoy any of it.* Ahab said it like this:

> *This lovely light, it lights not me; all loveliness is anguish to me, since I can ne'er enjoy. Gifted with the high perception, I lack the low enjoying power; damned in the midst of Paradise!*

I hate that "ne'er enjoy" part. And considered in that light, I truly *am* an outsider. I once interviewed Colin Wilson via e-mail for the *Wild Heart Journal*. Here is our conversation, verbatim:

> **Me:** Please elaborate on the connection between the artist's impulse toward creativity and expression and the religious person's yearning for spiritual freedom or union.
>
> **Colin:** Ooof! I don't feel like writing you an essay to answer that question. Norman Mailer once said to me that he got fed up with people who, after a lecture, asked ten-cent questions that required ten-dollar answers, and this is an example. I just don't have time to write you pages and pages on religion and creativity. Ask more down-to-earth questions, like how old are you, have you ever had syphilis, etc. and I'll answer. (The answer to those is 67 and no.)

It was a very short interview. (And FYI, that conversation was about nine years ago, so Wilson would be 76 now, and hopefully, still free of sexually transmitted diseases.)

Jewish people in America and elsewhere are almost always given two names at birth—one in their native language, and one in Hebrew. My English name is Elliot, and I used it most of my life. Eliezer is my Hebrew name. It's pronounced *eh-lee-eh*—(as in bed)—*zer*. Rhymes with Nebuchadnezzar, the infamous Babylonian king. "Eli" means God and "ezer" means help, so Eliezer means "God is my help." I was upset that all of my friends on a spiritual path had been given new spiritual names by their teachers at some point, to help them shift their primary identities away from their limited personalities over to their True Nature. Most of the names were Hindu, like Krishna, Arjuna, Ananda, and so on. Generally the names meant something along the lines of "Blissful Consciousness," and it was thought that even if you were totally miserable and depressed, your spiritual name would help you remember that your real Self was nevertheless still having a gay old time of it.

Interestingly, in Judaism, one of the last-ditch methods for healing someone is to change their name, thus tricking God, who might otherwise have had their name inscribed in the "Sayonara Sucker" column of the Book of Life. I once took a workshop in which we were asked to take on a new name just for the weekend. People chose names like "Fun," "Gentle Being," and "Millionairess," trying to cultivate specific desired qualities. I became "Crescent Jewel." My friend Eddie chose the name "Jim."

By the way, ordinarily Jews write the word God as G-d, never spelling it out on paper. This avoids the possibility of being suddenly burdened by a piece of paper that is considered sacred because it contains the Holy Name, and which you therefore can never throw away; but since you don't really want this scrap of paper, you wind up with a box of them in the attic. What's more, if we avoid spelling out "God" and the document in question *does* get thrown away, we've only thrown out a hyphenated word, and not the actual name of God. Predicated on the prior assumption, I guess, that if we *did* spell it out and the paper got thrown away, it would be akin to trashing our G-d, the presumably Untrashable One.

There's a great definition of heaven and hell I read somewhere: after death, you are shown a film of your life as you lived it, as well as a film of your life as you could have lived it, given your highest possibilities and potential. The closer the two films match, the closer you are to heaven. The greater the distance, the more hellish. I'm shown those two films every day in my own mind. And I'm trapped in the theater, like some surreal cinema in *The Twilight Zone* that shows the same two movies for all eternity. At least they're both comedies.

When a friend's house burnt down, I asked him what he missed the most, and he said the photos, and I completely understood. I went out that day and bought a fireproof safe and put all my favorite photos in it.

And now I never get to see them anymore.

The morning dew flees away
Is no more
What remains
In this world of ours?
—Ikkyu

I've always been interested in reading the enigmatic dying words of great people—particularly Zen masters. My favorite was Suzuki-roshi, whose last words to those assembled at his deathbed were simply, "I don't want to die." There was no hidden meaning, which is the essence of Zen.

Allen Ginsberg, who spent his life writing so many meaningful words and wonderful lines of poetry, apparently ended his life with only one word. But it was a great word, one of his best ever: "Tootles." (It's possible I'm completely misinformed about this, but I like the story whether it's true or not.)

Timothy Leary's last words were "Why not?" And his last words to William Burroughs were, "I hope someday I'm as funny as you."

My friend Karen's father was shoveling snow when his wife came out on the porch, screaming, "STOP SHOVELING, OR YOU'RE GOING TO HAVE A HEART ATTACK!" to which he responded, "IF I HAVE A HEART ATTACK, IT'S GOING TO BE FROM YOU SCREAMING AT ME!" Then he dropped dead.

Another friend of mine was standing around having a conversation with a 55-ish male acquaintance, and in the middle of a sentence he too just dropped to the ground, dead. His last words, she told me, were "Hey, it was good seeing you."

Finally, they say that Gandhi was such an evolved devotee of the Lord that at the moment of his death—when he was shot—he had the presence of mind to utter his sacred mantra, one of the Hindu names for God: "Ram." But when they depicted this in the film, it was in English, and came across more like the way it probably happened: when Gandhi was shot in the film, he said, "Oh God," which is more or less what any ordinary schlub like you or me would say if we were shot.

I was an interfaith, nondenominational hospital chaplain some years ago. My colleagues in the hospital were a Presbyterian reverend, a Mennonite minister, a Seventh Day Adventist pastor—I never learned the difference between a minister, a reverend, and a pastor—an Episcopalian seminarian, and an Apostles of Christ Holy Roller Pentacostalist. Plus, a Methodist, a Baptist, and a minister of the United Church of Christ. The hospital was in the Bible Belt, and all the patients were Christian, meaning they were followers of the teachings of Jesus Christ, son of Mr. and Mrs. Joseph Christ, not to mention the Son of God. As a Jewish Buddhist Sufi New Age pot-smoking aging hippie, it wasn't exactly a perfect fit for me.

(However, I secretly believe Jesus Christ was also a Jewish Buddhist Sufi New Age hippie, albeit probably without the use of pot. Although some claim he spent a lot of time in India before starting his Son of Man career, and if that's true, then he easily *might* have smoked some hashish chillums with the local Shiva babas—what young guy backpacking through India on a spiritual quest *wouldn't*?)

Milarepa's "lightning of death" struck the people I ministered to in the hospital all the time. But in that situation nobody ever had the opportunity to say their last words, because they were always on morphine, fentanyl, and various other medications, which allowed them to remain unconscious and without pain as they made their passage to the Great Beyond. When I saw this again and again, I quickly made out a living will in which I asked that I not be sedated at the time of death, that I'd rather be awake, even if in pain, so I could at least come up with some pithy, enigmatic last words. My wife Shari laughed when she heard this, pointing out that I tend to take five Advil for the slightest headache, so intolerant am I of enduring pain of any sort.

But what a disappointment it would be if, in addition to whatever else was causing me to be on my deathbed, I also suffered from writer's block, just when it was time for my last words. As a writer, if I am to take death seriously, I must always remain aware that *these* may very well be my last words.

Chapter 1

Ram Dass

Iwas in my car with a friend, driving on the streets of New York City one Sunday morning in December of 1975, listening to Ram Dass on WBAI's *In the Spirit*. I had read his book, *Be Here Now*, and it had resonated deeply within me. "I've got to meet this guy," I said to my friend, and he guided us to WBAI's church-front studio in the East Village. We got out of the car, I pressed the buzzer, and a female voice said, "Who is it?" I said, "Elliot." "Who are you here to see?" "Ram Dass." She buzzed us in, and it became apparent that apart from the engineer and Ram Dass sitting in a glass booth, we were the only people in the entire building. Within a few minutes, the show was over, and Ram Dass came out to greet us. He shook my friend's hand; he and I hugged.

Hugging strange men was a completely uncommon event for me back then; this was prior to going through the Human Potential Movement, when *not* hugging strange men would be suspect.

So like thousands of other people who had formed a profoundly intimate connection with Ram Dass in a relatively short time, I instantly had the uncanny sense that we knew each other deeply.

Prior to going to India and returning as Ram Dass, Richard Alpert had been a professor of psychology at Harvard, a colleague of Timothy Leary's. They were both kicked out for conducting experiments with graduate students on the effects of psilocybin, or magic mushrooms. The day the story made the front page of the *New York Times*, Ram Dass has said that he never felt more alive and whole, knowing he was on the right track for himself, even as his reputation was going down the tubes in full view of the public. Leary would go on to notoriety as an outlaw and champion of LSD, eventually staging his own "designer death" on the Internet which never quite happened the way he planned it, but he nevertheless went out in the trickster style for which he was famous.

(I once reached Leary on the phone, requesting an interview for *The New Sun* magazine. There was a moment of silence on the other end, and then he said: "Nah, I don't see any fun potential in that, no fun potential at all." He apparently based all of his choices in life on their fun potential. This was in direct contrast to his more serious-minded former colleague and drug partner, Ram Dass, who used to say, "If I have any more fun I think I'm going to throw up." For Ram Dass, it was time to get on with the spiritual journey, which, as he put it, was no longer about "getting high," but rather about "being high," a state that could be arrived at through arduous spiritual discipline or perhaps dumb luck, but certainly not through the pursuit of fun or pleasure.)

Alpert went off to India, embarking on a spiritual quest that over the years would make him a leading countercultural hero of the spirit whose greatest contribution may well have been the three simple words that formed the title of his first book, and which have since become a spiritual cliche: *Be Here Now*. I still have a muslin prayer flag with the cover of *Be Here Now* imprinted on it that I use to drape across my color printer. At times I have a Ram Dass screensaver.

Alpert returned to the States spreading the simple message of his wild and wonderful guru, Neem Karoli Baba: "Love people,

Serve people, and Remember God." (Neem Karoli Baba died about 35 years ago. My mother once saw a photo of him on my wall and thought it was the actor Ed Asner. And I'm certain there is somebody somewhere who would insist that Ed Asner *is* Neem Karoli Baba.)

After our hug, Ram Dass asked about my spiritual practices. Since I didn't have any, I mentioned that I had recently taken the *est* training. "And now you want to be a young Werner Erhard?" he asked. I wasn't sure what he meant. (Had I been honest, however, I might have replied, "Yes, I *do* want to be a young Werner Erhard." Who wouldn't have? Werner, the creator of *est,* was powerful, smart, rich, charismatic, doing transformational work that often had a profound impact on people's lives, and probably had lots of women anxious to sleep with him. Now I realize that Ram Dass by that time had undoubtedly met many, many people who had taken *est* and come out vaguely resembling Erhard in style and manner.)

Ram Dass invited me to visit him later that same day at his home on Riverside Drive and 112th Street. My anticipation of the meeting put me in a mind-spinning tizzy, wondering which deep secrets of my soul might get dredged up into the light of day. By the time I was ready to head uptown, I was in such a panic that I could not remember where my car was parked, so I jumped into a cab only to drive right past my car about four seconds later. When I arrived, Ram Dass escorted me into a candle-lit inner chamber that featured a huge altar filled with photos of saints and gurus, statues of various deities, fruit, incense, prayer shawls, and other ritual objects. We sat opposite each other, cross-legged on meditation cushions before the altar, and, exactly as I had been anticipating all day with dread, he said: "The game is, keep your eyes open, focus right between my eyes, and any thought that comes into your mind that you don't want to share with me, share with me."

You have no idea of the kind of crap our minds can come up with in response to an instruction like that. Ram Dass's notion was that private and secret thoughts are what keep people separate from one another, and since the true spiritual reality is one of unity—that we are all literally One Being—in sharing one's most hidden thoughts, the illusion of the separate self and ego would dissolve and oneness would be restored.

One of my most private and fearful preoccupations at age 23 was the size of my penis, and so I mentioned this to Ram Dass. His response? "Take off your pants."

So I did. And then, after seeing my penis, he said, "You could satisfy any woman."

I totally trusted Ram Dass, and had no idea at the time that he was bisexual, leaning toward homosexual, and quite possibly might have enjoyed having young men take their pants off for him. But I somehow knew in my heart that he sincerely wanted to help me free myself from the prison of separation and fear that I lived in, and if that meant taking my pants off, well then, so be it, off with them!

However, I ended the exercise by opting *not* to share with him the next forbidden thought that arose within me. . . . God knows how *that* would have turned out.

One of the consequences of that single encounter was that I gradually developed the capacity and willingness to share virtually anything about myself to anyone—apart from my parents, naturally—so great was my desire to live in a world with no strangers. (I was actually in a perpetual state of confession in which I felt compelled to reveal every little thing I thought or felt, usually to everyone's great dismay.) Allen Ginsberg had a poetic way of saying it:

Candor ends paranoia.

Except sometimes. That's the part Ginsberg left out. Werner Erhard would later supply the missing piece: "Tell the truth, but don't tell your grandmother you fucked the dog."

That put me back on the right track: withholding the details of my canine sexual encounters from elderly relatives became a useful exercise in restraint.

But through Ram Dass's candid, open-hearted blend of spiritual teachings, cosmological insight, and Jewish-bisexual-ex-Harvard-psychology-professor-stand-up comedy, he succeeded, time and again, at getting people all over the world to laugh at themselves and to exit packed auditoriums feeling inspired, their spirits renewed and faith restored. He was—and remains—unique among spiritual teachers in his willingness to publicly reveal his personal truth in all its flawed humanity, providing for people a mirror of their own neurotic foibles, yet simultaneously generating a context of something greater, ineffable and shared by all: our true identity in the empty fullness of God, eternally being here now. He generated and inspired a spiritual recognition of a great possibility, an inner glimpse of love's caressing presence, a glimpse that was often sufficient to radically alter one's entire life forever.

Many years later, after participating in a seven-day retreat with Ram Dass at the Lama Foundation in New Mexico, I was one of the last to return to my rustic monk's cell to gather my belongings. But as it turned out, I wasn't the last: as I left, I passed an open door and there was Ram Dass, sweeping his room before leaving.

That's only significant because most spiritual teachers don't go anywhere without an entourage of about 25 people attending to their every need, night and day. Find a teacher who sweeps his own room and I believe you're on to someone authentic.

So once my pants were on again, Ram Dass just sat there, looking at me with great love, warmth and compassion, and said, "You are like a fish. The Guru has got his hook in you now, and He's slowly reeling you in. You might splash around and kick your feet and resist, but the process is inevitable: you're being pulled in, brought back home to God."

That was probably true on some level, although 30 years of splashing and kicking later, I'm thinking, *the Guru must think he landed some big mother of a fish.*

Ram Dass asked me to write him in three weeks from my home in Boston. An interesting thing happened when I wrote the letter: it seemed ordinary enough at first, but then it suddenly occurred to me that I was writing in the private voice I ordinarily reserved for my personal journal. It was as if the bare mind of my inner world suddenly had company. Ram Dass and I were a united consciousness in which we were witnessing my own mind together from a space that surrounded it.

The content of the letter was every perverse and scuzzy thought that had ever run through my head, and that I had neglected to mention when we were looking into one another's eyes. Apparently Ram Dass had heard all of it before: lots of people had participated in the same exercise with him over the years, and many of those people had also revealed to him their inner pervert.

An aside on perversion: I once took a five-day course in spontaneous painting at Esalen Institute in Big Sur, California. As the week progressed, the walls filled with art, and I noticed there were some very obvious patterns and motifs. A majority of the paintings often contained images of one or more of the following: huge erect penises; dark, bloody vaginas; and snakes, often coming out of the dark, bloody vaginas. Why was there so much of this coming from an otherwise rather tame-looking group? Did we all share the identical shadow, and just didn't ordinarily recognize that perhaps it was nothing personal?

Perhaps. You'd think Ram Dass would lean that way, after all he's listened to. But I also discovered another explanation. There was a rule that you couldn't officially declare that your painting was finished and take it down until having a conversation with one of the facilitators. Their experience was that people were almost never really finished when they thought they were, and with a little coaching, would continue to add entirely new ideas and dimensions of meaning to their paintings that were just waiting to emerge. And it was true.

So they would stand with you and ask you a series of questions, hoping that one of them would serve as the impetus for further work. Questions like: "If an insane person escaped from the asylum, broke in here, and defaced your painting, what would it look like? What are five more possible images or colors you could add to the painting? What could you do that might completely ruin your picture?" And so forth. Questions to catalyze the artist to leap out of the merely predictable, which was an incredibly liberating occasion. One's "nice" picture often began to reflect shadows lurking in the corners.

However, I gradually discovered a pattern to the facilitators' interactions with us. They all went something like this:

"Well," a student might say, "I could put a rainbow in it."

"Uh-huh," the instructor might reply.

"Or . . . I could put a little bucket here next to the barn."

"Uh-huh."

"Maybe . . . I could add a dash of red to the sun rays."

"Uh-huh."

"I guess I could put a huge erect penis standing there in the field."

"Well *that* feels like it has a lot of energy, why don't you go with that one?"

So that's another possible explanation for why everyone's paintings often looked like wallpaper from Dante's *Inferno*.

Ram Dass responded to my letter by inviting me into a small weekly class with him, and so I guess I had been officially accepted as a student by my first spiritual teacher.

Fortunately there were no grades, because I was a terrible student. He asked us to follow a regime that included a maximum of six hours of sleep per night, an hour of meditation morning and evening, a weekly 24-hour fast, daily yoga, and a few other practices and austerities I've forgotten. (Basically, I didn't really do any of it—I'm not a big self-discipline guy.) But the classes with him were ecstatic occasions that usually included meditation, *pranayama* (breathing exercises), and lots of highly energized and passionate chanting to various Gods in the Hindu pantheon: Ram, Hanuman, Krishna, Kali, Sita, and others. Ram Dass brought charisma and a powerful energy to the room, and we were all in awe of him, and more or less under the impression that he was God's right-hand man.

I still think he's at least *one* of God's right-hand people. I used to think I was as well. But now I recognize that I'm way too self-absorbed to pretend I'm doing God's work, unless He happens to be on a new campaign promoting narcissism. How are *you* doing in this matter? I hope *somebody* is doing God's work or we're all in big trouble. God help us.

One day in class, Ram Dass was speaking about how we were all evolving. Suddenly, he whirled around, pointed at me and said emphatically, "You're not going to believe who you're going to be!"

When you hear something like that from someone like him and you're someone like me, it will form the underpinning and context for virtually the rest of your life, as you wait for the prophecy to come true. Finally, a few years ago, it did:

I was doing an approaching-50 retrospective of my life and realized that despite all my youthful years of believing and expecting I was bound for greatness and the extraordinary, I had pretty much turned out to be a fairly regular guy, doing not-always-my best as I trudged along. I was *not*, apparently, the next Kerouac, John Lennon, or Ram Dass of my generation. (As a young child it would have been the next Batman, Superman, or Green Hornet of my generation. Later, Mays, McCovey, or Marichal. Then Ginsberg, Kesey, or Leary. To simply be myself never even crossed my mind, although it is true: I actually *am* the Eliezer Sobel of my generation.)

And I suddenly realized that Ram Dass's prediction over 25 years earlier had been uncannily accurate:

I couldn't believe who I turned out to be.

After attending a public evening with Ram Dass one night in Boston, I felt my heart opening in a great love, bordering on ecstasy, and so I decided to wait in line after the event in order to greet him personally, and to ask him what I thought was a vitally crucial question:

"Are you my guru?" I asked when I got to the front of the line. Now a less scrupulous New Age teacher might have taken that

opportunity to say "Yes, my son" and quickly scooped up another
unsuspecting seeker/sucker and added him to his devotee list. But
Ram Dass gave me a great gift that night. He just looked at me somewhat scornfully and said:

"Grow up."

To which I responded, perhaps demonstrating the truth of
his answer, with my own erudite, philosophical retort:

"Fuck you."

You don't usually read about those kinds of teacher-student
interactions in the literature, but it was perhaps one of the more
useful conversations I've ever had with a spiritual "authority."

Recently, I overheard my good friend Yolanda singing a Hindu chant.
These chants have moved from their authentic religious source in
India, through people like Ram Dass to the States, through people
like me who sang them with people like Ram Dass, through people
who have chanted with me, and so on down the line. Or any similar chain, all resulting in, say, someone at the local fitness center
teaching yoga and including a Hindu chant as part of the class, while
lacking any authentic or deep spiritual connection to its original religious source whatsoever. It's because somewhere along the chain
something breaks down: it's like playing spiritual telephone.

For example, this is what I overheard Yolanda chanting:

Oya, joya, sock it to me boya, om namah shivaya.

One day, when I was 24, I met with Ram Dass privately to discuss
what to do with my life. He said, "You can spend the next 10 years

becoming successful, or you can spend them going to God." Coming from a guy with a long white beard who had given up Harvard for spirituality, it was a rhetorical choice. (On another occasion when I was again weighing a crucial life decision and asked his advice, his response was, "It doesn't really matter what you do. I use a coin a lot." It was an off-the-cuff remark, but being impressionable, I took it to heart and literally used the toss of a coin to make most of my decisions for the next 30 years. "Heads I get married, tails I'm gay. Heads I go with scrambled, tails fried over easy. Heads graduate school, tails gigolo." I simply could never figure out what I really wanted or should do in any situation, and I can no longer even imagine how my life would have turned out had the heads come up tails over the years, or the tails heads. I could easily have been a dental hygienist by now, or a cold cuts entrepreneur. It was only recently that I finally tossed a coin to decide whether or not to continue using a coin toss for my decisions. It came up tails for no, so I went for two out of three, but I finally had to let the method go. And now I never have the foggiest idea of what I want to do, or even where to look to find out.)

But when Ram Dass suggested I had to choose between being successful in the world or "going to God," I now believe that he was setting up a false dichotomy. Who said you can't become successful *and* go to God? And who said God was something to *go to* at all? But I nevertheless let go of worldly ambition, and after 10 years flew by, I realized with horror that most of my peers had homes, jobs, and families, and I had none of those things, nor had God shown up in any substantial way (this, in spite of my somewhat hazy understanding that He or She or It doesn't actually come and go, has never left, and can therefore never return).

I was a little pissed off at Ram Dass that day, because it meant my mother had been right about everything.

He was doing a lecture tour around then entitled "Nothing

New by Nobody Special." Nothing new, because he was essentially communicating wisdom from ancient traditions. Nobody special, because specialness is the ego's domain, and the true, spiritually realized human has presumably transcended identification with the ego. One of the highest spiritual compliments you can say about a particular teacher is that "there is nobody home." No ego, no self, just some vast cosmic spacious awareness of pure essential Being that emanates as naturally, effortlessly, and spontaneously as a ray of sunshine.

Or something.

Nobody special. "Easy for you to say," I thought, "because you're *somebody.* It's a lot easier for somebody to become nobody if they're somebody . . . but what about us nobodies?" And Ram Dass agreed, pointing out that you *couldn't* become nobody until you *had* become somebody. And that's where I ran into my difficulties. I met Ram Dass too early in the game, and together we short-circuited my path to somebody-hood and tried to advance me directly to nobo-dyland, and it was premature. It took me 10 years to fully realize that I was, in a word, *screwed.*

Chapter 2

Primal Therapy

My spiritual search actually began in about 10th grade, when I took a book out of the library called *How to Develop a Million-Dollar Personality*. I thought the one I had stunk. My quest became more active in college, when I first heard about Primal Therapy. My professor mentioned Arthur Janov's book, *The Primal Scream*, in the margins of a paper I wrote in which I had quoted the lyrics of a John Lennon song, "God." Apparently, John had written the song in response to his own experience of Primal Therapy. The lyrics consisted of a long list of people and things Lennon no longer believed in. Like this:

> *I don't believe in magic,*
> *I don't believe in I-Ching,*
> *I don't believe in Bible,*
> *I don't believe in Tarot,*

and so forth. He also didn't believe in Hitler, Jesus, Kennedy, Buddha, mantra, Gita, yoga, kings, Elvis, Zimmerman, or even the Beatles.

I believed in John Lennon, and still do. He ended the song with,

> *I just believe in me.*
> *Yoko and me.*
> *And that's reality.*

Another song from the same album, entitled "Mother," consisted of John essentially screaming his head off. Within a year, I had dropped out of college and entered Primal Therapy—this was two years prior to meeting Ram Dass—in order to scream *my* head off. Not with Janov, but in New York City with Dr. Sidney Rose, who assured my parents that in exchange for their $4,000, he would "turn me into a *mensch*."

(*Mensch* is a Yiddish word that means roughly the opposite of "scared little wimpy neurotic depressed Jewish kid," which, at age 21, was the self-image I delivered to Rose for repairs.)

Janov's theory was that all of us, during our infancy and early childhood, stopped being real, spontaneous, feeling creatures. He said that we learned to suppress our deep responses of rage, grief, and terror, and stored them in a hidden inner pool of Primal Pain. And that we subsequently took on an unreal social persona in order to survive and adapt to our environment. Through techniques of regression, the patient would re-experience those original, suppressed feelings, finally let them out, reconnect to the real and naturally-feeling, long-lost child one had once been, and emerge from the therapy healed and whole, "the post-Primal patient."

The initial costs for the therapy were roughly the equivalent of a year's college tuition at that time. I convinced my parents to spring for it, dropped out of school, and in November of 1973 I checked into a room at the Pickwick Arms Hotel in New York City. I was not to see or speak to anyone for three weeks, nor was I to read. I could keep a journal and go for walks. That first night I was told to fast for 24 hours and remain awake all night, to help take the edge off my defenses. Every day during the three-week intensive, I was to spend up to three hours a day in a dark, padded room with Rose. On my first day he had me lie there in the dark for three hours, calling out the words "Mommy" and "Daddy."

And sometimes, "I hate you."

Not much happened. I felt nothing, except a little stupid. On the second day, however, as I lay there in the dark, something happened. Rose unintentionally made a sudden move, and it triggered a "primal," a spontaneous regression to an earlier incident. I involuntarily screamed in fear, and found myself writhing about on the floor in terror. Rose realized what had happened, and so for the remainder of the session, whenever I calmed down, from somewhere in the darkness he simply said one word and it set me off again, screaming and writhing, reliving a nightmarish memory.

The word Rose kept repeating was: "Boo."

> *I'm back in our first home, at about age three. Mom is out somewhere, and Dad is playing his version of hide-and-seek with my brother and me. He turns all the lights out, and hides himself in closets or behind chairs. We wander around in the dark until at some point he jumps out from his hiding place roaring like a monster and scaring the shit out of us. To my older brother and him, it's a harmless and fun game. They have no idea that if the game came in a box, it would be labeled, "Ages 7 and up."*

Every time Rose said "Boo," I saw a large, shadowy figure coming after me, and I freaked out. In the world of Primal Therapy, this was incredible progress on only the second day.

For the next three weeks, I continued to relive countless long-forgotten scenes from childhood, either screaming in terror, sobbing with a wrenching sense of grief, or madly beating the stuffing out of pillows in rage. I was not *trying* to remember things; scenes just kept spontaneously appearing in my consciousness, as if an inner projector was showing previously unreleased home movies of my life. Despite the pain, it was actually exciting to feel reunited with that old self of mine, a familiar and beloved "me" I thought had been lost forever.

(This was a time in the self-help zeitgeist when it was still permissible to blame everything on your parents, if for no other reason than to trigger the repressed feelings that would otherwise be merrily doing cancer research in your body. It would take most of us a few more years to truly recognize that blame is not the optimum strategy for a happy life, and that taking complete responsibility for one's life, of necessity, retroactively forgives everyone everything, *especially* one's parents.)

Thanksgiving fell during this three-week Primal intensive, and since I was still in isolation, I had a turkey sandwich, sitting alone at the counter of Stark's Deli on Lexington Avenue, feeling lonely and sorry for myself. When I think about it now, I feel lonely and sorry for the guy who was working behind the counter at Stark's Deli on Thanksgiving Day, the guy who served me the turkey sandwich.

After the three-week period was complete, I continued going to Rose's office up to five days a week for over a year, for "group." This was not a typical therapy group where people sat in a circle and talked. This was simply a larger, dark, padded room, filled with patients lying on mats "primaling"—crying and screaming their guts out. The idea was that once we had learned how to access our feelings, we could now get into it on our own, while Rose and his assistants wandered from mat to mat to check in with people.

It sounded and looked like a loony bin, the air filled with wailing and screaming, piercing shrieks and heartbreaking sobs. Sometimes people threw up. Sometimes they took their clothes off. There was a lot of swearing, kicking, banging the walls. Everyone lost their voices. We all emerged from those sessions looking like POWs.

Eventually a lot of us left Rose to go to a new guy up the block that we heard was more "present reality-based" and confrontational. His name was Gavin Barnes, a former belt manufacturer without real credentials who hung out a Primal shingle down in the Village, and who, when he wasn't running therapy groups, rented his space out to porno production companies. Imagine my surprise one day when I spontaneously dropped in to see him, and my friend Jeanie from our group waved hello to me from across the room, where she was naked, on all fours, and engaged with two men in various acts that were probably illegal in some states. I turned down their invitation to play a Hasid at a whorehouse. In any event, Gavin would eventually kick me out of therapy because I wouldn't take my pants off in the group. It seems people were always asking me to take my pants off.

The Primal process made me extremely vulnerable for a while: I remember reading a *Peanuts* comic strip and bursting into tears. I remember seeing a young mother on the street holding her little boy's hand and bursting into tears.

I was always bursting into tears.

Apart from becoming, temporarily, a more feeling and sensitive person, the main benefit I received from Primal Therapy was that it enabled me to cease my practice of carrying a bottle of Pepto-Bismol with me wherever I went, because my stomach had always been in knots before. The therapy had untied the knots.

As for making me a "post-Primal," real, feeling *mensch* of a person, within a year of stopping therapy, I felt pretty much like the same neurotic mess I had been before I started, as unfeeling as the next guy: I was no longer moved by *Peanuts*. I was back to my familiar, unreal self again, as if my pool of Primal Pain was continuously fed by a seemingly endless underground stream.

Chapter 3

Werner Erhard & the *est* Training

In 1975, at the age of 23, I enrolled in the *est* training, short for "Erhard Seminars Training" as well as Latin for "it is." Founder Werner Erhard had experienced a powerful transformation of his very identity one morning while driving across the Oakland Bay Bridge, and the *est* training evolved from his attempts to communicate and re-create that transformation in the lives of other people. It was a two-weekend course in which about 250 people sat in a hotel ballroom each day from 8:00 A.M. until 1:00 in the morning or often later, guided by powerful and charismatic trainers in front of the room, all of whom looked and sounded more or less like Erhard. For a while, after completing the training, I, too, sounded more or less like Erhard.

est received a lot of negative media attention over the years: Erhard had a messy past and a controversial reputation, and depending on whom you spoke to, you might have learned that he was either a brilliant and beneficent humanitarian who could do no wrong—I was more or less in that camp—or else a power-hungry, abusive megalomaniac who demanded fierce personal loyalty from his staff while raking in oodles of cash at the expense of naive seekers looking for a quick fix. Numerous books and articles have appeared over the years that present convincing evidence of both sides of that equation, and resolving it is way beyond the scope of the present work. I can only speak here of my personal experience in the training itself, as well as some of the dynamics of Erhard's leadership style that had a direct impact on me, while acknowledging at the same time that there may well have been shadows lurking behind the scenes. (In the early '90s, Erhard went into voluntary exile from the U.S. after a questionable and highly disputed exposé was aired on *60 Minutes*, and to my knowledge, has not appeared publicly in this country since.)

The training had a reputation for being confrontational. People who hadn't experienced it directly only heard that the trainers called you an asshole and wouldn't let you go to the bathroom, and assumed that it was simply a random, watered-down amalgamation of many growth exercises, thrown together into a slick package for the masses, who would have to sit for long hours on hard chairs and not be allowed to pee. But in fact, Erhard had a much more sophisticated vision. I considered the training to be a brilliantly conceived Zen koan, effectively tricking the mind into seeing itself, and in thus seeing, to be simultaneously aware of *who* was doing the seeing. This inner observer was—*is*—a spacious and transcendent level of consciousness, clearly distinct from the tired story our minds perpetually tell us about who we are, and with which we ordinarily identify. Getting in direct and startling contact with this place within was the first real awakening of my spiritual journey.

And it was also true that the trainers called us assholes, and I eventually had to agree: we are. Who do you think got the world in the miserable shape it's in? A bunch of assholes.

I recently heard that my friend Rabbi David Cooper was intending to do yet another three-month meditation retreat. He is an avid "sitter," and has done many, many months of rigorous retreat, during which he rises as early as 2 or 3 in the morning and meditates continuously until 10 or 11 at night, adhering to this schedule for up to 100 days or more at a time. He is the author of about half a dozen books on meditation, Kabbalah, and contemplative Judaism, and travels the country leading silent Jewish meditation retreats, often with his wife, Shoshana. They are both well-loved and respected teachers to many.

When I heard he was about to do another three-month sit, I e-mailed him: "I can no longer remember the motivation for doing such a thing—is it to become more aware or conscious or something? I think I'm about as evolved as I'm going to get this time around." I loved his response, which was: "I do it because I have the vague notion that I could be less of an asshole more of the time."

So there's something to this asshole thing.

I came out of the *est* training renewed and restored, and helped found *The New Sun* magazine, dedicated to spreading the good news of transformation. In it I described my experience of *est*:

> *On a Sunday evening in November of 1975, I stood in the lobby of the Statler Hilton Hotel in Boston, struggling to remember where I had parked my car. I kept pacing back and forth in the lobby. I was absolutely unable to remember where my car was. Suddenly, in a burst of insight, I said to myself: "Well I know one thing for sure . . . I KNOW I didn't park it in the lobby!"*

It was kind of like that old Sufi story about the man who loses his key down the road but is searching for it under a streetlight because that's where the light is. When I went out on the street and stopped looking for my car in the hotel lobby, I had much better results.

My article continued:

> *I walked out of the training with my mind on "tilt." All my wires had gotten crossed. Everything I had always thought about myself and about my world—all of my*

ideas, opinions, thoughts, attitudes, memories, hopes, worries, beliefs—all of it had suddenly revealed itself to be a hopeless tangle of chattering, machine-like voices. All that stuff which had made up "me," suddenly wasn't me. My view of myself had shifted dramatically. "I" was somehow now the space, or context, or awareness, or Self, within which that old "me" occurred.

This was perhaps the most important teaching from the *est* training that has stayed with me 30 years later: the incessant voice that lives inside my head, calling itself "I" and "me" and constantly narrating the story of my life, is not who I really am. Rather, that constant mental chattering I normally think of as "my mind" was revealed in the training to be nothing more than an automatic and mechanistic *thinking machine*. It sometimes has great ideas, but more often than not it simply perpetuates a problem-riddled, grim interpretation of life, and is ill-equipped to be in charge of me and my decisions.

I once heard an *est* trainer, Ron Bynum, tell the story of his first wedding, and how, as he stood at the altar, about to say "I do," he heard himself thinking, "You're making a huge mistake." The words haunted him and the marriage didn't last. Several years later, following his own transformation—i.e., the transformation of his relationship with his own mind—he remarried, and as he stood at the altar, he again heard the inner voice say, "You're making a huge mistake." This time, however, he simply replied to his mind internally, "Thank you for sharing," and moved confidently forward into a happy marriage.

The voice had not changed or gone away, but his relationship to it had fundamentally altered. The trainers likened this situation to driving a car, trying to steer with our hands on the rear-view mirror, continuously crashing into things. Shifting dominion over

our lives from the predictable, machine-like, chattering mind back
to one's authentic, spacious Self was to get our hands back on the
steering wheel. One began to have an intimation of this Self as the
context in which the *content* of one's previous identity and ongoing
life-story appeared; "I" itself was observed as an object *within* one's
consciousness, rather than as the sole, ruling subject.

This is in fact the singular shift that launches one onto the
spiritual path—which the *est* training actually did for thousands of
people—for it calls into question as well as illuminates the fundamental nature of the very "I" that has been posing as us. Such a
distinction is likewise the domain of most spiritual traditions and
"Ways," whose common purpose could be described as the awakening of consciousness from the tyrannical rule of the ego, or "I."
(In the Gurdjieff system, for example, one is taught to recognize the
multiplicity of "I"s within us that believe they are in charge, when
in fact our lives are being run by committee! This is easily made
clear to anyone who has vowed in all sincerity to get up at 4:00 A.M.
to meditate or go for a run and yet when the alarm goes off, it is
quite a different member of the inner circle who hits the snooze
alarm and blows it off. The same is true for the "I" committed to
staying off sugar, who must contend with the "I" who happily puts
away half a strawberry shortcake, or yet a third "I" who tries to me-
diate between the two.)

The stated purpose of the *est* training was to "transform
your ability to *experience living* [my emphasis] so that the problems or situations in life that you are trying to solve or are putting
up with will clear up just in the process of life itself." What would
shift, they promised, was how we *experienced* things, not the things
themselves. Life, the trainers said, would be exactly the same after
the two-weekend course as before. The same bills would need to be
paid, we'd be dealing with the same issues and problems. But we
would experience them differently, "be with" them in such a way

that they would essentially solve themselves, or at the very least be seen as opportunities.

And what was this other way of experiencing? To engage life exactly as it is, unfiltered by our likes and dislikes, our preferences and aversions, our strongly held beliefs and opinions about how things should be or could be. It was to unconditionally accept the way things are. For if the training was finally about one thing, it was about "what is": cultivating the Zen-like ability to "be with" and align oneself with things as they are, allowing life to be exactly as it is—and as it isn't—and likewise allowing oneself and other people to be exactly who they are and who they aren't. In fact, known for developing its own somewhat cultish and ultimately tiresome language, perhaps the most essential catchphrase of the *est* training was, "What is, is; and what isn't, isn't."

When that statement is truly grasped and considered seriously rather than dismissed as sheer psychobabble, the world itself stops for a moment, and the mind becomes silent. There isn't anything to fix or change. In this moment of now, all is exactly as it is, and as it isn't, and it can be no other way. This was *est*'s definition of "perfect." But as philosopher Alan Watts pointed out, lest one think that this point of view in some way equals happiness, it doesn't; for one's own unhappiness is merely another set of phenomena to witness impassively. No experience, high or low, can be left out of the equation. "Be unhappy when you're unhappy," a trainer might have said, a variation of the Zen notion, "eat when hungry, sleep when tired." Applied to sexuality later in the training, this became "when you're hot, you're hot; when you're not, you're not."

How does this idea manifest in a personal, practical way? If one reported feeling sad, for example, a trainer might have responded in a matter of fact manner:

"Rocks are hard, water is wet, and you're feeling sad." You don't try to fix or get rid of the sadness any more than you would try to make water less wet. It is simply part of the perfect "what is-ness" of the current moment of your experience. Your reaction to it, trying to push it away, effectively roots it more firmly in place.

"When you allow *it* to be," Erhard used to say—and he meant *anything,* even cancer—"it will allow *you* to be." And the flip side: "What you resist, persists." (Some of these early *est*-isms have since been mainstreamed into the therapeutic/New Age community, their source long forgotten.) For when we consciously choose for things to be as they are, we are in harmony with existence, or as noted author Byron Katie says, we are "no longer in an argument with Reality," and it places us in the God-like position of looking out on all of Creation and saying, "Let there be *this,*" and presto, life manifests exactly that way.

I vividly remember trainer Randy MacNamara's dramatic explanation of what we were to expect when we left the *est* training: the possibility of believing we'd lost whatever it was we had gotten there and that things were worse than ever and everything was falling apart and the training hadn't worked. Then, after allowing us to contemplate that grim possibility in silence for a moment, his deep, booming voice filled the room:

"YOU . . . FORGOT . . . TO CHOOSE!"

Choose what?

"WHAT YOU GOT! Choose what you got, choose what you got, choose what you got," he explained, and eventually you'd be out of the water. Or not even *eventually,* which implies that time is required for transformation: the *est* training was in the spirit of "sudden Zen," for the possibility of "choosing what you got" exists now and always. And in the very moment you really make that choice, you come unstuck, for you had merely been resisting the "is-ness" of the moment you were given.

This was directly opposite to the prevailing self-help party line of those me-decade times that proclaimed, "Get what you want, for you can have it all," which was often a New Age disguise for greed. Rather, *est* turned it around, pointing out that if you instead "want what you get," then you'll realize that you already have it all, and can stop searching for it and start the real work of giving it away, through contributing your vision to the world. "If you're not sharing it," Erhard would declare, "then you never got it."

One unfortunate side effect of this maxim was to turn graduates of the training into what became known as "estholes," obnoxiously hell-bent on getting everyone and their grandmothers into the program. (One enrollment technique used with the graduates in follow-up seminars was to ask everyone in the room who had already enrolled in the next 10-week program to turn their nametags upside-down and then essentially browbeat into submission all those with right-side-up nametags. My friend Dave and I beat the system by *not* enrolling, reversing our nametags anyway, and then delighting in the fun of browbeating people who were resisting. And we knew all the lines. If someone said, "I just don't have the time or money," we would be in their face, answering, "Those are *exactly* the things that stop you from getting what you want in your life. You are run by time and money. That will start to turn around for you as soon as you register yourself in the seminar."

Dave and I were excellent enrollers. We ourselves never signed on for the next program, however; we didn't have the time or money.)

One of the fringe benefits of allowing others to "be as they are, and as they aren't" is to come to the recognition that underneath all the emotional baggage people carry about one another, beneath all the hurts and resentments, there lives a fundamental quality of unconditional love.

Among the exercises *est* graduates often did to help uncover this quality was one called a "be with." You'd sit opposite someone for long periods of time, gazing into one another's eyes in silence, observing the enormous internal chatter produced by the mind in such a situation, and becoming aware of all the stuff one normally does to avoid and complicate the simple matter of actually just being with somebody. It was a powerful exercise that seemed to cultivate and reveal the love that is inherently present between people, and I continued to do it with friends over the years, outside of *est* seminars. Eventually, however, I got to the point where I was actually able to avoid being intimate with people *while* gazing silently into their eyes, even more so than during conversation, and so I came full circle, back to actually speaking as a way to either be with *or* avoid people.

But it became crystal clear to me during the *est* training that at bottom, people love each other, if they're given half a chance. Love is what is waiting to emerge when everything that is in the way of love is let go and cleared away. I remember one woman at a relationships course with Werner protesting, "But my father never told me he loved me," to which Werner responded, "Your father loved you, and the way he expressed it was by never telling you." In this light, perhaps the most valuable moment of the four-day training occurred for me when it tearfully dawned on me that despite all the difficulties I had gone through with my parents over the years—I was a miserable teenager—that in fact, they still loved me unconditionally, and even more to the point, I recognized how much I loved them, beneath my lifelong list of grievances and complaints.

The most astounding personal example of ubiquitous love occurred for me at the end of the training, when I found myself standing in front of my 250 fellow participants—complete strangers only one weekend previous—and announcing that I was in need of a place to live and would be happy to live with *anyone* in the room! This coming from someone who, before then—as well as since—could count on one hand the number of people alive on the planet with whom I would choose to cohabit. So although I was perhaps experiencing only a temporary euphoria of love and connection that would fade soon enough, it nevertheless revealed to me a "space of possibility," a way of being in the world I would forever after aspire to, and would re-experience periodically over the years through various situations and stimuli. (Although nobody offered me a place to live that night, I did wind up moving into a house with other *est* graduates soon after.)

At the end of the first weekend of *est*, the trainer sent us home with an inquiry to ponder until the following week: "Who would be wrong if your life got better?" And the answer, for me, was plain: I would. I would be wrong about everything I had ever blamed for my unhappiness. For one of *est's* most fundamental axioms was that people are not the victim of their circumstances in life, and that which they are seeking is not to be found by manipulating those circumstances. A more satisfying life is not dependent upon finding a different relationship, a better job, a new location, a better situation or more money, physical healing, or anything in the domain of what Werner called, "more, better and different." Rather, he preached, "At *any* time and in *any* situation, *no matter what* the circumstances, you have the ability to transform your life." Rather than persisting in the futile attempt to wring satisfaction *out of* life, one could choose to bring one's satisfaction *into* life. (A variation on this theme was, "You don't need to go looking for love when love is where you come from." Another was, "You've already won; now let's play.")

I received this particular teaching from the horse's mouth. I was interviewing Werner about all these matters for *The New Sun* in

1978, and he stated quite unequivocally and forcefully, "Listen Elliot: Until you get that NOTHING is going to do it for you, that there isn't ANYTHING that's going to come along and make you happy, you are unprepared to get at where the truth is . . . The truth is always and only found *now*," he said, "in the circumstances you've got."

In other words, the bare-bones existential fact of the matter, now and always, is that *this is it*. And its concomitant is also true:

"All suffering," Werner said, "is a function of 'this *isn't* it.'"

This is a variant of Buddha's Second Noble Truth: "The cause of suffering is desire." For what is desire, but the wanting for something—*anything,* inner or outer—to be different than it is? "Stop waiting for your life to 'turn out'"—another of Werner's popular refrains—"because *this* is how it turned out." The problem becomes, for most of us, that the present moment of our lives, just as it is, is not all it's cracked up to be, so if "this is it," we conclude, basically, that "this" sucks! But that's only because we are never truly seeing "this," for we are always looking at life through the distorting lens of our desire for it to be different and our commitment to change it and improve it, all predicated on the unexamined, prior assumption that "this" *can't possibly be it!* And yet all it takes is the right drug at the right time—or the *est* training, a meditation retreat, or any requisite stimulus and fortuitous condition—to instantly stop us in our tracks and allow us to behold the dazzling beauty and self-evident perfection of the present moment seen through clear eyes. Or as William Blake put it, "If the doors of perception were cleansed every thing would appear to man as it is, infinite."

And yet the fruition of one's quest, *est* insisted, was not necessarily the dramatic event the typical spiritual seeker hopes for. Enlightenment does not arrive with lightning flashes, bells and whistles, or the sudden appearance of a choir of angels; it simply requires a slight shift in position, a "getting off of" whatever point of view one is stuck in, grimly attached to, or feels "right" about.

So if there is any person or situation I believe is the cause of my unhappiness, it is possible to relinquish that point of view, even if I am "right," even if someone *did* do whatever it was I believed they did to me. Regardless of the circumstances, I can "get off it," let go of being right about my position and point of view, and choose instead to be "at cause in the matter," rather than "at the effect of," and thus be fully responsible for the quality of my experience of living, moment to moment. It is a wresting of the power over our lives back into our own hands, rather than merely being buffeted about by the winds of constant change around us.

Unfortunately, this idea was often stretched by *est* graduates into what became the oft-used pop-psychology phrase, "I create my own reality," which in turn rapidly devolved to a realm of magical thinking in which one could be stricken with what former *est*-trainer Stewart Emery once called the Super Source Syndrome: "*est* participants used to come up to me after the training, shouting 'I am God, I am God!' and I would say, 'Wonderful, here's a loaf of bread and a fish, now go feed the hungry masses.'"

And yes, as empowering as the *est* philosophy could be, I also discovered over time that it instilled in me the potentially damaging notion that if I wasn't saving the world and being a Gandhi or a Martin Luther King—or a Werner Erhard—I wasn't truly living. The bar was placed so high that who among us would not constantly fall short? The trainers' repeated, impassioned exhortation that "who you are matters and what you do makes a difference" could inspire either greatness or paralysis, and I experienced both ends of the spectrum over the years. There tended to be a built-in shame response when one's life wasn't working, for after all, one was "at cause in the matter," completely responsible. But it was not only one's own life; one started to feel ashamed that life *anywhere* was not working, that one was personally responsible for the whole world not working, for not having ended war, poverty, hunger and starvation on the planet. It was a bit much to take on. Werner did, or tried to, and we were enrolled in his vision.

(Being "completely responsible" was especially empha-sized in terms of "agreements" that *est* participants were required to make, one of which was absolute punctuality. If you showed up even two seconds late after a lunch break, you would be confronted at the door by an assistant who would demand to know, "Who's re-sponsible for you being late?"

If you responded with "I had a flat," or "My child had to be rushed to the hospital," or "My watch is running slow," or any other conceivable excuse, you'd never get back into the room. You had to simply say, "I am. I am responsible for being late." Which would be followed by, "Are you willing to re-create your agreement to always be on time?"

A "yes" would get you back in the room. Once my friend Cheryl and I arrived late for a seminar and when asked who was responsible for our being late, without having planned it, we both pointed at each other and simultaneously said, "He is" and "She is." It didn't fly.)

For three months following the *est* training, I experienced my daily life with the kind of enthusiasm I hadn't known since the age of five. I was no longer preoccupied with my search in life—I didn't view myself as someone needing further improvements and hard work and changes and more enlightenment—I saw that the Self was already enlightened, and that I was already the Self. My life became a fascinating movie, unfolding frame by frame before my eyes. The inevitability and perfection of the sequence of scenes in the film left me filled with a kind of childlike awe and wonder. The universe emerged before me as an exquisitely designed, flawless mechanism. And my particular life—the ongoing story of "me"—was simply a part of it all. And in some unspeakable way, I knew that my Self, or, more accurately, *the* Self, was all of it.

Alas, 99 percent of spiritual aspirants who have such a peak experience or awakening will inevitably fall back asleep and seemingly lose, or forget somehow, what had seemed suddenly obvious, true, and liberating. It is akin to spiritual amnesia, like finally getting the Cosmic Punch Line (referred to in *est* as "getting it"), but later being unable to remember the joke. This was a maddening position to be in. Erhard used to say it was as if a person was in Baltimore but didn't know it, and was trying to get *to* Baltimore. Any move in any direction would only take the person further away from Baltimore.

Eventually I felt desperate to get back to Baltimore. And for the next three decades I would try everything to get "it" back again. Perhaps the most eloquent and concise description of "it" that I have ever come across is from an Alan Watts essay, "This Is It," from a collection of the same name:

> To the individual thus enlightened it appears as a vivid and overwhelming certainty that the universe, precisely as it is at this moment, as a whole and in every one of its parts, is so completely right as to need no explanation or justification beyond what it simply is. . . . The mind is so wonder-struck at the self-evident and self-sufficient fitness of things as they are, including what would ordinarily be thought the very worst, that it cannot find any word strong enough to express the perfection and beauty of the experience. . . . The central core of the experience seems to be the conviction, or insight, that the immediate now, whatever its nature, is the goal and fulfillment of all living.

That, in a nutshell, is "it," and as Watts indicates, it occurs *now*. The tricky part is where he indicates that the perfection of everything as it is includes "what would ordinarily be thought the very worst." He is referring to the "perfection" of genocide, tragedy, pain and suffering of all kinds. It is a perfection, therefore, not in the sense that everything in life is exactly how we *want* it, but rather, that the present moment of existence is the only possible—hence perfect—result of all the causes and conditions out of which it has inevitably appeared.

It could also be said that "it" is the real subject of this book. And that *is* what I got at the *est* training, in the now-back-then, and subsequently seemed to lose, in the now-later-on. And having once tasted the freedom of such an awakening, even for a moment, one can never again get a truly good night's sleep, for it's as if a perpetual restlessness of the soul is set in motion to retrieve what has been seemingly lost, through any and all means possible.

Thus began the endless cycle I have been caught in, of retreats, workshops, meditation techniques, and other consciousness-altering methods, including psychedelic drugs, all manner of bodywork, therapeutic release, fasting, diets, New Age psychics, healers, channels and shamans, immersion in religious traditions, on and on and on. Werner once said that "People will do *anything* and give up *anything* to get enlightened, except the *one* thing required, which almost no one will give up: *people will not give up that they are not enlightened!*"

He was right. I am living proof, the 99th Monkey, hell-bent on proving over and over again that I am still not enlightened. Truth be told, it is actually much easier to continue striving to *become* enlightened, which often involves all sorts of entertaining and exotic pursuits and travels, than to actually *be* enlightened, which would likely put an end to all that and leave me face-to-face with the enormous responsibility of having to live an enlightened life in the world, characterized by loving service and hard work. Or perhaps, as Timothy Leary might have suggested, characterized by more *fun* as well, since to remain a spiritual seeker requires, at the very least, that one continue to be miserably dissatisfied with virtually everything all the time. (Not a lot of fun potential.)

And for those of us who continue to believe that getting enlightened will provide some sort of free ride and final relief from suffering through the experience of blissful, mystical divine union, author Andrew Boyd has pointed out that this very moment of epiphany can in fact be a "a crushing experience from which we never fully recover." Echoing *est*'s view, Boyd continues: "When you feel connected with everything, you also feel responsible for everything." I've always puzzled over the way people describe the Buddha as having "unbearable compassion," because most people seem to go on and on about his compassion and completely gloss over the unbearable part. But surely, the more we open our hearts in love, the more sensitized we become to the enormous pain and suffering all around us. Or as Boyd concludes: "I am One with the Universe, and it hurts."

Near the end of the second weekend of *est*, the trainer quoted a passage from the Ramayana, a Hindu scripture, in which Hanuman (the embodiment of selfless service to God) says to Ram (God): "When I don't know who I am, I *serve* You; when I know who I am, I *am* You." He was pointing out that one age-old method of getting from there to here—from being asleep to awake, from ego/mind to Self—is through selfless service, which tends to take one's attention off the relentless pursuits of the personal ego. (Although ex-trainer Stewart Emery, bless his heart, once declared—shouted, really—as people were gushing their gratitude for his "service" to them: "DON'T YOU GET IT? IT *SERVES ME* TO SERVE YOU—THERE ARE NO NOBLE MOTIVES!")

Nevertheless, *est* took the idea a step further: They pointed out that the very highest form of service was to "serve one who serves." While presumably this could have been referring to any number of possible "servers," it was obvious that Werner himself was such a one, and opportunities for volunteering one's time to serve his cause were abundantly available. To nail the point, at the very conclusion of the 60-hour seminar, Randy MacNamara's last words to us were to declare, "There are now at least three people alive on the planet who know who you are: You know who you are, I know who you are, and Werner knows who you are."

Sitting in an expanded state of newly awakened consciousness, one tends to be vulnerable to suggestion, much like ducklings can be imprinted. In that moment, my heightened experience of Self was inextricably linked to Werner, and I had the uncanny (and naive?) sense that Werner himself really *was* the Source of my spiritual awakening, and I felt a deep kinship and profound gratitude towards this man I had never met.

But this idea of Werner as Source, together with the notion that one must "serve one who serves," combined to set in motion a potentially cultish commitment to serve Werner, believing it to be both one's best shot at personally progressing towards the Grand Spiritual Prize, as well as being a truly benign way to forward the noble cause of transforming the entire planet, one *est* graduate at a time, until we had a "world that works for everyone, with nobody and nothing left out." It was a very heady adventure.

(By the way, the "What Would Jesus Do?" fad had a precedent long ago: when I would volunteer my time at the *est* office, we were frequently told to ask ourselves the question, "What Would Werner Do?" And we were also asked to "Re-create Werner." The *est* trainers, in fact, were masters at re-creating Werner, and as a result, were often seen as Werner-clones, speaking his words with identical rhythms and inflections and dressing alike—it was a bit scary.

My personal response, after asking myself the question, "What Would Werner Do?" was usually, "How the fuck should I know?"

But the real answer, I think, was that Werner would do things *consciously*. He was committed to a sense of immaculate order, and doing things completely and wholeheartedly. In the men's restroom at the *est* office was a sign: "Please leave this bathroom more conscious than how you found it." To this day, I find myself cleaning up restrooms at gas stations, in restaurants, on airplanes. It's my—and Werner's—little contribution to a more conscious world.)

I recently attended a Zen retreat where each person was given a daily chore that served both a necessary function—chopping vegetables for salad—as well as provided an opportunity to practice "meditation in action," to bring mindfulness and presence into mundane daily activities, so that one's deepening meditative awareness was not confined to the cushion alone.

So there I was, at 52, paying $450 for the opportunity to clean the toilets, which had the added bonus of stripping away any last vestige of self-importance to which I might have still been clinging. (For this reason, some Zen enthusiasts consider it the best job.) Along these lines, there is a long tradition in the arena of guru-disciple relationships of giving up all one's personal rights, and simply serving the Master and doing what one is told, no matter how unreasonable. In fact, the more unreasonable the better, for it is precisely the most unreasonable demands that most quickly bring to the surface our protestations, resistance, and, ultimately, the opportunity to "get off it," to be released from the stranglehold of our own addiction to being right and to "doing it our way," and thus discover the inner freedom and spaciousness of being detached from our own egocentric point of view.

Yet from the outside, this can look like madness and manipulation. I once volunteered to answer the phone at the *est* office, for example, and I got yelled at for not making the phone ring!
"What's between you and having that phone ring?" my superior
asked, in a confronting tone. "Why are you resisting creating the
phone ringing?" (I could have beaten her at her own game had I
said, "And what's going on with *you* that you've created having a guy
like me in your office who doesn't get the phone to ring?")

For when one signed on to work for Werner, it was made
clear that one had no rights, and was expected to meet unreasonable demands without protest. I once assisted at an advanced *est*
course called "The 6-Day," which involved volunteering nine con-
secutive 20-hour days, an opportunity for which we *paid* $150. If
there was a marine boot camp of the Human Potential Movement,
this was it. It was so exhausting that each morning it was actually
somebody's job to make sure all of us volunteers were really getting
out of bed. Someone would knock on every door each morning and
say, with a clipped, drill-sergeant tone, "YOU HAVE AN AGREE-
MENT TO HAVE YOUR FEET ON THE FLOOR. ARE YOUR FEET
ON THE FLOOR?" (One volunteer assistant eventually cracked after about five days of this and spontaneously began running away.
The staff chased after him, calling, "We just want to talk to you." He
yelled back, "Then you're going to have to catch me!")

An important aspect of The 6-Day was an outdoor ropes
course in a mountain range in the Berkshires, the best part of which
was literally stepping off a mountain into thin air, flying down a
half-mile zip line. It was meant to instill in us the cellular experience of stepping forward into life and the unknown with a sense
of trust and adventure. But for me, jumping off a cliff did not at all
prepare me for the *really* challenging moments in life: getting up
in the morning, or having a job. Leaping off mountains into empty
space was kids' stuff.

In any event, after spending the day helping out on the ropes course, we had to haul all this heavy equipment about a half-hour down the mountain, which took three trips. As I lay collapsed at the foot of the trail following the third trip, sleep-deprived and beat, I was informed there was one more load that needed to be brought down.

That was the moment I truly grasped what working for Werner Erhard was about: just when you've reached utter and total exhaustion and believe you've reached your absolute limit and can do no more, you're literally asked to run up a mountain.

Which is a good experience to have . . . once! My superhuman efforts at The 6-Day existed for me outside of the ordinary stream of my conscious experience, like a dream of functioning way beyond what I usually insist are my limits. It revealed what is possible, and I would never do it again.

By the end of our nine days together at the 6-Day, our group of assistants had naturally bonded and we sat in a closing circle with the trainer, sharing "something you've never told anyone before." One of the women confessed to having worked as a prostitute for several years in her 20s. We all acknowledged her courage with applause. We went around the circle until we reached this guy Jim, who kind of took us by surprise: "Okay," he said meekly, as if he was about to sheepishly confess to raiding the cookie jar, "I killed a guy once." We applauded hesitantly, everyone nervously looking around the circle to see if anyone else was going to clap.

Then to close, the trainer read us a canned acknowledgment—Werner scripted virtually everything that his trainers said. What the trainer said to us was this:

"I want to acknowledge you, not merely for doing a *good* job, as if that's *all* you did. I want to acknowledge you as if I had come to you this morning and asked you to take the roof off the building by noon, and you did it. I want to acknowledge you for taking the roof off the building."

Several years later, *est* had evolved into "The Forum," which continues to flourish around the world today under the auspices of Landmark Education. I volunteered in San Francisco to assist at an event called "Openings" in which several hundred people paid $600 to observe Werner meet with his Forum Leaders, some of whom were former *est* trainers. Werner never showed up, but surprisingly few people accepted the offer of their money back, and chose instead to stay and watch the Forum Leaders meet amongst themselves. It was thought that these folks communicated in such a powerful way that if one knew the proper way to listen, much could be gleaned. I lacked this ability, apparently, because as far as I could tell, there were about 200 people sitting in expensive bleacher seats watching what seemed to me to be a somewhat boring corporate business meeting, and no refreshments.

But I heard something that weekend that would forever raise a red flag in my mind about that organization. One of the Forum Leaders was discussing his commitment to what they all referred to as "the Work," and he said, "I want you to know that the nature of my commitment to the Work is such that, if my kids were dying, I'd still be here leading this event."

My inner fanatic alarms went off, and it was the last time I would ever volunteer. When the weekend was over, those of us who had assisted had a meeting with our supervisor, who said this to us, as if spontaneously thinking it up himself:

"I want to acknowledge you, not merely for doing a *good* job, as if that's *all* you did. I want to acknowledge you as if I had come to you this morning and asked you to take the roof off the building by noon, and you did it. I want to acknowledge you for taking the roof off the building."

❀   ❊   ❀

To be fair, though, what looks like possibly cultish devotion from the outside can in fact be a consciously chosen path of liberation from the inside. The classic example of surrender in the spiritual literature of the Tibetan tradition describes Marpa ordering his student Milarepa to build a house, stone by back-breaking stone, and upon completing it, commanding him to tear it down and rebuild it in another location. This cycle repeats itself until Milarepa's ego is completely broken, and he is enlightened.

Now suppose that scenario were to be played out in today's world? Imagine the headlines: "INNOCENT YOUTH ENSLAVED TO POWER-CRAZED TIBETAN CULT LEADER!" So how is one to judge? I joined countless others who were thrilled with the value and benefits we received from Werner's training, understood the personal advantage to be gained through engaging in the practice of service—in fact, we were asked to "agree" to "get more out of it than you put in"—and joyfully volunteered millions of collective hours of free labor in support of Werner's mission, which was to spread the possibility of transformation far and wide, through "sharing the training" with others—i.e., gathering up new recruits. Was this an elaborate, abusive scheme to feed more money and power back to the "Source," or a legitimate avenue of spiritual development? Or could it have been both? Could one get the enlightening benefits of selfless service through serving a person or system revealed in the end to be possibly corrupt? I would say yes, recalling the old teaching adage that "it is the purity of the disciple that determines the outcome."

When something blows our mind, it is because it completely confounds our habitual way of thinking and our taken-for-granted belief systems. It only takes one seemingly miraculous or non-ordinary event to call our entire framework of reality into question. Whether it be Jesus walking on water, Sathya Sai Baba materializing holy ash from his fingertips, or Uri Geller bending a spoon from across the room, we instantly realize that there is more to this life than has heretofore met our eyes, and once we have been thus awakened—and mind-blown—we are suddenly open, from that point on, to witnessing further non-ordinary events. And naturally, once we're so predisposed, we tend to see what we're looking for, much as when we learn a strange new word and it suddenly appears in our world two or three times that same week. Hence, *est* graduates were "creating miracles" in their lives on a daily basis.

But actually, though *est* was mind-blowing, it was not through witnessing a non-ordinary event, but more in the manner, as I've said, of an awakening in consciousness: the very core of one's personal reality was altered, the center from which sprang all prior beliefs, opinions, attitudes, and what one had learned to expect from life, what one knew to be "possible." Hence, Werner spoke, in his unique and careful language, of his work as "creating a clearing for the possibility of possibility." In a flash of transformation, one's previous limitations were annihilated in the recognition of the limitless nature of the true, unbound Self. Everything became possible, including miracles—one needed to rely only on the power of one's personal intention to make it happen.

So yes, the *est* training blew my mind and opened me to a new world of possibility, but it also came with a whole new set of unexamined beliefs and assumptions (i.e. "I create my reality") that would eventually be in need of blowing again. One gets out of a box to breathe the fresh air of freedom, only to eventually bump up against the walls of a bigger box. But this is actually built into the very fabric of transformation, for *est* never implied that transforming one's life was a one-time only, final event. Rather, to be transformed is to enter into a life that *keeps* transforming: blow your mind once, and you have a permanent suspicion of any fixed notions of reality. You come to view life as a series of Chinese boxes, with bigger and bigger boundaries.

Does anyone ever bust through fully, out of some final box into pure and permanent Space itself? I don't know. There are powerful enlightened masters who might claim that to be the case, and there are equally powerful debunkers who insist such emperors have no clothes. True believers will insist on the pure, liberated state of their master and absolutely "know" it to be the case. To the critic of such believers, that is simply the symptom of their disease, and never the twain shall meet.

Those of us on this journey of awakening were at first firmly entrenched in our individuality, with its egocentric, me-first, solo existence, often largely colored by greed, competition, lust, and the drive for power. Then at some point that position was challenged—we had that mind-set blown—and we awakened to a higher organizing principle, characterized by unity, holistic interconnectedness, oneness, love, enlightenment, and God.

My question is, what happens when the blown mind is blown again? What happens when the explosion of Eastern spirituality and New Age paths of the past 30 years explodes again? Where will we land next time? Is the Perennial Philosophy a known given, a static truth, predictable and identical to its historical antecedents, or is it rather an evolving, transforming philosophy, one that will reveal hitherto unknown dimensions of experience? Of course, leave it to Werner, who once said, "When you find the place where no one has ever been before—where it is *impossible* for anyone to go—look for my footprints."

❀   ❀   ❀

About 10 years ago I was exiting the main terminal at Dulles Airport when I spotted a familiar face:

"Randy MacNamara?" I exclaimed.

"November '75, Boston," I told him, by way of identifying myself. After a few remarks back and forth, I said, "Well, it was a great weekend you put on, 20 years ago." And in true trainer form, he instantly got to the point:

"Does it still impact your life?"

"Well . . . sure, yes," I replied. And then he hit me with what I thought to be an astonishing question:

"Daily?" he asked.

I was a bit tongue-tied. Daily? How many different workshops, therapies, psychedelic journeys, meditation retreats, and Prozac had I done over the years, all geared toward, if not getting it again, or getting more of it, than certainly maintaining and reinforcing it? With such a mix of experiences over the years, how could I possibly be sure what had created which results in my life? I tried to explain this, and added, "But in terms of the training marking a departure point and altering the direction of my life from that moment on, it certainly impacts me daily." I'm not sure that was good enough for him, but we reached the walkway and parted company.

His question reminded me that from Werner's point of view, the training was *not* intended to merely generate some "first experience" for people, like a spiritual sneak preview. For Werner, this was to be the defining turning point in people's lives, from which they would never go back; an epiphany in consciousness that would still be impacting them 20 years later, as they strolled through Dulles Airport.

The paradox of the path to enlightenment is that the only place to go is here, and the only time to go is now, and yet to truly be fully present in the here and now may require years of striving to seemingly get somewhere. The two play off each other and keep the game going. The *est* training, in a sense, was saying, "it's more fun to try to become enlightened if you're already enlightened; otherwise you may have to wait forever."

This approach fueled one of the main arguments that opponents voiced against Erhard's work, that "you can't package and sell enlightenment in a few days, because people spend years and years doing austere spiritual practices, and often still fail to 'get it.'" Werner's response to this was, "No, people spend years and years *not* getting enlightened—when they finally get it, it happens in a flash, it takes no time at all, it happens outside of time." In other words, enlightenment could just as well occur in *this* moment of now, after some 40 hours of sitting in a hotel ballroom, as in the moment of now that occurs after 40 years of sitting in a Zen monastery.

But a glimpse of the Promised Land is not a permanent residence. After mulling all this over for 32 years, I've concluded that whatever occurred after two weekends for the half a million or more *est* graduates was obviously a far cry from an abiding state of enlightenment. For many, the experience opened a door of possibility in consciousness, revealing a grand and ecstatic vista, but to live in that place requires practices, discipline, commitment, perseverance, and grace. And probably more than 40 years.

But I definitely got it, and I definitely lost it, and paradoxically, we are speaking of that which can never be gotten *or* lost, for it is always already present. And for three months following the training, I lived in a somewhat remarkable, powerful, and completely unfamiliar state to me: this new me was genuinely happy, committed to life, passionately alive, and deeply connected to everyone he encountered. Normally I was more accustomed to living in a state of isolation, complaint, unhappiness, mental/emotional pain, and ordinary, generic suffering. To this day, these two identities continue their struggle to take charge and run my life. (In fact, it may well be, in the end, after years and years of searching, I will die and someone up there will tell me: "By the way, you were bipolar. It was never about enlightenment. You were just mood-swinging through life." I actually came up with my own diagnosis of my condition: Incarnational Disorder.) Nevertheless, the *est* training had revealed to me what it's like to truly stand and live as and express my true Self authentically, and simultaneously experiencing my more familiar identity with a certain detachment and even humor. It was clearly the beginning of my spiritual search.

Chapter 4

Hilda Charlton
& *The New Sun*

Hilda Charlton was definitely not an ordinary woman by any stretch of the imagination. She had spent her early years as a modern dancer, and once, during an important performance in India for visiting dignitaries, she managed to dance her way backward into a swimming pool, an event that precipitated a shift in her focus from the artist's life to the spiritual path. She wound up remaining in India for 18 years, hobnobbing with God's top people in the East—Bhagawan Nityananda, Sathya Sai Baba, Paramahansa Yogananda and others. When she returned to the sex, drugs, and rock and roll world of '60s America, she began holding court in New York, teaching people—or "kids," as she referred to everyone—about God. Eventually her classes moved to the Cathedral of St. John the Divine, where over 300 people would show up every Thursday night and Hilda would infuse the room with such a sense of mystery and the sacred that everyone would leave feeling utterly stoned and in love. And believing in miracles, healings, God, Guru, and Hilda.

This was long before everyone and their mother had become channels. Hilda was a pioneer in that area, claiming to see, hear, and converse with Jesus, Mary, Joan of Arc, Pericles, and innumerable other figures from spiritual history. Plus, she had this extraordinary way of filling the cathedral with otherworldly, high-pitched, haunting, chanting sounds that bounced off the ceiling so that they sounded like they were coming from Heaven itself.

Now *that's* when the spiritual path was fun.

She also told outrageous stories of her personal journey with God, such as the time she lost her library card and was so upset she commenced haranguing God about it nonstop, until finally He apparently grew tired of her kvetching, and one morning as she walked down a New York City street, she noticed something come floating down from the sky and drop at her feet: the library card. She was so convincing in her delivery, and filled with such child-like delight and excitement, that most people took her at her word and their own lives subsequently took on a magical quality as well, filled with daily miracles, healings and divine interventions that they would attest to each week at Hilda's gatherings.

I discovered Hilda's clairvoyant abilities the first time I went to one of her meetings at the cathedral. I had just moved to New York with the intention of writing a book. After a few days of writing, however, I had gotten completely depressed and was just lying around a lot, staring into space. I went to the cathedral to hear Hilda teach, and afterward a lot of people were crowding around her to greet her personally. I was waiting my turn, intending to tell her of my depression and failed attempts to write a book. As I was rehearsing what to say, she suddenly marched through the crowd and walked right over to me, a complete stranger, tapped me on the chest three times and said: "Whattsa matter, kid? Depressed? Why don't you write a book?" I thought that was pretty good.

Her response to me the next time I was depressed was even better. She told me: "Bake a cake, kid!"

Which I did, and it definitely worked. I continue to use that technique to this day. I've become quite the baker, albeit with a bit of a paunch.

Hilda would keep you on your toes with seemingly incidental remarks that indicated she somehow knew about your private world and therefore there was nowhere and nothing to hide. For example, when I informed Hilda that I was planning to lead a weekend workshop, she said to me, "What are you going to teach? I hope you're not going to teach meditation, kid, because you don't meditate."

She was also very anti-drug, and wanted all of us to find God instead. I once raised my hand to speak at one of her public gatherings: "Hilda, before meeting you I used to really enjoy smoking pot, but now I feel guilty about it." Her response: "Well that's good, kid—at least you feel guilty now. That's progress!"

It was at one of Hilda's meetings that I became editor of *The New Sun* magazine. Bruce Silvey, the publisher, stood up and announced that he was starting a New Age spiritual magazine and needed help. I hung around to meet him afterward and he said, "Okay, you're the editor." Thus began three years of meeting every guru, healer, and nutcase who passed through New York City selling spiritual goods.

My overexposure to such stuff eventually rendered me nearly unable to distinguish the wheat from the chaff, although I suspected that if it involved having to wear a pyramid on your head, it was probably bogus.

The good news was that Hilda became a monthly columnist for *The New Sun*, and I had the unique opportunity to go to her home each month to pick up her column. She would always have me read it back to her aloud—not so that she could hear it, but so that the meaning of her words would get through my thick skull and imprint on my consciousness. She would usually bop me on the head while I was reading in order to help the process along. God knows where I'd be today if Hilda hadn't bopped me on the head so much.

One time she spontaneously entered a trance state and said she kept hearing the name "William Blake, William Blake" and saw an image of me lying in the grass, writing. She thought maybe it meant I should read Blake.

Which I tried to do, but I never really had the patience to unravel all the imagery and words Blake uses that I didn't understand. Then an interesting thing happened about a year later:

I went to cover an appearance by the Reverend Keith Milton Rhinehart for *The New Sun*. The reverend was an albino, and wore nothing but white, down to his sandals. Apart from periodically weeping and having jewels drop from his eyes (a feat I only witnessed on video), his main routine was to have the audience drop cards in a hat containing the name of a dead person, their own name, and a question for someone who had passed on to the other side. Rhinehart was thoroughly blindfolded by someone in the audience with both cloth and duct tape; he then entered a trance state and his voice changed as he became a discarnate doctor with a thick British accent who would serve as a go-between for the living and the dead.

Rhinehart reached into the hat blindfolded, pulled out a card, held it to his forehead, and began to speak to someone in the audience. Like this: "Is there a Joey in the room?" Someone assented. "Ah yes—your Aunt Sarah says yes, you should finish your dissertation, and she also wants you to know that your Uncle Larry is very sick." And Joey's jaw dropped, because he hadn't even mentioned his Uncle Larry on the card! It was pretty impressive.

I wrote my name, the name of William Blake, and asked Blake if he had a message for me. When Rhinehart got to my card he said, "The music of the spheres is filling the room, and William Blake is here. Is there a Philip present?" I had not mentioned on my card that Philip is my middle name. "That's my middle name," I said. "Ah yes. You were known as Philip in your last life."

But then came the kicker: "William Blake says he tried to contact you through another medium about a year ago, but you were skeptical—are you still skeptical?" In shock I remembered that day at Hilda's and stammered: "Uh . . . " "He says your pen is mighty. That right now your writings are reaching thousands, is that accurate?" "Yes." *The New Sun* had a circulation of 8,000 or so. "But someday your writings will reach millions."

That's my best supernatural, occult, otherworldly story. I've never heard anything about Reverend Rhinehart again, I still can't make heads or tails out of most of Blake's poetry, but maybe this book will reach millions; buy one for a friend.

❀   ❀   ❀

Working for *The New Sun* provided me with lots of good material that I used to think would make for a quirky book someday. This is that book.

Like the time I went to interview Leonard Orr, the founder of "Rebirthing," a technique in which the client is submerged under womb-like warm water, breathes through a snorkel, and relives their birth in such a way that their pattern of breathing is released from a lifetime of tension and holding on, and once again becomes the deep, oxygen-replenishing event it once was, prior to contracting in terror. Eventually rebirthers stopped putting people in water because they discovered that "dry rebirthing" was equally effective. Leonard Orr was also preaching the possibility of physical immortality through choosing a path of "youthing" instead of aging. Leonard was becoming a year younger every year. If my calculations are correct, by now he should be about six months old.

Naturally, my several rebirthing sessions revealed only that, for all intents and purposes, I had never taken a truly deep and full breath my entire life, and was unlikely to do so in the future. My wife Shari was a breath worker when we met, and she said that I was her only failure, which would eventually precipitate her changing careers. But for the first year of our marriage, all day long, everyday, she reminded me to breathe. You have no idea how annoying that is. I was convinced that I would remember to breathe with or without her help.

But Leonard Orr was onto another kick the night I met him and heard him speak. He said he had an idea for sale that was worth millions of dollars, but that he was willing to part with for the price of admission to his lecture, which that night was $50. Here is his idea, which was in the nature of an affirmation, and which I can let you have for only $16.95:

> *My personal connection to Infinite Intelligence*
> *is sufficient to yield me a huge, personal fortune.*

Ironically, sometime later I happened to get hold of one of Leonard's newsletters that he sent out to his rebirthing community, in which he angrily complained that they were not tithing him enough of their monthly incomes and, as a result, he was flat broke.

And then I heard him speak many years later in Santa Fe, shortly after he had returned from India. He was wearing an orange robe and had shaved his head, and said he was in contact with the immortal Godman named Babaji who, according to Leonard, was in fact the voice in the burning bush that had spoken to Moses, and was in fact the "Father" Jesus had been referring to when He said, "I and my Father are One." In other words, Babaji was/is the whole proverbial ball of wax, the Creator of the Universe.

Truthfully, Leonard seemed to me to have become a bit of a crackpot. Although, the longer I worked on *The New Sun*, the more I came to suspect that virtually *everyone* I encountered through the magazine was more or less a crackpot, including, and perhaps especially, me. But what do I know? Maybe Babaji really *is* the whole enchilada. Had I met him, I would have said, "That first day, when you created the heavens and the earth? Good thinking. Oh, and thanks for the firmament—nice touch."

I may sound cynical and closed, but it's truly the exact opposite. In actual fact, I really have no idea whatsoever if Babaji exists or doesn't, is the Creator of the Universe or isn't, or if Leonard really is a crackpot or God's best friend. Truly I don't. I'm not just saying that. In Zen, they speak very highly of the state of mind called "don't know," because it leaves one open to seeing new worlds of possibility, whereas when you are convinced you already know something, you are never in a position to discover that perhaps you don't, because as Werner Erhard used to say, "you don't know that you don't know."

It frees us up when we can adopt the innocent "beginner's mind" attitude of a child, open to any and all possibilities, unfiltered by a lifetime of preconceived notions and what we believe are certitudes. The only drawback to this approach is that people like me wind up being open to some very bizarre ideas. Maybe Babaji really *does* dematerialize and teletransport his body across time and space, and possibly the Virgin Mary really *does* have a predilection for appearing as an apparition on Mexican barn doors and to little Yugoslavian kids, and perhaps I really *am* the reincarnation of a 4th-century stone mason with bad allergies named Hippolyte, as revealed to me by a psychic once. She also told me there was a dead woman who was watching over me and chuckling, and who, by the way, resembled Bea Arthur. How should I know what's possible in this existence?

Someone wiser than I am could probably maintain the "don't know" attitude while still discriminating the true from the false, but I'm stuck gaping at the universe completely clueless and dumbstruck. I believe neither in the God of religion nor the non-God of science, and nor do I disbelieve in either. And I really don't believe in agnosticism either. It can be a very difficult way to live, without a lot of handholds. My exposure to so many paths and traditions has left me with a not-uncommon New Age amalgamation of a spiritual life in which the Brahma of Hinduism, the Unnamable God of Judaism, Buddha Nature, Islam's Allah and the Christian Father in Heaven are all one and the same, exactly, identically, and all equally existent or non-existent, so I am simultaneously a born-again Hindu, a Jubu, a contemplative Christian, a singing Sufi, and a secular humanist.

But I learned something about True Believers during my stint with *The New Sun*, because on any given day I would be having a conversation with, say, a representative of the Sai Baba organization, who would make it plain that he took it for granted that "everyone knows" Sai Baba is *the one and only true living avatar of humanity* for these times. Of course. Not five minutes later, I would be on the phone with the Muktananda people, who understood that their Guru is the most enlightened teacher on the planet. Then the Rajneesh devotees, and on and on it went. I published a piece about this in *The New Sun*, in the "My Guru Is Better Than Your Guru Department," describing a heavyweight boxing match between Sai Baba and Baba Muktananda, which made the True Believers very upset. I had Ram Dass doing the play-by-play in the manner of Howard Cosell: "Talk about *shaktipat!*"

I've always been mystified by the huge differences between the types of spiritual phenomena that people experience in various religious settings. Why is it, for example, that evangelical Christian Holy Rollers will spontaneously speak in tongues, and report that the spirit of the Lord Jesus has entered and taken them over, whereas a Muktananda devotee's body will just as suddenly express itself in sudden, jerky movements, called *kriyas* and *mudras*? And why will the Muktananda people also experience the *kundalini* rising up their spine, resulting in visions of a blue pearl, but that will never happen to a Hasidic Jew?

It is not uncommon for members of the Santo Daime religion in South America to perceive apparitions of Oxum, the Mother of the Waters. The average Buddhist meditator, on the other hand, can sit still for weeks and basically remain in a simple awareness of the breath moving in and out of the nostrils, with not much of anything unusual happening, and in their case, *that's* the point. You won't find anybody in a Buddhist meditation retreat speaking in tongues (although of course they are in silence!), and the Pentacostalist never beholds Krishna playing his flute. But it is the intensely personal nature of these very real experiences that make true believers of people, for they mistakenly assume that when something so healing, unusual, or even supernatural occurs for them, it must not only be The Truth, but they conclude that their own experience must be a universally true spiritual criterion for everyone else as well.

And that is simply not the case. As Hilda often repeated, there are many paths up the mountain, each one tailor-made for different cultures, religions, and individual souls.

As for me, my experiences with *The New Sun* left me in an undefined limbo of a detached spiritual reporter, an outsider among all those outsiders: in the 32 years that have since passed, I have met countless teachers, gurus, shamans, and healers, but I never once would feel that wholehearted, one-pointed devotion and confidence of the true believers who have found their One Teacher and Path. I suppose that's a good thing, since lots of them often turn out to be narrow-minded and intolerant jerks. Nevertheless, I've always been envious of their certainty amidst this very uncertain life. It must be nice to believe someone always has your back. When a devotee narrowly escapes a bad traffic accident, it is clearly "Baba's Grace," or else the more generic grace of God. But as Ram Dass would point out after suffering a debilitating stroke in his later years, grace takes many forms, some of them quite fierce. Surely if there is a force of grace in the universe, it covers not only those that are spared the car accident, but the ones who smash head-on as well. Any theological approach demands that God be an all-or-nothing proposition. She's either here or she isn't, *always*.

Chapter 5

Gurus & Saviors

Muktananda, Rajneesh, Maitreya, Adi Da & Sai Baba

I spent some time at Baba Muktananda's ashram in South Falls-burg, New York, in the late '70s. What was once an area jam-packed with Jewish-style Catskills hotels and bungalow colonies had been bought out and co-opted by an assortment of Eastern re-ligions. Shecky Greene, if he were dead, would be rolling over in his grave. At Muktananda's Siddha Yoga Dham, garish statues of Hindu deities now stood on what was once the shuffleboard courts; the cafeteria had shifted its cuisine from gefilte fish and potato pan-cakes to samosas and vegetable curries; and yarmulkes had been replaced by mala beads, incense, and little key chains and trinkets with Baba's picture on it. I guess no one thought to combine both worlds and put Muktananda's picture on a mah-jongg tile.

Thousands of people would come to chant, hear Baba speak, and wait on long *darshan* (spiritual audience) lines in order to bow at his feet, offer him a piece of fruit that they would pur-chase just outside the room, and receive his blessing, which in-volved him bopping each person on the head with a peacock feather as they lowered their heads before him. Offering fruit to the guru is a Hindu tradition, and coconuts in particular, with their hard shell, were said to represent the encrusted ego, the hope being that Baba would crack you wide open. The fruit was sold from a basket just outside the meditation hall, then carried by each devotee to the front of the line and offered to Baba, but actually grabbed by one of his swami sidekicks, who put it in another basket which, when full, would be carried back to the lobby to resell, so that each coconut or pear was bought and offered several times over. Recycled blessings, I thought, that's a pretty good racket!

While many people there experienced profound revelations in Baba's presence, I seemed to fall into a deep slumber whenever he entered the room. No matter how determined I was to remain alert and hear him speak, as soon as he made his appearance, I'd be out like a light, which everyone assured me was because I couldn't handle his energy and instead needed to "go unconscious." Which was probably accurate. I *did* like getting bopped on the head with the feather, though, and when I asked him once if he was my guru, he told me "That's for you to figure out," which was a reasonable reply.

But Baba was the first in a long list of spiritual masters in whose presence I somehow failed to get what everyone else seemed to be getting. At a weekend intensive where Baba officially transmitted "shaktipat"—spiritual energy—by pressing his thumb into everyone's "third eye," people all around me entered spontaneous bliss states, swooning and shaking, later reporting visions of Krishna, white light, and blue pearls. Me? As Charlie Brown would say, "I got a rock." Nothing, apart from extremely drowsy.

Meanwhile, life outside the meditation hall was primarily spent hanging out in the ashram's Amrit Café, guzzling chai in the days before it became a Starbucks staple, purchasing Muktananda knickknacks at the ashram gift shop, or else performing *seva*, the Sanskrit word for service, which was the way the ashram got their bathrooms cleaned while you thought you were "serving the Guru" and being part of a grand spiritual plan. Somehow, whether it was at *est*, Muktananda's, or your average *zendo*, it somehow always came down to cleaning bathrooms. I couldn't begin to imagine what would happen to thousands and thousands of spiritual seekers should some of these organizations ever spring for a cleaning service.

Muktananda's translator back then was a pretty young girl named Malti who had grown up in Baba's intimate circle. She was a very sweet and ordinary person who mixed with the rest of us, eating and conversing together. Then, when Baba was nearing death, he named her and her kid brother his co-successors. Within a short time, however, she basically told her brother to take a hike and became Baba's only successor. I observed in amazement as everyone's devotion to the guru was transferred instantly and without question over to Malti, who overnight became Gurumayi, and now couldn't walk two feet in the ashram without hundreds of people rushing to literally prostrate themselves at her feet. Talk about adjusting to a career change.

Nearly every person at the ashram was given a new Hindu name, and this usually occurred as part of the darshan experience. I always assumed that Gurumayi would look deeply into each person's soul and come up with the perfect new name for them. I discovered, however, that she merely reached into a jar and pulled out a slip of paper and read the name. Nevertheless, I had come to the decision—momentous, for me—that my time had finally come for a Hindu name, and I waited patiently on the darshan line, watching her give out names to many ahead of me, and intending to ask her for one. Which I did, but ironically—and this could only happen to the 99th Monkey—Gurumayi looked at me and said, "I think you should keep your own name."

Eventually it came out that in addition to Muktananda's ability to transmit spiritual energy with his thumb pressed between one's eyes, he had also learned how to do it with his penis pressed inside young girls in the ashram. Just one of the perks of the guru business.

One of my pilgrimages took me to Rajneeshpuram in Oregon, where Bhagwan Rajneesh and thousands of disciples had created a huge and bizarre community that included an airstrip for Rajneesh Airlines, newspaper hawkers on the street selling the *Rajneesh Times*, a bookstore that only sold books by Rajneesh, and a boutique that only sold clothes in the Rajneesh colors, which at that time had transitioned from bright orange to a mellower burgundy shade. It was all Rajneesh, all the time.

I got there just as the ashram was entering an advanced stage of utter paranoia due to bomb threats and ugly politics in the nearby town, which would all explode in scandal before long and shut them down. (Apparently, they had bused in homeless people from around the country with the promise of the good life, but really to get them to vote in the local elections in order to elect one of Rajneesh's followers as mayor. Needless to say, it did not go over big with the townsfolk.) In the meantime, there were about three security checkpoints to get to the main gate of the ashram, armed "peace officers" roamed the grounds, and my luggage was searched down to the last aspirin bottle and sniffed by German shepherds. I also had to sign about 10 release forms, and I was given a color-coded bracelet that determined where on the ashram I was permitted to go. As I was being frisked I remember thinking that somehow this didn't feel the way it usually felt when I visited a spiritual community.

Bhagwan was notoriously controversial for encouraging sexual freedom, and his followers were known to be extremely promiscuous. I was jealous as hell, but as usual, I missed the party.

I had shown up just in time for the AIDS scare, which they were determined to keep out of their community. Upon checking in, my girlfriend and I were each given a little portable sex kit: a box containing condoms, rubber gloves, a dental dam, and an instruction booklet outlining the local customs of the tribe: "No kissing on the lips anywhere on these grounds. No oral, genital or anal contact whatsoever. Wash hands thoroughly before and after any sexual contact, and wear rubber gloves for all intimate touching." (Later I would go to their ashram in Pune, India, where all visitors actually had to first go to the hospital next door to get an AIDS test, just to get in the front door.)

Every day Bhagwan would drive down the main drag in one of his much-publicized hundred or so Rolls Royces, waving to his ecstatic followers who lined both sides of the street, a sea of reds and burgundies, strewing rose petals and chanting in Hindi or Sanskrit. Jeeps with armed guards would surround the Rolls, and a helicopter would hover just above, containing a marksman with a machine gun pointed at the devotees. The three days I was there, however, Bhagwan had a cold, and I was told that this was the first time he had ever failed to appear for the daily procession, which actually went on without him, only with somebody else driving the Rolls—Bhagwan's understudy, I guess.

By the time I visited Bhagwan's ashram in India some years later, he had recently died, claiming that Reagan and the CIA had poisoned him as he was being deported from the States after all hell broke loose at the Oregon ashram. Several things were revealed in the process, among them that some of Bhagwan's people had tried to put salmonella in the water supply, there appeared to have been at least one attempted murder, and apparently Bhagwan himself was a big fan of nitrous oxide, which might explain why he always looked stoned. And according to several women followers, he was a terrible lay.

About five years later, in India, I discovered that to gain entrance to the Pune ashram, in addition to an AIDS test, I was also asked to purchase a mandatory maroon robe for daytime use, and a white one for evening gatherings. Thus properly equipped with my clean sexual bill of health and my robes, I entered what I thought of as Rajneeshland.

Like the ashram in Oregon, this too was essentially a New Age theme park, with possibly the cleanest bathrooms and healthiest food in all of India. (There was no toilet paper; the toilets had built-in bidet spouts so there was a simultaneity of flushing down and spraying up that was quite startling at first.) Everyone—meaning thousands of people—wore the identical floor-length maroon robes. In the evenings, we all changed into pristine white ones for the gathering in Buddha Hall.

Buddha Hall was a huge structure the size of several football fields, with a vast marble floor surrounded by 30-foot-high mesh walls giving an open-air feel. Bhagwan had suffered extreme allergies to scents of any kind—perfumes, soaps, shampoos—and so when he was alive, there had always been official "sniffers" who would smell each person before admitting them to the hall. I found it puzzling that even though Bhagwan was dead, the sniffers were still at it. They were two beautiful young women, however, and when they came in close to me from either side to smell me, it was actually quite a sensuous and pleasurable experience.

Then we had to go through a metal detector. Again, when Bhagwan was alive, there had been threats to his life, but we were merely going to watch a *video* of one of his lectures.

Once inside, a rock and roll band was playing, 5,000 devotees in white robes were dancing, and as several people dusted off Bhagwan's throne in front of the room, a Rolls Royce pulled up, the door was opened for the phantom guru, they escorted the invisible figure to the throne and then at just the right moment, a video screen descended from the ceiling and there was Bhagwan, bigger than life, as the music and dancing reached a frenzied peak and all 5,000 devotees lifted up their arms and chanted "Osho" in unison.

Bhagwan changed his name in the very last days of his life. Several times in fact. But he finally settled on Osho. And call me paranoid, but being in the midst of 5,000 people dressed identically—a good percentage of whom were German—raising their arms and chanting "OSHO!" in unison to a video image of a deceased guru gave me the heebie-jeebies, and I got out of there the next morning.

For every spiritual teacher or path that I might appear to be dismissing on some level, I have at least one and usually several close, respected, and highly intelligent friends who are devotees and have received enormous benefit. For example, every true Rajneesh devotee I've ever met has seemed to emanate a certain unmistakable wild and free spirit. (Could be all the sex.) And none other than author Tom Robbins, for example, has written about Bhagwan's 100 Rolls Royces as being not at all akin to the type of perverse indulgence of such corrupt spiritual leaders as Jim Bakker with his gold-plated toilet, but rather, as an ironic statement of Rajneesh's fierce stand *against* materialism, a living piece of performance art making a mockery of America's consumer culture. As the 99th Monkey, therefore, all these tales are meant to reflect primarily on my own persistent inability to receive what's being offered. As for what's actually out there, you're on your own.

My time at *The New Sun* seemed to have prepared me to be a bridge between two very distinct worlds: the lunatic fringe and the main-stream normal. To this day, I have a foot in both worlds, and am equally at home with all sorts of people who would never be able to tolerate one another. I acquired this skill while hitchhiking in my late teens: in order to feel safe in the vehicle with whoever picked me up, I learned to adapt my conversations to the level of my driver, and found myself able to converse with racist truck drivers about niggers and kikes, with Republicans about hippies and the evil of drugs, New Agers about the photon shift and the Mayan prophe-cies, and so on. Pro-life or pro-choice, depending on the ride, like Woody Allen's Zelig, the chameleon-man who literally became the people he encountered. As a result, there are a whole lot of people out there who pretty much assume I share their worldviews—both the bizarre and the "straight"—just by virtue of the fact that I hang out and listen to them. I've subtly trained most of them to never ask me what *I* think or feel, because I am much more comfortable in my journalist's role as an interviewer, even with friends, especially if they happen to be crackpots. And some of my best friends are.

It was actually one of the crackpots that pushed me over the edge and got me to fold *The New Sun* after about three years: I re-ceived a call at six in the morning from a woman with a very shrill voice, clearly in a panic, wanting us to print a warning to everyone that humans were being monitored from outer space, and we only had six weeks left to choose between Good and Evil. I promised her we'd print it, but we didn't. Instead, we simply stopped publish-ing, which meant that nobody received her warning, and for all I know, the majority of us wound up choosing Evil and the world is currently experiencing the miserable consequences of that collec-tive choice. So it could be argued that as the 99th Monkey, I am not only responsible for *preventing* the Golden New Age of Peace, but, in failing to pass along that woman's message, I essentially *caused* the onset of Armageddon.

Because the individual *does* matter. One person *can* change the world. The fact is, we are each of us secretly big enough to be the Messiah, and yet obviously small as a meaningless speck of dust in an incomprehensively infinite universe. I like the way the ancient Jewish sages depicted this dichotomy. They said that every Jew should carry a scrap of paper in each pocket. On one it should say, "I am dust and ashes." On the other, "And for me was the world created." Some theologians have actually come up with a description of God that also derives from this idea: Everything/Nothing.

And if we are made in God's image, we, too, are Everything/ Nothing. But there's also this persistent idea that despite our equality in spirit, one of us will in fact emerge as the Big Cheese of the Millennium, that a single person will step forward and guide the entire globe out of the mess we've made.

I was once in a human potential seminar in which the leader asked, "How many of you have ever believed yourself to be Christ?" He meant it in the specific, incarnational form of Jesus returned, rather than the more generic "Christ within each of us." Eleven of the sixteen people in the room, including the leader, raised their hands. *Our* hands, I should say: count me in.

In the Jewish Renewal movement, there is talk of the Messiah coming not as a person at all, but as a collective rising up to "Messianic consciousness"—a state of loving, enlightened awareness to which we all must aspire in order to usher in the Messianic times. But there are many people who would still prefer God to show up in person—that is, in some *other* person, besides themselves, and for folks of that persuasion, there is no shortage of contestants for the position of World Savior:

Messiah #1: Maitreya

Maitreya is said to be a dark-skinned man who is already among

us, presumably living as "an apparently ordinary man" in the
Pakistani community of London—you'd think that shouldn't be so
hard to track—awaiting "an invitation from humanity to enter into
full public life." His way has been prepared and announced by an
80-ish British gent named Benjamin Creme. About 30 years ago,
Creme was convinced that his man was about to reveal Himself to
the whole world at once via simulcast satellite television, speaking
to everyone in their own language. So confident was Creme that his
organization shelled out a zillion simoleans to take out full-page
ads in nearly every major newspaper of the world, specifying an actual date and time for the Greatest Show on Earth. Needless to say,
Maitreya pulled a no-show and got bumped from prime time.

    Creme is still lecturing and touring, still promising that
Maitreya will make his grand appearance to humanity any day now,
along with a group of fellow Master Souls, together guiding the
world to an age of peaceful, harmonious and balanced living for all.
Creme's literature describes Maitreya as "the head of the Spiritual
Hierarchy, who is known to esotericists as the World Teacher. Expected by the world's major religions as the Christ, the Messiah,
Krishna, Imam Mahdi, and Maitreya Buddha . . . [who] returned to
the everyday world in July 1977."

    A monthly newsletter reports recent appearances by Mai-
treya in Salt Lake City, Cairo, Krakow, villages in Argentina, Ven-
ezuela, and many others, often followed by the phrase, "Water was
charged in the area." Exact locations are never given. Their monthly
news analysis also reveals the uncanny accuracy of Maitreya's many
predictions. For example, He once said, "You will see me on TV,"
and sure enough, the newsletter points out, *TV Guide* recently devoted "an amazing 20 pages" to reviewing shows that had a spiritual
orientation. (Perhaps a sign of *something*, but not *necessarily* the
presence of Our Lord on Earth in human form.)

    Another example offered of this sort is the story of a 14-

year-old Muslim girl in England who cut open a tomato to find that
the veins of the fruit spelled out the messages "Mohammed is the
messenger" and "There is only one God," in perfect Arabic letters.
Sure enough, in 1988, Maitreya said "I will flood the world with
such happenings that the mind can never comprehend it." (If only
He had said, "And I will speak to you inside of tomatoes." Now *that*
would have been impressive.) And so on: Maitreya is pointed to as
the source of any and all phenomena in the news, from the mundane
to the supernatural. A woman writes that, "A strange man appeared
out of nowhere and changed my flat tire." Maitreya responds, via
Creme: "Yeah, that was me."

But if this guy is really alive and living in London, how does
a Messiah spend his time while waiting around to save the world?
Does He hang out in singles bars?

"What do you do?"

"I'm a World Savior—but I'm not working right now."

Does he apply for temp work in the meantime? (Skills: typ-
ing, steno, redemption.) In any event, since He is said to be awaiting an invitation from humanity—though you'd think the Messiah
wouldn't stand on ceremony—I would like to take this opportunity
on behalf of humanity to extend a warm invitation to Maitreya to
begin His public work. Seriously.

Messiah #2: Adi Da

Next candidate is Adi Da Samraj, the "Ruchira Avatar," formerly
known as Da Avabhasa, Da Kalki, Da Love-Ananda, Da Free John,
Bubba Free John, and Franklin Jones, originally of Jamaica, Queens,
who commutes between his secluded hermitage in Fiji and his community in northern California. In addition to changing his name
every few years, Da also has a penchant for publishing huge white
tomes of what are clearly intended to be contemporary scripture
containing the word of God, e.g., "The Dawn Horse Testament." I

picked up several such Da works in Barnes & Noble recently and found that nearly every word is capitalized for sacred emphasis. An example chosen at random:

> *The Self-Existing and Self-Radiant Transcendental Divine Being Resides in the Speech and in every Body Part of the True Heart-Master. Therefore, devotees Awaken to the Great One via the True Heart-Master's Word, and Silence, and Thought, and Glance, and Touch, and Deeds. One should meditate on the True Heart-Master's Bodily (Human) Form, His Spiritual (and Always Blessing) Presence, and His Very (and Inherently Perfect) State at all times.*

If there's any doubt about Who He Is, he lays it to rest elsewhere when he states, "I do not simply recommend or turn men and women to Truth. I AM Truth. I Draw men and women to my Self. I am the Present God."

Being the Present God was not sufficient for him, however, for elsewhere he asserts that he is actually the one and only God of all human history, appearing now in our midst. Now *that's* chutzpah.

Adi Da is said to have been born as "the Bright"—that is, already enlightened, the avatar of our age. Although horror stories of abuse, manipulation, sexploitation, harems, and drug use have been alleged over the years, he has managed to come through it all with his kingdom relatively in tact. I followed his guru career carefully from the beginning, reading all of his early written works until he stopped using small letters, and until I could no longer handle the sheer weightiness of his scriptural proclamations. Plus a friend of mine, a close "inner circle" devotee, told me the nightmarish tale of how Master Da attempted to seduce his wife and break up their marriage, and warned me away from someone he considered to be "a dangerous megalomaniac."

Unlike many modern gurus who thrive on public adulation and sheer quantity of followers, Da has made it nearly impossible for the merely curious to get near him. An elaborate, tiered structure surrounds his teachings, and apart from a few special occasions over the years, only those demonstrating a significant degree of commitment to His Way are permitted to actually meet Him, for only the True Devotee that is in Right Relationship to The Heart-Master can benefit from His Divine Company. The rest of us slobs can only speculate from a distance. For a self-proclaimed World Teacher, this is a bit limiting, though perhaps preferable to collecting devotees indiscriminately.

I was actually invited to one of those special occasions where ordinary non-devotees from the public were granted visitation rights, and I spent a few days at Adi Da's Mountain of Attention Sanctuary in northern California. Hindu in style and flavor, the grounds have numerous temples, stupas, and holy spots that tend to cause the residents to be in a perpetual up and down bowing motion as they walk about. I tried to politely go along with the local customs, but had to draw the line when I was offered a sip of the water that had been used that morning to bathe the Master's Sandals. Others around me greedily gulped the blessed shoe beverage down, but I heard an inner voice saying, "Uh, I don't think so."

Adi Da tends to keep his devotees on edge all day, all of them wondering if or when he will deign to make an appearance. They were in cell phone contact throughout the day I was there, to learn of updates: "We heard that Beloved might walk to the bathhouse at three o'clock." Excitement would permeate the ashram and devotees would drop what they were doing and start heading over to line the path to the bathhouse, until the next update came through: "Ix-nay on the athhouse-bay. Beloved has a cold." The next rumor to circulate was that "Beloved has said he might return to Fiji because He's displeased with our service to Him." I wouldn't have been at all surprised to hear that "Beloved is having a bowel movement at 3:30."

Meanwhile, the residents kept us visitors entertained with tours of the Fear-No-More Zoo, where we got to meet Yes and No, Da's pet giant land tortoises. We also paid our respects at the gravesites of Jingle Baba the Camel, and Da's first teacher, Robert the Cat. But most intriguing was being treated to a viewing of Adi Da's astounding and powerful photography work, housed in its own gallery. Some of his photos fill huge walls, composed of many smaller pieces, joining to create a magical whole. He may or may not be God, but he is clearly an artist of the highest order.

Finally, after waiting all day, the call came through: darshan with the Master would be granted, but not in the meditation hall as usual. Instead, because of His illness, He would sit just inside the doorway to His home and we would line up outside and each have a moment in His Presence, to hold His gaze and offer a flower.

And despite my cynicism, I must report that my 30-second encounter with the Godman—despite the fact that he was blowing his nose—was actually quite a powerful and profound experience, in which I felt myself gazing into a vast and radiant empty space, my heart dissolving in tender love, coupled with a sense that I never wanted to step away from the meeting. And for an old, jaded, and cynical spiritual seeker, 30 seconds of that is nothing to sneeze at.

Nevertheless, Adi Da himself has made it clear that when someone from the public experiences such phenomena in His Presence, it is at best "spiritual entertainment," but ultimately meaningless and useless unless the person enters into True Relationship with Him as a formal devotee. And I learned that in order to merely get your foot in the door—meaning, to become a member of His "Third Congregation," the outermost, least committed level of His community—requires nothing less than an Eternal Vow of Devotion to Him, coupled with a renouncing of all prior vows, teachers, and teachings, not to mention tithing 5% of one's income, which increases to 15% as you progress on "The Way of Adidam."

All of which left me out. For one thing, as a Jew, I have a prior commitment, a previous Eternal Vow, namely, not to bow down or "place other Gods before Me." And actually, in order to be invited to Adi Da's sanctuary, I had to agree in advance that I'd be willing to do a full-body prostration before The Master, a process they actually trained us in ahead of time once we got there, using a life-sized photo of him in order to practice. I complied, but as I went down to the floor, I had my spiritual fingers crossed, internally explaining to the Jewish God that I was essentially just play-acting, and not to take it personally. Fortunately, since our darshan occurred at Da's house instead of the meditation hall, I never had to do the real thing.

Adi Da actually garnered the respect of various religious thinkers during his earlier years of teaching, among them philosophers Alan Watts and Ken Wilber. And this is because his core message in those years, before he went off the deep end into the One-and-Only-Eternal-God-of-All-Human-History bit, was theologically sophisticated and spiritually sound: that the human ego falsely presumes itself to be imprisoned, separate from God, and seeks a way out. Therefore, the search for freedom, predicated on a false assumption, is *itself* the problem, and effectively *prevents* the experience of present freedom. In truth, one is "always already free," Da says, and any effort to *become* free is born of and perpetuates the illusion of a separate, suffering, independent ego. He compares this self-centered, contracted seeker to the mythological figure of Narcissus, who dies looking at his own reflection. In Adi Da's "Way of the Heart," the way to remember and cultivate one's True Identity is through contemplation of, and surrender to, "Such a One" as Adi Da, in the traditional guru-disciple relationship. As a Messiah, however, Da is apt to be a huge disappointment: he promises no mass salvation, no golden age of peace, and nothing special in this new Millennium, apart from the ongoing horror show in which we presently find ourselves. Although, come to think of it, he did say in *The Promised God-Man Is Here*, "Mark my words: You are about to see God move in your generation." (Of course, it could be argued that all of us see God move every time we lift our little finger, but he was clearly indicating more dramatic, Cecile B. DeMille-type events.)

Messiah #3: Sathya Sai Baba

At the other end of the spectrum in the devotee department is Sathya Sai Baba of Puttaparthi, India, who boasts of some 30 million followers, or more, worldwide. So if it ever comes down to a vote, he's a shoo-in. Baba is famous for his wild frizzy hair, orange robe, and the fact that he can wave his hand around and make *vibhuti*—holy ash—materialize and pour from his fingertips. He'll occasionally pop for ring, necklace, or trinket manifestations in this manner as well. Ram Dass once said that he was informed by a close devotee of Sai Baba's that "Baba doesn't *create* these things; he simply *transports* them from his warehouse." Ram Dass also reported that Baba, knowing he was dealing with a Western academic and skeptic, rolled up his sleeves and placed his open palm right under Ram Dass's eyes, who then witnessed a blue shimmering light suddenly congeal into a little trinket. (But just consider that warehouse for a moment, piled floor to ceiling with rings and trinkets that Baba probably gets wholesale. Some of them may still even have the label on: Materialize with Care.)

I spent three weeks at Sai Baba's ashram in 1990, along with about 20,000 others, reduced from the two million who had just been present for Baba's 65th birthday celebration. (That would make him about 83 now.) His method of granting darshan to the gathered millions had been to fly over the crowd in a helicopter and wave. So if it's personal intimacy you're after, He's not the Messiah for you, unless you happen to be young and male, but more on that in a bit. Time at the ashram was organized around two main events daily: each morning we'd rise at 4:30, dress in white, and wait in long lines for hours until being admitted into the temple compound. Lottery determined the order of entry; the first line inside got to sit in the front row and have a better look at Baba when he would finally emerge and slowly perambulate the grounds for all of 10 minutes. A similar routine was repeated in the late afternoon, except the lottery winners got to go inside a small temple and chant with Baba. I sat in the first or second row several times, just a few feet from him, sharing direct eye contact for minutes at a time, so I figured that if there was a transmission to be delivered, I was in the optimum position. But alas. Other than that, there wasn't much to do all day except sit around and listen to people attribute all of their daily life experiences to Baba's Grace: "I was standing at the corner, and Baba made the light turn green." "I have dysentery—Baba's cleaning me out." And so on.

Like Da and Maitreya, Baba is also considered by his followers to be the Absolute Living Avatar of our age, a direct appearance of God in our midst. He promises massive, apocalyptic changes in the near future, putting many parts of the planet underwater. I, like countless others, witnessed his most well-known and frequent miracle: standing less than 10 feet from me, sleeveless, I watched him wave his hand in the air and make huge quantities of *vibhuti* come streaming from his fingertips. Debunkers, on the other hand, claim that slow-motion videos will reveal Sai's masterful sleight-of-hand maneuvers. Most interesting, perhaps, are those, like Ram Dass, who will say that the materializations are real but completely superfluous when it comes to what's important in spiritual life. Baba himself says the miracles are his "calling card," and that "I give you what you want until you want what I have to give."

The ashram had a museum of world religions, which included state-of-the-art displays, behind glass, about Hinduism, Buddhism, Christianity, Islam, and a few others, perhaps Jainism and Zoroastrianism. Tucked away in a corner, as if it was an afterthought, was a little thrown-together exhibit of Judaism. Essentially it consisted of a table with a few ritual items tossed on it, mislabeled in someone's scribbled handwriting on index cards. The tefillin were identified as a menorah, the menorah as a yarmulke, and the yarmulke as a tallis. (Tefillin are small leather boxes containing passages from scripture that Jews strap to the arm and head for daily prayer. It is considered by Orthodox Jews to be a mystical two-way radio of sorts, providing a direct line to God. A tallis is a prayer shawl, and a yarmulke a skull cap.) I switched all the little cards around, as if I was playing the Jewish version of three-card monte: "Watch the cards, follow my hands, which one is the tallis?"

Sai Baba's "logo" is a symbolic representation of all the world's major religions—an Om, a cross, etc. Someone once asked him why Judaism wasn't represented, and Baba's response—this from the Avatar of our Age, God to over 30 million followers—was to say, "I thought Judaism was included in the cross." Of course to devotees, who believe Baba to be infallible, this was a cryptic response with a hidden teaching. Given what I saw in his museum, I didn't think so.

While millions of people worship Baba as God, he himself says that "You are God, you just don't know it. I also am God, but I know it." And yet the feeling at the ashram was definitely that Baba was the *real* God and the rest of us 20,000 schleppers had to hope and pray that he might hear our prayers and pick us out of the mob one morning for the daily small-group interviews, where the truly blessed received a ring or necklace that Baba would materialize.

Devotees will tell you miracle story upon miracle story about Sai Baba, from *vibhuti* appearing on their photographs of him to tales of raising the dead. Perhaps the most outlandish story

I heard is that he has 12 disciples living far up in a Himalayan cave with only a magical crockpot for sustenance, which Baba fills from afar with their daily meals, and he occasionally teletransports to appear before them and deliver further instructions. Now *that's* Messiah material, if you ask me.

To be fair, some rather remarkable coincidences and startling events did happen to me there. Out of the 10,000 or so male visitors at the ashram, I found myself assigned to a bed across from Alan Levy, a follower of Hilda Charlton's from the old days whom I hadn't seen in perhaps 12 years. He just happened to be traveling with copies of a just-released book I knew nothing about, entitled *The New Sun*, a collection of Hilda's articles from my own magazine! And there on the first page of the introduction my own name was mentioned. Hilda had been very fond and respectful of Sai Baba, and to receive her book from Alan over a decade later, sitting in the bed across from me at Baba's ashram, a 1 in 10,000 chance—well, it gave me pause, to say the least. Another even more remarkable thing happened to me at Baba's that I will get to later. But for now, these fortuitous events notwithstanding, the day I was to depart from the ashram, the small group of new friends I had been hanging out with had figured out that I was not a real devotee, not sold on Baba after three weeks there. One of them laughed confidently and said to me, "Just wait and see—there are always stories like this. Someone comes here and doesn't really connect to Baba, and then as soon as they leave, something happens. You could be walking in Bangalore and a complete stranger could come up to you on the street and say something about Baba, and you'll just get it." He and the others bid me an affectionate farewell, not a doubt in their minds that Baba would triumph over my resistance in the end.

Ordinarily, I enjoy getting out of the hustle of a city into the quiet repose of a spiritual ashram. In this case, though, when I got into Bangalore I felt amazingly liberated, as if the ashram had been a cage and I was free again. And then, sure enough, as everyone predicted, I was wandering the streets when a total stranger—an Indian—approached me completely out of the blue, and said, "You have just come from Sai Baba's?" Boing! My heart jumped. "Well," he went on, "I just want to tell you that I lived there with my wife and children for 15 years and we finally had to leave in disgust because we found out all his materializations are a fake, they're just magic tricks, and we also found out he is a homosexual and makes love to the little schoolboys who come to meet him."

I have no idea if any of that is true. I hope it isn't, but a Google search will reveal an enormous can of worms; an assortment of scandals and accusations, including murder; and certain Christian fundamentalist groups have identified him as the Antichrist. My response upon hearing this stranger's report on the street was to *pranam*—bow with my hands in the prayer position—and say, "Thank you." For it freed me, and enabled me to stop thinking about Baba and whether once again I had just met God Himself incarnate and missed the Ultimate Boat due to my sheer inability to surrender, see the light, whatever. Being the 99th Monkey is an incredibly tough job: you even get to meet the Avatar of our Age face to face and remain impervious.

There is a book I never read called *The Three Christs of Ypsilanti*, which tells of a mental ward in which were housed three patients all believing themselves to be Christ. I don't know if or how they worked things out, but I'd give anything to sit in on a meeting with Maitreya, Adi Da, and Sai Baba, or probably even more entertaining, to sit with a group of all their devotees. To make it really interesting, I would add a few Lubavitcher Hasidim, the black-garbed, Brooklyn-based Jewish sect that patrols Manhattan in a "Mitzvah

Mobile" in search of lost members of the tribe. They believe their
late rebbe, Menachem Schneerson, was/is the Messiah. His death
several years ago didn't put them off of this notion, and many now
await his resurrection. Since it was known that his Messianic reign
wouldn't officially commence until he set foot on the Holy Land
(Schneerson never made it to Israel), his followers built him a
house in Jerusalem, an exact replica of his Brooklyn home, so that
the Messiah, when he comes, will feel at home and not get disori-
ented. The rebbe's main selling point, I thought, was that he looked
like Moses.

   And I haven't even touched on all the female candidates
for the job: there are an abundance of "perfect incarnations of the
Divine Mother" walking the streets. These include: Mother Meera,
a young Indian woman living in Frankfurt, Germany, made popular by writer/devotee Andrew Harvey in several books, and subsequently denounced and exposed by Harvey as homophobic when
she wouldn't support his homosexual marriage; our own Ma Jaya in
Florida, a Brooklyn housewife who was doing intense *pranayama*
(breathing exercises) in her bathtub when India's long-deceased
Bhagavan Nityananda appeared on the edge of her tub. She was
later made famous by Ram Dass's public confession of being sexually seduced by her in the guise of Tantric teachings; and Ma Amri-
tanandamayi, known affectionately as Ammachi, in southern India,
famous for individually hugging thousands of people in rituals of
mass affection/darshan. She hugged me, pulling my head down
into her lap, smothering me between her breasts as she murmured
"My son, my son" in my ear. It felt pretty good; certainly way better
than merely getting bopped on the head by Muktananda's peacock
feather, plus Ammachi required no coconuts.

❋   ❋   ❋

And the list goes on and on. I have a friend who serves as my "man in the field." He has traveled the world and literally met every guru, yogi, and holy person alive today, and keeps coming up with new ones, making even me seem like a neophyte. He actually said this to me once: "If you want to get in on the ground floor with someone, there's a new guru starting up in L.A.—a non-dualist." He's like my spiritual broker, advising me where to invest my karma on the spiritual stock market—I'd have made a killing had I bought in early to Muktananda, though had I owned a lot of Rajneesh options at the wrong time, I would have lost everything when he went belly up.

Chapter 6

Chareeva, Actualizations, Michael Wyman & the Moonies

very workshop I took had a first-aid kit on hand, in the event of minor cuts or bruises. I should have known that a weekend workshop called Chareeva was in a different league when I learned that their first-aid kit included splints, crutches, and slings. When I entered the room and looked around the first night, I turned to my girlfriend and said, "Piece of cake," based on my assessment of who was there. Nobody looked very threatening.

Of course, the various workshop assistants hadn't arrived yet, including the three giant, scary linebacker-type guys who, in order to help me release my repressed rage, would at some point surround me and begin pushing me back and forth like a ping-pong ball, ripping off my shirt, while the leader arranged to have both my girlfriend and an ex-girlfriend stand on the sidelines and scream, "YOU HAVE NO BALLS, WIMP! FIGHT!" and so on. I later learned that one of these big galoots wound up incarcerated in a mental asylum.

One member of our group decided that Chareeva wasn't for him, and decided to leave. He got tackled by the big guys before getting near the door. He stayed. Then I watched timidly as the leader sent one of his henchmen after my girlfriend, simulating a rape scene that left her wailing and sobbing, which they considered a good result. Or, as the leader put it, in observing my girlfriend writhe in terror beneath the weight of his assistant, "Touchdown."

At one point a participant was in front of the room, in the "hot seat," discussing his life. The leader challenged me to respond, saying, "What do you have to say, Elliot? You're the editor of a spiritual magazine." I felt pressured to come up with something suitably enlightened, and said to the man in front, "Well, why do you hold these things as a problem?" The man's response was to leap out of the hot seat and come after me with both fists, and for a moment I feared I would need Chareeva's unique first-aid kit. What followed was all a blur to me, but apparently I stood up and fought back, a situation I had spent my entire life consciously avoiding, but I guess I did the right thing because I was praised afterward for not backing down.

The last night was Primal Night. The leader walked around the room snapping a rubber band against his wrist to keep him alert, as the rest of us screamed and cried through the night, and in my case, threw up a lot. By morning, paper and paints were distributed and most everyone had come through some sort of emotional tunnel and painted joyful and bright sunrise pictures. My painting was totally black. A beautiful young Israeli girl came up to me after seeing my painting and said, "Dere is not only ze darkness, Elyot, dere is also ze light." I vanted to kill her. The leader would later leave his wife to marry her.

To send us home on a positive note, each person took a turn placing a big sheet of drawing paper in front of the room and the group was asked to contribute adjectives to write on the paper that would capture a sense of the person. Mine contained things like: "Hates himself; angry; depressed; unfriendly; pompous; arrogant; selfish; withholding; passive-aggressive; hostile; fearful;" on and on—this is what we were to take home and hang on our walls in order to help us stay in touch with the value of the workshop. My girlfriend's chart was similar. We got home, ceremonially burned our papers, and then got into bed and stayed there for a week, in our pajamas.

As I write of all these experiences, I keep hearing that song from *A Chorus Line* in my head: "What I did for love . . . what I did for love."

Because love, finally, in the end, is what everyone is craving. Not to be *loved*, but to be *loving*. That became clear to me in Stewart Emery's Actualizations workshop. Stewart had been the first trainer besides Werner Erhard to lead the *est* trainings, and he eventually split off to do his own thing. Actualizations was considered to be a lot gentler than *est*—basically, all that meant was that when Stewart called you an asshole, his Australian accent made it sound less offensive.

The format was simple: one after the other, each of the 100 participants got up in front of the room and told their story or discussed some issue in their lives. Stewart stood in the back and pretty much made mincemeat of each person's story, but in a masterfully loving and humorous way, so that it became increasingly difficult for people to believe in their own suffering-laden soap operas. Stewart's responses ranged from gentle and nurturing to flinging his shoe at people. Those of us in the audience visually observed person after person literally emerging from the heaviness of their own dramas and self-imposed mental prisons and regaining their sense of humor, dignity, and presence.

I remember standing up there, looking and acting like my usual, morose self, informing Stewart that I was the editor of *The New Sun* magazine. "*The New Sun?*" he exclaimed in disbelief. "From the looks of you I should think you'd change the name of the magazine to *Journey into Darkness!*" He said I needed to lighten up, and prescribed a "weekly regimen of Saturday morning cartoons and six months in Disneyland."

By the end of four days, the 100 of us found ourselves in a sacred and holy space of profound love that is difficult to describe. There was a sense of utter safety and a tangible, physical relaxation of all the ordinary tensions that might normally arise for people in a social situation with a group they hardly know. And while that New York hotel conference room felt far more spiritually vital and alive than any church, synagogue, or mosque I'd ever set foot in, it was balanced as well by a sort of cosmic, underlying sense of humor. Our personal soap operas, with their tedious tales of woe and suffering, had been exposed and the conclusion we had each come to was, as Stewart put it, that "the situation is hopeless, but not serious."

I think Emery would have readily agreed with novelist Tom Robbins's spiritual advice: he suggests one begin each day by staring into the mirror and repeating three times: "It's not about me." Stewart likewise insisted that life was "nothing personal." Even love, he said, was not personal, for it is something that simply flows out from one person and lands on whoever happens to be there. Genuine, conscious love simply loves without discrimination. "I love you," he explained, technically translates to, "I love, and you're there." Romantic love, on the other hand, is a dramatically different story, rooted in the illusion of specialness as well as the exclusive exchange of what is misnamed love for the short time its flame flickers.

At one point someone asked Stewart what the purpose of life is, and he replied, "I don't know what the purpose of life is . . . but FOR SURE, IT ISN'T TO HAVE A BAD TIME!!" Stewart was truly a master magician in working with people, and it was an awesome privilege just to be in the room and watch him work. And in the end the lesson for me was that while ordinarily I was desperately looking to be loved, admired, approved of, noticed, and acknowledged, in my heart of hearts, my true self was actually dying to be the one *doing* the loving and admiring, the approving and noticing and acknowledging of others. What I was longing to get was what I most needed to be giving. After all, if everyone is craving love, *somebody* has to dole it out.

I went on to become part of a team of people trained to help share the spirit of Actualizations with newcomers. As part of our training, we were put through a series of "intensives." The first one dealt with our physical presentation of ourselves, and each of us took a turn standing in front of the room and receiving feedback. In my case, it was, "The beard doesn't work . . . lose the wallet in the back pocket" and "Who can take him shopping?" By the end of the week, I still felt like the same guy, but I looked a whole lot more actualized.

Another of the intensives had to do with our ability to "enroll" other people—particularly into Actualizations, but "enrollment" in the Human Potential Movement was a buzzword that referred to your ability to share your life energy in such a way as to inspire another to join you—in a project, in their own commitment to living, in whatever. So the exercise involved each of us pulling an instruction out of a hat: mine said I was to "enroll the group in doing the alley-cat or bunny-hop."

The group was instructed to not only refrain from being "nice" or responsive, but to actively resist joining in, to heckle and taunt the enroller, and only allow ourselves to be enrolled if we felt genuinely inspired. It took the eight of us about twelve hours to get through the exercise. Not surprisingly, one of the things we discovered as the day wore on was that sex usually seemed to work. If all else failed, a woman could remove an article of clothing and usually seduce at least one of the men to join her and then the rest would soon follow. Humor also worked. Being totally outrageous worked the best. You've never seen an alley-cat like the one I came up with—I did my combination Tony Bennett/vaudeville alley-cat, with a dash of Maurice Chevalier.

There was a gorgeous Hollywood starlet in our group whose

beauty was useless to her in this exercise. She wound up sitting in a corner weeping at our lack of response, clearly an actress's worst fear. And the group was ruthless. Certainly weeping didn't work on us. And nobody was leaving until we all "got it." She eventually managed to get over herself, and discovered that when trying to get a group to play leapfrog, tickling was a successful maneuver.

At the end of our team's three-month commitment, we gave each other awards. I was named "Most Lightened Up." But what they didn't know was that I had used my secret workshop technique in order to land that prize. Whenever I took a workshop, I would begin it wearing my glasses. Sometime on the last day, I would put my contact lenses in, and invariably I would receive the same feedback: "Wow, you look so transformed. You're so out here with us. You're not hiding anymore. Stay out here and play with us. You look so clear." Putting in my contacts was the surest guarantee that other people, at least, would think I got something out of a workshop.

The only part about Actualizations I had difficulty with was that everyone was always kissing everyone else on the lips, regardless of gender or sexual preference. My friend Dave and I, homophobic to begin with, realized that to *refuse* to kiss men on the lips would call attention to us, and everyone would think we were gay. So using this odd logic, we would brace ourselves and go around the room, cheerfully kissing men on the lips as a way of demonstrating how secure we were in our identities as heterosexuals.

Michael Wyman was one of the dearest friends I met at Actualizations, and sadly, several years ago he died suddenly of an asthma attack at age 55. Michael was an extraordinary person who created his own workshop called "The Power of Acknowledgment" that was popular in New York during those early workshop years in the late

'70s and '80s. Michael was always acknowledging people, saying things like "You are a magnificent spiritual being, and I want to acknowledge you for how powerful you are, and how much you have given of yourself to the people in your life." But he really meant it. It was the Power of Acknowledgment workshop that I spoke of earlier, in which everyone took on new names for the weekend: I was Crescent Jewel, and in the advanced course became Matthew. At the end of the advanced course, we were all given nametags to wear that said "God."

It was also the Power of Acknowledgment I was referring to earlier where the participants were asked to raise their hands in response to Michael's query, "How many of you have ever believed yourself to be Christ?"

Whenever I was in New York, I'd ring Michael's buzzer on McDougal Street and the two of us would go off to a coffee shop if it was during the day, or a tavern at night, and spend hours and hours talking about God, reality, and the cosmos, Michael always pushing me in the direction of my dreams while putting away huge amounts of food and/or half a dozen martinis, and laughing uproariously. He was overweight, and had a deep and infectious belly laugh.

No matter what we were discussing, he invariably found a way to use his favorite demonstration, which involved pouring various liquids from one glass to another. "If this glass of water is your mind, and this soy sauce is negative thinking, watch what happens when I pour the soy sauce into the water. See how muddy everything gets? Now watch when I add the Power of Acknowledgement from this pitcher of fresh clear water. . . ." And he would pour clear water into the mix, causing the brackish liquid to overflow all over the table. And the next time it might be, "Okay, so this glass is your relationship with your primary partner, your home and hearth, your security. This other glass is your passion, your desire, your animal sexuality. Now watch." And he'd simultaneously pour both glasses into a third glass and sit back triumphantly, as if he'd just finally solved all my relationship problems in one simple move.

One New Year's Eve, a few of us were sitting around a table at two in the morning, inebriated. In the center of the table was a cream pie, and I commented that I had always wanted to throw a pie in someone's face. Michael, whose business card identified him as a "Master Empowerer," masterfully empowered me to "go for it." I smashed the pie in his face, and as whipped cream dripped off of him in all directions, he shook my hand and said, "I want to acknowledge you for going for what you want in life." Unfortunately, his wife didn't share his enthusiasm, considering that a good percentage of the whipped cream landed on her new red velvet shoes. It cost me a hundred bucks and a profuse apology to clean that one up.

Shari was planning to join us in a bar one night in the Village, where she would be meeting Michael for the first time. I had told her, "Be prepared: he's going to acknowledge you." She didn't exactly know what that meant, but within three minutes of introducing them, Michael looked into her eyes and with his customary passionate intensity, said, "Shari, I have worked with hundreds of beautiful and extraordinary women in my life, all over the world—in seminars, in workshops, with private clients—in New York, in California, nurses, lawyers, housewives, college girls, Pakistani women, you name it, and without a doubt, I want you to know that you are absolutely the most radiantly beautiful, spiritual, sexy, and powerful woman I have ever laid eyes on and if Elliot doesn't marry you he's an asshole." That was Michael's way with people. And so I married her.

I asked him to start calling me Eliezer, and he agreed, if I would start calling him St. Michael, which I did, humoring him. One time St. Michael called me at my home in Batesville, Virginia, asking for a 50-dollar donation towards a peace-making trip he was taking to Israel and Palestine. I said "Sure, I'll stick a check in the mail today."

"No," he said, "I need it sooner than that, would you please send it via Federal Express."

"No Michael," I replied, "You don't understand where I live. I'm out in the country here, in the sticks, the nearest town is 30 minutes away, and I can't just pick up and go—not that I even know if or where there is a Federal Express outlet."

Just then I looked out my window, and a Federal Express truck pulled up. "Okay, they're here," I told him, and he said "Thank you," as if I had let go of my resistance and caused the truck to show up. He also took responsibility for bringing the Berlin Wall down, because it happened the day after one of his groups visualized it happening. We all humored him about that sort of stuff because we knew that even if it was a grandiose delusion, he was nevertheless a true lover and a genuine spiritual disciple. There really *is* a power in acknowledgment, and in Michael's presence nearly everyone he met felt special, seen and noticed, and loved. Maybe he *did* bring the Berlin Wall down.

One of his favorite teaching tools, apart from pouring liquids from glass to glass, was collage. Whatever someone was wanting for themselves, Michael recommended they visualize its manifestation through making a collage. So if someone was struggling financially, their collage might include pictures of a country house, a speedboat, and so forth. Since I was actively seeking a partner at the time, my collage featured a variety of beautiful women. But I happened to run into Michael at a party one night, and when I indicated that I was on the lookout, hoping to meet someone there, he actually scolded me gently, saying I was wasting my time and that I would have had a much better chance of meeting someone had I stayed home alone and worked on my collage.

At his funeral, person after person stood up and said they were Michael's best friend, and had spent hours and hours talking with him in coffee shops and bars. "No wonder he was overweight and always struggling financially," I thought, "the guy spent his whole life in restaurants." But in fact it was a testimony to Michael's sheer presence, his unique ability to focus his attention—and acknowledgment—completely upon whomever he was with in such a way that everyone who ever met him remembered the encounter and considered themselves his best friend.

Sadly, at our last meeting, in a restaurant, Michael confessed, in a sober moment, that despite all the workshops and seminars that he had taken as a participant and that he had led himself, and despite all the people whose lives and hearts he had touched with great love and humor, and who treasured him dearly, the real truth of the matter, he said, was that he had never been truly happy his whole life. Soon after that lunch I learned of his death. *May his soul be free and at peace. Amen.*

Just as I was departing for a summer jaunt in California, one of the *New Sun* columnists happened to call, and said, "Beware of the Creative Community Project while you're out there—they're Moonies in disguise."

Sure enough, a week later I was sitting in the San Francisco Greyhound Terminal with my backpack, studying a map, having no particular destination in mind. As I was considering Fresno, I was approached by two extremely attractive young women. Apparently single guys with backpacks were prime targets. They were from the Creative Community Project and invited me home with them to "the Center" for dinner. Inwardly, I imagined myself on an undercover assignment for *The New Sun* and agreed to go with them; truthfully, their appearance was so striking that had they asked me to attend a toe fungus conference for bald ex-haberdashers I would have eagerly accepted.

The Center was a two-story house, and I sat on the living room floor along with about 15 other wandering stragglers who had been recruited that day. We were served a grayish concoction that could only be termed gruel, and which Oliver Twist would have politely declined. Someone delivered a pep talk about creating a new world community of harmony and peace, while a slide show depicted happy people playing volleyball in a beautiful setting. There was no mention of the Reverend Moon.

After dinner we were loaded onto "The Elephant Bus," which would take us to their camp a few hours north of San Francisco to spend the weekend. I was acutely aware that none of the recruits were permitted to sit together on the bus—each of us had been assigned a "big brother" or sister who kept us separated from the other newcomers for the duration of the journey. En route, we were invited to join in singing rousing and somewhat sickening renditions of "God Bless America" and "Swing Low, Sweet Chariot," the latter altered to include our names, as in: "I know a brother whose name is Elliot, coming for to carry me home. . . ." *What I put myself through to get a story*, I was thinking. I also made an inner vow, in fear of brainwashing: *no matter what I may be thinking or feeling by the end of this weekend, I will leave this place Monday morning.*

Once at the camp, we were settled into the floor space in a barn, alongside perhaps 30 others. I attempted to steal a moment with another recruit in the men's room, but was thwarted even there: my "big brother" stood next to me as I brushed my teeth and waited outside the stall while I used the toilet.

I was awakened at the crack of dawn by the unlikely appearance of a man with a guitar looming over me and the others, singing "When the red red robin goes bob bob bobbin' along . . . wake up you sleepy head, get up get out of bed . . ." The day was filled with a series of lectures about the Divine Plan for Humanity, strangely choreographed in such a way that everyone in the room respond-

ed in unison at precise moments of the talk with enthusiastic re-
hearsed phrases and patriotic songs. The actual content of the talk
was not unreasonable.

Mealtimes were particularly bizarre. We sat out on the grass
in a circle, newcomers again separated, took hands and said the
grace before meals, which went like this: "Choo choo choo, choo
choo choo, choo choo choo, yay yay pow!" Then food was distributed and in some grotesque charade of forced "giving," each of the
big brothers immediately placed half of their food on their recruit's
plate. So I had one and a half grilled cheese sandwiches, while my
host had only a half.

After lunch we were taken on a hike up a mountain and
when we got to the top, we were asked to stand in a line, facing out
over the valley below, and sing "Climb Every Mountain" at the top
of our lungs, accompanied by a solo trumpeter. I kept glancing over
my shoulder to see if Allen Funt would finally appear and we would
all get the joke. But nobody was laughing. Some were crying.

On our last night we gathered around a campfire and I finally learned a little about some of the people. In each case, I discovered that the community members, like me, had been traveling
hippies, many of them foreigners, who had been picked up on the
street and came up for a weekend just like the one I was having, and
never left. I gathered that they had more or less disappeared from
their own lives, never returning to jobs and families back home.
I was encouraged to do the same. One of the leaders was a Jewish
woman from Long Island named Beth who was particularly tuned
into me. When I finally decided to let down my "cover" and mentioned that I was the editor of a New Age magazine back East, she
said quite matter of factly: "The New Age is not about putting out
some magazine, it's about being here and really living your dream
in community. You better pray very carefully to Heavenly Father to
guide you about whether you're supposed to stay here with us." Ap-

parently Stage II, a week-long experience, would begin the following morning. Still never a mention of Moon.

Each of us was asked to offer a song or story to the circle
around the fire, and in perhaps one of the most unlikely juxtaposi-
tions of energy I've ever participated in, I picked up a guitar and
did a deep and soulful rendition of "Kali Durga," a Hindu chant to
the goddess Kali, destroyer of impurities, who is a fierce-looking
creature usually depicted holding skulls dripping with blood. It
wasn't quite in the same vein as "Kumbaya" and "Michael Row the
Boat Ashore."

Monday morning arrived and I realized that despite the utter weirdness and silliness of the place, I also understood how one
could be seduced: we had been treated like five-year-olds—sung to,
fed, our hands literally held throughout most of the day. One's hungry inner child responds to that stuff on a primal, emotional level,
in spite of one's better judgment. Before I left, I finally confronted
one of the leaders about being a Moonie. He didn't deny it, and said
that Moon would have been introduced in my next weekend, were I
staying. "Do you think he's the Messiah?" I asked. "Without a shadow of doubt," he said.

I was true to my vow to leave, and discovered that as friendly and welcoming as the "Creative Community Project" had been in
getting me up to this camp in the middle of nowhere, I was completely on my own to get out. I walked five miles to find a main
road, and hitchhiked back down to San Francisco. Some years later
I would see a film called *Ticket to Heaven*, the first half of which described my experience almost exactly. The second half showed what
happened to the people who didn't leave Monday morning. It was
not a pretty picture.

Chapter 7

Haiti

I got it into my head that it would be a good idea for me to experience the Third World, but I wasn't quite ready for India, so I decided to go to Haiti for a week. People, meaning me, who are professional truth seekers on a perpetual quest, will find a way to turn any and every life circumstance into a personal growth experience. I was actually looking at life in such a way that it was impossible for anything *not* to be a personal growth experience. My whole existence was a chess game being played with God in which anything and everything that happened to me was carefully designed and executed by the Divine for my personal education and edification. Life, as it unfolded moment to moment, was God's Divine Message to me, disguised as the flow of my own experience. Even someone else dying would ultimately be more about *my* experience of death than it would be about the end of *their* life. So now it was time for my Third World experiential seminar.

My first night in Haiti, I sat in my hotel's courtyard listening to a local trio of musicians. In my honor, they sang the only English song they knew, which went like this:

Hey baby,
Hey baby,
I love you
you love me.

They repeated this lyric 43 times. I actually counted.

Upon awakening on my first morning there, I heard a lot of commotion coming from the courtyard. I peered through my hotel room window and saw perhaps 70 or 80 men screaming and shouting at one another. I wondered if I had unwittingly walked into the center of a political coup, that perhaps my hotel was actually the meeting place for a rebel guerilla group. But then I learned from the woman who ran the hotel what all the fuss was about: *me.*

Word had gotten out that a white man, an American, had arrived, and these men were fighting over who would get to be my guide, whether or not I wanted a guide. The owner called a cab for me and then escorted me through the crowd, yelling at the men to clear a path and stay away. She was tough. A whole crowd of screaming maniacs actually did what she asked. She got me to the curb, and as I got into the cab, she warned me not to let anyone jump in with me. The cab sped away, went around the corner, pulled over to the curb, and Henry got in.

Henry became my guide. And it didn't take very long before I realized not only that I *did* want a guide after all, but that I'd actually be hopelessly and totally lost without one. Very few people spoke English, there were no newspapers or public phones, no little tourist maps or information counters. And most conspicuous, not a single other white face, which explained all the commotion at the hotel. Henry, in effect, had struck oil: I paid him $20 a day to take me around. He told me that he used to have his own apartment in Port-au-Prince, the capital, but could no longer afford the monthly rent, and so was living with his family again. His monthly rent had been $20.

I found no bottled water in Haiti, and lived on 7-Up all week. It was only this year, in telling this story to Shari, that she pointed out that the 7-Up was probably bottled in Haiti using the same water I was afraid to drink. "But don't they boil it when they make 7-Up?" I countered. Neither of us actually had a clue as to how 7-Up is made, so we left it at that.

Haiti is an amazing place. The public buses in Port-au-Prince are hand-painted in wild, colorful, detailed folk-art, and whenever I, or anyone, boarded a bus, the entire busload of passengers stopped their reading or chatting and said, in unison: "*Bon jour, monsieur.*" Just that in itself tells the whole story. The natural Haitian assumption of connection was so diametrically opposed to New York City's built-in paranoia and fear that boarding a bus became a moving, tearful occasion for me. This makes sense, I thought. This is as it should be: people are *friendly.*

I went with Henry to visit his family. They lived in a one-room, 12-foot square shack, shared by his parents, two brothers with their wives and kids, and his sister's family, for a total of 13. Their living space resembled the average Middle-American's backyard storage shed, although the latter are of a much higher quality and construction.

I brought a big bottle of Coke for them, and after a futile search for some sort of cup or vessel to serve it in, Henry's eight-year-old nephew produced a rusty old Mobil oil can, into which they poured the coke and passed it around. I drank from the bottle.

One night I asked Henry to take me to a club to hear some music. I wanted a taste of the nightlife in Port-au-Prince, imagining crowds of dancing figures, a pulsing Caribbean beat, torchlight over the shimmering water. Henry took me to a small, dark, dank bar in a deserted part of town, where there was a jukebox, no other customers, and a hooker named Francesca, with whom I danced. I had Henry buy us all a bottle of rum to share, and I watched as he pocketed the change and pretended there was none. Given that I was paying him the equivalent of a month's rent per day, I didn't want him to be cheating me as well. So once we were sufficiently drunk, I tried to tell him about this, based on the principle of the matter. We had the following exchange about it:

"Henry, when you do something like that, it makes me no longer trust you."

And he replied: "And Monsieur El-Yot, I trust you completely." We clinked glasses and that was that. I had to say "no thank you" to Francesca about six times before she gave up on me as her trick for the night, and Henry escorted me to my hotel where I threw up and went to bed. Now that's nightlife.

Another evening he encouraged me to attend a voodoo ceremony. I gathered it was some sort of tourist show and only agreed to go with some reluctance. We joined a dark circle of people in a clearing somewhere, not too far off the main drag. A group of men and women were dancing frenetically around a fire to the rhythmic pounding of multiple drums, driving themselves into a trance state. Right before my eyes one of the men reached into the fire, pulled out a red-hot burning ember and took a big bite out of it, and then spit sparks at us. Next a woman hypnotized a chicken by swinging it around as she danced, until it lay limply in her hand, at which point she rewarded it by biting its head off and drinking the chicken blood that was spurting everywhere. That sort of thing.

It felt like a "real" voodoo ceremony to me, despite the fact that I noticed several of the performers were on the bus with us when it was over, and they just looked like tired workers on their way home after another gig, as if the ceremony was roughly equivalent to those Wild West shows in American theme parks, where cowboys get shot off the roof of the saloon. Another day, another chicken.

I rented a bike and rode through the countryside one day, without Henry. Some of the people along the way stared, but most waved and called out *"Bonjour."* The children, mostly naked, were among the most radiant beings I had ever seen. Perhaps all children are, but these kids seemed to shine even brighter in the midst of such poverty. Almost all the kids knew four words of English, which I heard all day long, every day: "Hello" and "Give me money."

I had discovered the day before that some of the adults knew those words as well. Henry had taken me down to the docks where, unlike the gentle country folk I had met, I experienced a mob of people—all men—surrounding me, pushing and shoving, and one guy was literally two inches from my face, screaming very, very loudly: "GIVE ME MONEY! GIVE ME MONEY!" A much more direct approach to panhandling than the obsequious "spare change?" method of American street people. I gave him money.

As I pedaled along on my bicycle, a young boy, who knew a little more English than most, came up alongside me on his bike. His name was Willie; we spoke for a bit, and he invited me home to meet his family. His mother, like many other women I had seen along the road, was sweeping their dirt porch. Within literally five minutes of meeting her and the other kids, the following conversation ensued:

> Willie: "You will take me with you to America."
> Me: [*laughing*] "No, I can't do that."
> Willie's mother: "You take him."
> Me: [*confused*] "Oh, I'm so sorry, I cannot do that."
> Willie: "Yes, I go with you."
> Willie's mother: "You take him."
> Me: "I'm sorry. I can't. I must go."

I rode off, everyone sad.

At one point I came to some sort of tourist attraction that

required me to leave my bicycle behind and go on foot. A young boy hanging around offered to watch the bike for me, and I didn't think twice about it. It wasn't like those guys in Tijuana who offer to watch your car for a fee, and if you want to have four tires and a windshield when you return, you have no choice but to agree. This kid just offered to watch my bike, and I trusted him implicitly. And indeed he was standing there waiting for me with my bike when I returned three hours later. I tipped him, and looked at photographs of his entire extended family.

I began to feel wistful or something. I wasn't sure what the feeling was at first. Then I realized it was *envy*. All those people who shared primitive dwellings and had to walk a mile to lug a bucket of water back for bathing, who drank out of rusty oil cans, had something I deeply wanted, needed, and missed: a sense of intimate family, community, and belonging. For sure, nobody there would have even begun to understand my contemporary, upper-middle-class American neurosis of wondering who I am, what to do with my life, who to do it with, or what it all means.

I know that what I'm about to say is not an original revelation, but it was to me: I could actually feel in my very soul that existential angst is the privilege of the leisure class. I would remember this later, back in the States, when I stood in a drugstore aisle trying to decide which of 32 different ointments, lotions, creams, gels, and unguents I should choose for relief of rectal itch.

The day I left, Henry's mood markedly dropped. I had tried to explain to him that 1) he and his family have some things few of us in

America have, and that we long for, and 2) that I am by no means a rich man. Nevertheless, I saw in Henry's forlorn face at the airport that in his mind I was a departing King returning to my palace in Paradise. And it was true, my apartment in Washington Heights that I shared with a friend for $580 a month, extremely modest and low-end by Manhattan standards, still represented a monthly rent that was 29 times the amount ($20) that Henry could *not afford*. Just before I boarded the plane, he asked me to either come back for him or send him money to join me in the States.

The plane was filled with wealthier Haitians traveling to the U.S., and it was reminiscent of the public bus rides, in that all the passengers were interacting with one another, including me, sharing food and so forth. We landed in New York's Kennedy Airport, got on line for customs, everyone still chattering excitedly, and no sooner did I pass through customs and officially re-enter these United States of America than I felt a tangible wall descend upon me—a wall of fear, paranoia, and separation, in which instead of smiling and greeting people and making eye contact, I instinctively avoided any semblance of human connection and went on self-protective alert. The contrast was so startling that I felt deeply sorrowful for a few weeks about what passed for normal in our culture (at least in New York), and all the more so because I also realized it was invisible to most of us. And sad, too, because I knew it wouldn't take me long to re-adapt to this atmosphere of isolation and forget that it could be any other way.

Chapter 8

The Manual, the School & the Workshop

Towards the end of my tenure with *The New Sun*, I received a call one day from a man in Brooklyn looking for a writer. He sold mail-order how-to books that he published in his basement and advertised through the classifieds in the *National Enquirer*. He had just run an ad, as a test, for a book that didn't yet exist, and received thousands of orders. So he needed someone to write a book for him, pronto. I took it on.

The ad he ran said something like, "Change Your Luck Overnight: Send for Free Introductory Material." The free introductory material was a four-page leaflet that had also been produced previously in order to sell a product that did not yet exist. The leaflet declared that "This material has emerged from the Ancient Secrets of the Essenes. Don't make a financial move until you've read it." The name of the phantom book was *The Manual of Good Luck*, for which thousands of people paid $17.95. They were all waiting to receive their book at about the same time I was hired to write it.

I was actually not at all well versed in the Ancient Secret of the Essenes, so I dropped that idea, and to produce the manual, I sequestered myself in a Tibetan Buddhist Monastery in Woodstock,

New York, for seven days. I spent the first three days in writer's ago-
ny, crumpling page after page. And then I hit on it: I would create the
home-game version of the *est* training, for all those people—I was
thinking mostly of my own family—who I truly thought would enjoy
and benefit greatly from *est* but who I knew would never do it. So like
est, the manual began with a set of agreements, asking readers to set
aside a full day of their lives in order to create an experiential workshop for themselves, orchestrated moment to moment by me.

And then I did my best to directly communicate to readers the basic, eye-opening insight that the *est* training had provided
me: that our fundamental identity is not the separate, familiar "I"
that ordinarily seems to be in charge of our lives, but is rather that
spacious, creative awareness, prior to "I," that lives in a world of
inherent Unity with All That Is and Is Not. (You had to Be there.)

As of 1987, which is the last time I checked, *The Manual of
Good Luck* had sold over 40,000 copies, and was still selling. I received only the agreed-upon flat fee of $1,000. It never occurred to
me to negotiate for a percentage. A thousand dollars seemed like
a good deal to me then. The reason I haven't checked back since
1987 is because I'm too embarrassed by a letter I sent the publisher
at that time. A friend had calculated that this guy must have made
about half a million dollars or more on my work, and that I had
nothing to lose by writing him and requesting $25,000. So I did.

My friend was right: I lost nothing.

Interestingly, just recently, out of the blue, a stranger
tracked me down through e-mail, desperately trying to get hold of
The Manual of Good Luck. It seems her daughter had discovered a
copy of it in the Peace Corps library in Ethiopia, and it had changed
her life. I sent her one of the six remaining copies I keep in a box.
I also recently discovered a book with the same title for sale on the
Internet, so I ordered one. Imagine my surprise when I discovered
my own book, reduced from 175 pages to a disjointed 20, but they

were all my words, verbatim, including aspects of my personal life story told in the first person, being sold by an unscrupulous plagiarist. I wrote him and accused him of being an unscrupulous plagiarist and he promised to stop.

And once, in 1981, I received a letter from a Mr. Rajani in India who had read the book and more or less acknowledged me as his guru. He wrote me to say that he and his family would be escorting his wife to the States the following month for a serious operation, and could they possibly visit me en route to receive my blessing? I was teaching at an alternative high school in East Orange, New Jersey, at the time. On the day of the visit, I put on my white embroidered Nepalese shirt, and found myself greeting not only Mr. Rajani with his wife and children, but also his brother's family and several cousins. In all, 14 visitors from India showed up in East Orange to meet me. My students brought trays of drinks and cookies, and as I had requested, stood by like dutiful servants as I blessed his wife.

This was before my training as a chaplain, and I had never blessed anyone before. I put my hands on her head and closed my eyes and silently counted to 10, "one Misssissippi, two Mississipi," etc. But I realized something: blessings are in the heart of the receiver.

Mr. Rajani was perhaps my one and only potential devotee in this lifetime, but I blew it when I accidentally stole his special gold pen. He had handed it to me to autograph his copy of *The Manual of Good Luck*, and I had unconsciously, I figured out later, stuck it in my pocket. When he asked for it back, I was genuinely puzzled, and patted both my pockets to indicate I didn't have it. I found it after he left and would have mailed it back, but in telling the story to one of my ninth grade students, he asked to see the pen, and then very casually stuck it in *his* pocket and walked away, a deft and crafty move to which I could only bow and surrender. And in the end, it was probably best that Mr. Rajani left feeling disillusioned and my faux guru career got nipped in the bud.

How did I wind up teaching at an alternative high school in East Orange, New Jersey? One morning I received a call out of the blue from the prettiest girl in my high school class, whom I had not seen nor heard from in the 10 years since we graduated. Had she phoned me during our school years together, when she was clearly in my "unobtainable" category, and I was surely in her "irrelevant" group, I would have been ecstatic, and the resulting boost in my self-esteem could easily have eliminated the reasons for just about everything I subsequently did with my life and am retelling here. But having grown and matured in those 10 years, hearing from her was no longer a cause for ecstasy, but rather, simply made me entirely reassess and alter my life overnight! She was calling to let me know of a job opening at an alternative high school that, for whatever reason, she thought I might enjoy. So I thought about it for at least a few seconds, phoned the school, took the job, and left New York for a year of teaching.

The school was unique. Located in two adjacent old houses, the four faculty members lived in one of them, and the 24 students attended classes in the other. The classrooms were just the rooms in the house, furnished with old beat-up couches and armchairs. There were no attendance rules or grades, so you had to be a really good teacher for kids to keep showing up to your classes. I taught theater, poetry, music, sex-ed for boys (the blind leading the blind), a class on personal transformation using *The Manual of Good Luck* as a text, a class on service using *Be Here Now,* and Algebra II, using a textbook my father wrote in which I was featured in the verbal problems, usually mowing a lawn in 1.3 hours. My father taught *me* Algebra II over the phone each night, keeping me one chapter ahead of the class. On the first day of my theater class, I ran through my repertoire of about 15 activities in the first six minutes, as the kids just shrugged their shoulders and said, "I ain't doin' that." I had to think on my feet, but by the end of the year we managed to put together a great production of *Godspell*, albeit without using the actual script.

These were kids who had quit the public school system for one reason or another. The two scariest ones were Mike and Paul, who habitually showed up tripping on acid. I could always tell. It was a dead giveaway when I asked Paul, "Hey, how ya' doin'?" and he responded, "Fire. It's the primordial element." Or if I stood up in the kitchen to, say, get the salt, Paul might observe with self-satisfaction: "I know what you're up to! I see what you're doing with those triangles: going from the table to the cupboard and back. Sacred geometry." He outlined the path I had walked in the air with his hand, and I saw he was absolutely right: it *was* a right triangle, albeit with a slightly wobbly hypotenuse.

Mike was a little scarier. He often expressed his anger by literally putting his head through the plaster walls or banging incessantly on the piano. He spent the first two weeks of school quizzing me about all the foods in the staff refrigerator, wondering which items were communal and which belonged only to me. Weeks later, I learned that he and Paul had been hoping to slip me some LSD, and had concluded that my Vitamin B capsules were their best bet.

Mike expressed astonishment when I refused his invitation to attend a "secret ritual" at midnight on Halloween in the woods, and demanded an explanation.

This was my explanation: "For some reason when I consider your invitation, I feel a sense of fear welling up inside me."

Later that day he asked if he could see me privately: he came up to my room, stood before me and declared, "The only way you will ever rid yourself of this fear of me, is to kill me." And from behind his back he presented me with a huge kitchen knife. Inwardly I was as freaked out as he intended for me to be. But I calmly took the knife and asked, "Should I do it now, or should I take you by surprise?" "It's up to you," he said, and I said, "Well, I'd prefer to take you by surprise."

I finally won Mike over by sitting with him at the piano for hours every day, carefully transcribing to music paper every one of his random bangs in perfect musical notation, forcing him to make compositional decisions and to actually end up with a repeatable cacophony of sounds, complete with lyrics:

> *My Daddy's becoming*
> *a corporate executive.*
> *Never suspecting*
> *that he is a number.*

The melody would have made Frank Zappa proud.

Mike loved having his music taken seriously, and by the time the school year was over and I moved back to New York City, I had become his cool older friend in the Village, a status I had to pay for in spontaneous trips to CBGB's at all hours of the night to see some of his favorite performers screaming and smashing microphones on the stage. He turned up at my apartment one day when a friend and I were painting Easter eggs. Mike's approach, appropriate to the punk spirit of the times, was to mix various dyes into a little pool of color on the counter, and then smash the egg down into it.

Actually, Mike was an angry, terrified genius, and I didn't quite grasp that at the time, because I, too, was an angry, terrified genius, only more polite. Now I am no longer an angry, terrified genius. Now I'm just terrified.

✦   ✦   ✦

(Incidentally, one of the sub-themes of this book has to do with the utter terror of being a living human being on this planet. The whole idea makes me shudder and quake. Another way of saying this: I am afraid to be myself, and I am afraid of you, and if you looked deeply enough, you'd probably discover that you are afraid of me as well.

Fear, fear, fear makes the world go round.

At the conclusion of the first weekend of *est*, the trainer had all 250 of us lie on the floor, and visualize a scenario in which we were frightened of somebody. As in a bad dream, when we tried to run away, wherever we turned, there were more people to be afraid of. The guided imagery escalated to the point where there was no-where to run, nowhere to turn where there weren't more scary people, and by this point our entire group was shrieking and screaming in fear.

Then suddenly, we all stopped and were silent for a moment, and then slowly, one by one, we started to get the joke and began laughing hysterically.

Here's the joke: Everybody is scared of everybody.)

I created and led, with my friend Warren, a weekend workshop called "The Joy of Self-Expression," in which we came up with all sorts of creative, artistic, and sometimes silly ways for people to express themselves, including, at one point, having them sit face-to-face and say the word "doody" without laughing. We would look at each other in amazement across the room during this exercise, at the sight of these grown men and women saying "doody," just because we told them to.

I watched Warren at a party once, introducing himself to

people by sticking his hand out and saying, "Hi, my name is Warren and I am free to express myself," which was a clear indication that he wasn't, and made him instantly likeable.

We tried out an exercise in our first workshop derived from the game Ram Dass had played with me that day we met. Sitting in a circle, people were asked to complete the sentence aloud, "What I'm unwilling to share is . . ." The exercise backfired, however, because of what I myself was unwilling to share, but did so anyway: that I still harbored thoughts about going back with my previous girlfriend. My current girlfriend was in the circle, and was famous for her histrionics and dramatic public displays of anger. By the time we came to some resolution and she had calmed down, it was nearly 4:00 A.M., and one of the workshop participants said, "I paid to take a workshop, not to attend the Sobel Institute of Family Therapy."

I eventually learned that, despite Ram Dass's theory that revealing secrets brings people together, in certain situations, when there is something that one is unwilling to share, it is best interpreted as a Divine Message to keep one's mouth shut.

At the beginning of our workshop we asked people to say what they hoped they would get out of it: people usually said things you'd expect, like "to be more expressive." Or "to be free of fear." One man said he wanted "to learn Russian and grow a new set of teeth." He died a few years later, at 43, of liver cancer. His last words, I was told, were simply "*do svidanja*" (goodbye).

The Joy of Self-Expression used the arts as a primary tool for opening people to the depths and edges of their own creativity. We had the participants bring their sleeping bags and hole up together in a fairly small space from Friday evening until the wee hours of Monday morning, getting them dancing, singing, painting, writing, speaking in gibberish, talking about their sexuality, performing "Five Little Ducks," and, of course, saying the word "doody." All in a context of "social silence," meaning that apart from when an exercise invited speech, nobody spoke the entire time. Mostly I instituted the silence so that I wouldn't have to talk to anyone. Nevertheless, this combination of going inward in a monastic-like silence, and outward in outrageous and daring creative expression produced a remarkable, transformational effect resulting in a tangible, collective altered state by the end in which people were generally glowing, joyful, and in an ecstatic mood not unlike some of the "workshop highs" we ourselves had experienced in *est* and Actualizations. When Warren and I brought the workshop to Esalen Institute several years later it became one of the most popular weekends offered there for a while.

We had stumbled onto a technology of generating peak experiences for people, and it was naturally a big hit. What made it a peak experience was the utter sense of safety that would allow people to drop their social personae, usually fueled unconsciously by fear, and allow their natural expression of love and wholeness to emerge and be expressed, the arts merely being the vehicle. It was actually a very ordinary phenomenon: love becomes obvious and present when fear, judgment, and separation are dropped.

Our workshops generated a safe enough atmosphere for people to risk creative expressions that they'd never dared before. But they also put people in situations that terrified most of them, such as standing in front of a group of strangers and singing alone. And in order to be in a position to ask people to move through their terror, I had to confront my own, again and again. This usually occurred the week or so leading up to a workshop, which I would spend in states of abject fear to the point of feeling like I was going to throw up or die. It was impossible for anyone to be around me at those times. Eventually I decided I needed to find something to do that didn't scare me to death, despite all the New Age talk about "feel your fear and do it anyway." I felt my fear and did it anyway for about 15 years, on and off, and after running some 50 or more successful workshops, it never got any easier, so I eventually stopped. And ultimately, the truth is that ecstatic highs are not really worth a whole lot, with one major exception: the very first time it happens, it blows your mind and opens you to an alternate reality, revealing another way of being in life that is to ordinary living what Technicolor is to black and white. To taste this great possibility only once, through whatever means, is sufficient to launch one onto a path that then requires enormous effort, discipline, and commitment in order to cultivate that new realm of experience and have it gradually become not a one-time high, but a way of life. Some of us—including me—unfortunately, become more addicted to the rush of "peak experiences" rather than to the work they implicitly demand and set in motion. As Alan Watts put it, speaking of drug highs in this case: "Psychedelic experience is only a glimpse of genuine mystical insight, but a glimpse which can be matured and deepened by the various ways of meditation in which drugs are no longer necessary or useful. When you get the message, hang up the phone. For psychedelic drugs are simply instruments, like microscopes, telescopes, and telephones. The biologist does not sit with eyes permanently glued to the microscope; he goes away and works on what he has seen."

And ultimately, most workshops, including mine, were similar to a drug experience in that they provided an extraordinary and ecstatic, but temporary, high, and people usually went back to being the way they always were the next day or week. Or month. (Although, as temporary mind states go, an extraordinary and ecstatic high is definitely one of the best.) But if you've been through that roller-coaster ride hundreds of times, as I have, you gradually stop expecting yourself to ever really change permanently into that idealized self who is constantly living in the depth, fullness, and aliveness of the Self at its very best: wide open, joyful, full of love for everyone and everything.

A currently popular teacher named Adyashanti has said about his own intense spiritual search that no matter what profoundly altered mind states he experienced, he eventually came to realize that his consciousness always seemed to return to "this," just the ordinary present moment. The mind is inherently stubborn about change, and seems to snap back to its original position like an elastic band. But there's a catch: when we truly comprehend in our guts the finality and truth that This truly is It, right now, *no matter how our life is,* then we grasp what Werner Erhard was always screaming about: that no magic pill or workshop or experience of *any* sort is *ever* going to come along and finally "fix" you or me or make us permanently happy, and in that very moment of giving up the search for transformation, a transformation paradoxically does in fact occur. One recognizes that one was never broken in the first place, and suddenly all the energy previously devoted to seeking a way out of or through the problem of the unfulfilled self is freed up to power one's mission and vision, which is a gesture of giving and contribution rather than one of searching, waiting, and hoping. And that's a good thing, if a bit sobering, because it means we are asked to step up to the plate in life with what and who we already are. We have been given our piece in the game, and it only remains to play wholeheartedly.

But there's another catch: even *that* recognition doesn't necessarily last. There may seem to be a genuine letting go of the great search and a consequent waking up to the present power and beauty of one's actual true nature, but the next day might feel different, and one's inner seeker gets kicked back into action, looking for where the magic went. Presumably true enlightenment wakes us up from this endless cycle of seeking experiences, seeing clearly that *all* experiences, both miserable and blissful, are temporary. They arise and pass away, as the Buddhists would put it. So the seeker thus informed would be well advised to immediately cease looking for enlightenment within the realm of any experience that comes and goes, which pretty much rules out everything!

I can say no more . . . because if I truly look honestly at my own spiritual path historically, every experience I've ever had that felt like "it" has in fact passed, so by definition wasn't really it. That's why I didn't promise to change your life at the beginning of this book. I'm still addicted to changing my own. They should file this book far away from "Self-Help" in the bookstores, in a section called "No Help Whatsoever."

And yet, those moments when it *has* felt like I was truly living from the part of me that does "get it," the place from which I was looking at life was somehow prior to, and the witness of, the perpetual flow of my personal experiences through time, whether positive or negative. But even that wise, transcendental, partially enlightened persona within me seems to dematerialize daily as my mind churns up the dramatic events of my ongoing story and before you know it, I'm back in the fray.

As the 99th Monkey, committed to seeking rather than finding, it is very difficult to confront letting go of wanting some big or miraculous change to occur in my essential make-up. Yet after all the things I have done to grow, change, and improve myself over the years, I must confess that I still feel pretty much like the same person I was when I was about four years old. And there seems to be little reason to believe that this same me won't continue to persist into the future. I have a feeling I'm stuck with myself, in sickness and in health, now and forevermore.

Because the 99th Monkey *is* the ego, which is the seeker, thinking or pretending that it wants enlightenment, but actually programmed and completely committed to *avoiding* enlightenment at all costs, because its own survival is at stake in the matter. Oscar Wilde said that if God wanted to punish people He would answer their prayers, and it is true that the worst thing that can ever happen to a spiritual seeker is to find what he or she is looking for, because the "I" that is looking must give way to the "I" that has found, and those two are mutually exclusive. From the seeker's point of view, it is perceived as self-annihilation, and who in their right mind wants that?

In actual fact, however, "ego death" is not necessarily the dramatic or fearful spiritual event it's cracked up to be. We go through mini ego deaths all the time, and they are actually fun and liberating. Anyone who skis, for example, knows that in the actual moment of maneuvering a speedy and difficult spot, all of one's attention must be focused and present, leaving no room for the ordinary ruminations of the "I." That is an ego death. It is thrilling, but there is nobody there to say "I am thrilled"; there is only the raw, visceral experience of moving downhill through a splash of white in the wind. Almost any activity of sufficient concentration can produce such moments again and again, from playing a musical instrument to crocheting. The Dalai Lama's book, *A Flash of Lightning in the Dark of Night*, refers to a similar phenomenon: in the sudden glimpsing of a flash of lightning, or a shooting star, one's mind stops and only a direct, naked awareness remains, unfiltered by the ego. For a moment, we encounter life directly. Or anytime we are in a battle of wills with our spouse or lover and we are able to simply drop the need to win and be right, that simple gesture is a form of ego death. Sufi teacher E.J. Gold goes as far as to say that we actually have hundreds of such moments of awakening every day, but we fail to notice or appreciate them. Most of us prefer our enlightenment to be more special and dramatic, with, if not a choir of angels, then at the very least a little white light. Something, anything, besides simply *this*. And *this* is where God lives, with or without special effects.

Chapter 9

Gabrielle Roth, Esalen & Big Sur

I met Gabrielle Roth in 1980 and the whole texture of my spiritual/ seeking life shifted to another dimension. I heard her speak at the East-West Center in New York and she blew me away. No speaker in the ordinary sense, her body slinked and slithered across the stage as she spoke, communicating a freedom of soul and expression that cut through the room and landed right where I was sitting. Her words were a spontaneously choreographed prose poem that I found completely seductive and irresistible; I was being drawn, I now realize, to my next teacher.

Gabrielle was—is—an urban shaman and dancer, a hip, beat artist-spirit who went through her own intense spiritual search and experienced firsthand much of what the '60s and later the Human Potential Movement had to offer. Tired of all the head games and pseudo-enlightenments she saw around her, she was determined to get people back inside their bodies, to dance their way back to the "still point" in the "moving center" of their essential being.

She described most people as "nice, normal, neutral neurotics," suffering from "trizophrenia"—thinking one thing, feeling another, and doing a third. Her method was to catalyze a process in people through movement and dance that ultimately would en-

able them to be restored to their wholeness and authenticity, so that
body, heart, mind, soul, and spirit would again move and act as one
undivided Being. But it is always the person behind the method that
breathes life into any form of creative or transformational work,
and simply being around Gabrielle seemed to spontaneously stir
the sleepy psyche, as if taunted to come awake to meet this elusive,
sleek figure dancing on the periphery of consciousness, beckoning
one inward to unravel the soul on a rhythmic path toward silence
and stillness. Through her lithe and catlike movements and poetic,
street-wise speech, she seduced lethargic souls out of their inertia
onto life's dance floor, teaching us to "pray the body," and to *Sweat
Your Prayers*, as one of her book titles proclaimed.

Over the course of the next 15 years, I would take many,
many workshops with Gabrielle in New York and at Esalen Institute in Big Sur, California, along with hundreds of others, men and
women of all ages and shapes, all of us gyrating, writhing, shaking,
crawling, leaping, spinning, and cathartically letting ourselves go
deeply and freely into our own true dance, into raw, primal movement and sound, beyond all self-consciousness. Quoting Bhagwan
Rajneesh, she summed up her teaching in one phrase: "Dance until the dancer disappears and only the dance remains." Meaning,
move past the personality and all its self-conscious hesitations
and concerns, shake free of the ego's constraints on one's way of
being and moving through life, dance through and beyond the self,
so that there is only the unfiltered, unconditioned, spontaneous
moment of movement itself.

Gabrielle generated an atmosphere of "soul-permission,"
which allowed one to do just that, to disappear into the dance and
tap into a deep and personal sense of the primordial rhythms of
one's essential Being, and of life itself. And unlike high school,
everybody had a spot on the dance floor: old, young, overweight,
slim, stiff, loose, awkward, fluid. On a sheer physical level, Ga-

brielle worked us harder than any gym teacher or coach—one's commitment to healing was practically measured in buckets of sweat and physical exhaustion, along with extraordinary endorphine highs, emotional release, and explosions of creativity. For those who had spent way too long on the meditation cushion or in the therapist's office, this was a real, down-to-earth, *embodied* transformation that included the heart and mind but was ultimately rooted in the beat and the feet.

I became part of Gabrielle's closer circle for a few years; we were known as The Mirrors Ritual Theatre and Dance Troupe, and for a while we performed nearly every Saturday night in New York's Soho district. What made it "ritual theater" was that we performed our own lives.

None of us were professional actors. We had each approached Gabrielle as spiritual seekers, little knowing that her way of working with us would be to regularly place us onstage in front of up to 1,500 strangers! One of her methods of helping people recognize and detach from their ego was to expose it and express it in theater. So if in my normal life I had a tendency to be depressed, in the theater I became Danny D. Presso, starring in his own depressing drama, and leaving me out of it. Instead of my usual strategy of trying to rid myself of depression, which gave it power and reality, I learned to stand back as "The Holy Actor" and simply witness and dramatize my depression as merely one of my ego's possible scripts, along with Sam Special, Larry Look-at-me, Bitter Bob, and dozens more. Each of us revealed our psyche's assortment of dysfunctional characters in such a way that both the audience and us were able to view them from a place of detachment, poignancy, and humor. Connie Cling literally climbed up my body and I couldn't shake her

off. Everyone avoided Judy Judge with her hypercritical tongue.
Gladys Gorge ate a box of cookies on stage in about 12 seconds flat,
and Captain Control attempted to rule over the whole show, ordering us all about onstage. Gabrielle herself sang a solo:

> *I've given this body*
> *to men I wouldn't even*
> *lend my car to.*

Think of your own worst problem in life, and then imagine
that you suddenly are expected to appear in front of an audience in a
few days and make them look with interest—or laughter—at the very
issue that is most disturbing you. That is essentially the process we
went through every week in preparing our shows. We looked into
the truths of our relationships, careers, spiritual paths, fears, and
sexualities, and turned the whole ugly mess into theater. And were
transformed in the process.

Along with the ensemble work, I also wound up doing
stand-up comedy in the show, usually about my sex life:

"They say you have to love yourself first before you can love
another. So I tried. But I couldn't make a commitment—I needed to
have an open relationship with myself so that if it didn't work out
I'd be free to see other people."

"I sometimes say to a new partner, 'Do you want to have
sex? I'm terrible in bed.' And they say, 'So why would I want to have
sex with you?' And I say, 'I said *I'm* terrible in bed. Maybe you're
really good in bed. I certainly won't get in your way."

"I'm so paranoid of getting herpes or AIDS that my idea of
safe sex is for my partner and I to be in separate rooms, each of us
wearing an armor-plated full body suit, and then the magnetic pull
makes you both slam into the wall."

"Most women don't know how to touch a man. Men have
been trained in the intricate details of how to keep one finger

on the G-spot while rotating the clitoris counterclockwise, but my experience is that women tend to grab on to my sexual organ for dear life, like it's a gear shift, and anything over first hurts like hell. Some women like to peal out: FIRST SECOND THIRD FOURTH VROOOOOOOM. I'm screaming and she thinks I'm having a good time."

"I've never been very good with this whole giving and receiving thing, and who's supposed to be doing what to whom and when. I need to take turns having sex so that my responsibilities are absolutely spelled out, so I'm clear what's expected of me and what it's going to take to get the job done."

And finally, once I said to an audience: "The worst thing in the world for a guy to hear from a woman is, 'Let's just be friends.' Just once I'd like a woman to come up to me and say, 'Let's just be lovers. I don't really have the energy for a relationship right now.' It's never happened."

And then it happened, that same night. A woman approached me after the show and said, "Let's just be lovers." I made a date to see her, and when I went to her apartment, I discovered that she collected the Sunday *New York Times*, and all the rooms were piled floor to ceiling with years and years worth of newspapers. She then said to me, "If I ever get around to reading them, I would definitely start with all the Section Twos.'"

For whatever reason, I was not erotically charged by this information, and we proceeded to spend an awkward hour together before mutually concluding that this was a very terrible idea, and I went home.

Perhaps the best part of hanging out in Gabrielle's scene was that all the women wore these great outfits—tight leotards, brightly colored leg warmers, skimpy Balinese tops and sarongs, lots of purples and blacks—and dancing with them in that setting was, as Gabrielle herself put it, the closest thing to safe sex you could find that had no complications or strings attached. There was a highly charged sexual energy in Gabrielle's workshops, but it was contained and expressed in the dance. Sexual energy is life energy, and when the body is reawakened and turned on, it is no longer a private matter. Aliveness is not a tickle in the groin but a full-bodied, embracing Yes to embodiment itself.

And yet the social stuff was there too: I noticed that when a young, attractive woman was my dance partner, I turned up all the juice and exertion and did my best to match her pulsating, limitless energy, as if it were true of me as well. Then Gabrielle would thankfully call "switch" and I would make sure to choose an older, overweight man or woman as my next partner so I could catch my breath, clutch the stitch in my side, and dance the way an out-of-shape guy truly felt.

And that was more to the point: if you were sad and sluggish, the instructions were to dance sadly and sluggishly, but to dance. It was the physical expression of the Zen notion of being angry when angry, tired when tired. When you begin exactly where you are and start to move through the five fundamental rhythms that form the essential movement practice of Gabrielle's work, the dance takes you out of yourself, into a land of fluidity and mystery, and often extreme states of joy, sorrow, chaos, anger, fear, exhilaration, inspiration, and, ultimately, a sweet silence and stillness.

Some of the women in the troupe occasionally danced in topless bars to earn their living. I went to see them perform, and sat at the bar along with all the other men, feeling superior. Because I was in a peer relationship with the dancers, and I was only there to visit and support my friends, whereas the rest of those guys were just your average horny sleazebags off the street, just coming to gawk. The truth, however, was that I was both a personal friend of the dancers *and* a horny sleazebag.

Gawk city.

A significant part of Gabrielle's development as a teacher occurred at Esalen Institute, and it was she who first lured me out there. Taking me from my New York City life to Esalen in Big Sur in 1985 was like a New Age Fresh Air Fund, a spiritual Head Start program. I never returned to live in New York.

I was seeing a therapist at that time, and she shocked me one day by informing me that in her estimation I was a drug addict. I reeled with that notion for some time. It was very confusing because I was acquainted with a whole class of countercultural friends—and teachers!—for whom marijuana was either a holy sacrament or else a nonessential but pleasurable social event, much like a glass of wine with dinner. Rather than deal head on with my therapist's "accusation," I chose to move to Big Sur, California, where I knew that people who *didn't* smoke grass and do other drugs were considered to be an aberration.

Esalen Institute was formed in the '60s by Michael Murphy and Richard Price on an exquisite site right on the edge of the Big Sur cliffs, beneath a towering mountain range. The spot had been sacred to the Esselen Indians for thousands of years, due in part to the natural hot springs that bubble forth on the land, believed to have healing properties. Esalen was one of the first "growth centers" of its kind, where such notable figures as Fritz Perls, Abraham Maslow, Alan Watts, Aldous Huxley, and many other luminaries and radical thinkers came in the early days to share their breakthroughs and ideas. It was also among the first places to explore encounter groups, Gestalt Therapy, and numerous other therapeutic modalities, including massage, Rolfing, and other forms of bodywork.

Esalen continues to flourish today, and is still known for its glorious, natural hot springs, contained in stone tubs perched right atop a steep cliff overlooking the crashing Pacific, and beneath the towering mountains of Big Sur. Contrary to popular belief, these are not the site of wild sex orgies, but rather, depending on the time of day and who you are with, either a place of quiet, meditative reflection or a place for social conversation. I'm sure there have been many sexual exceptions over the years, particularly in the wee hours of the night (the only time the public was allowed in to use the baths), but I never witnessed or experienced anything like that over the course of many years.

Nothing was more exquisite than to sit in the Esalen tubs, alone or with a loved one, under the extraordinary expanse of the Big Sur starry night, listening to the waves crash about 100 feet below. If you hadn't found God in church, you had a pretty good shot at Divine Revelation right there in that magical spot, with the sparkly, infinite, black-beglittered sky, the salt-spray smell and sounds of ocean and otter, the looming, awesome presence of the ancient mountains towering above, and the natural hot sulphur spring water caressing your body as it bubbled forth from within the old Indian earth. With the proper attitude, to be there was itself a healing prayer without words.

And nothing was more annoying than to share such a moment with a group of newcomers to Esalen, attending some workshop or other, who disturbed the tranquility with the most inane conversations imaginable, covering every wacky New Age subject you could think of:

"I'm feeling the photon shift in my root chakra; I need some deep tissue and regression work."

And, given the many foreigners who came to Esalen, it was often in an accent:

"Vee vent on a shamanic journey and I saw zee earth moving out of zee house of Pisces."

Once in a while, you'd get a group singing "Amazing Grace," which was a little better. I myself was once the annoying party: I was sharing a tub with my friend Daniel, a therapist, and I was remarking on how malleable and willing everyone who participated in Esalen workshops were—you could ask them to do anything and they'd jump right in. So Daniel and I thought we could promote a new healing approach, to be called Chicken Therapy, in which people would be asked to flap their arms and squawk like chickens, and we even developed a theoretical underpinning for the practice, in terms of how the flapping stimulated certain acupuncture meridians, and the clucking used the vocal cords to transmute the energy, or something along those lines. Then, as we practiced flapping and squawking a few times right then and there, several people approached us from a neighboring tub and earnestly inquired, "Which workshop are you guys in? We would like to sign up." So we had our first converts to the chicken cult. And I have no doubt that had we pursued the idea and actually run such a workshop, not only would it have been well attended, but people would have reported receiving amazing benefits from it. You get what you pay for.

But the best part about Esalen Institute from my point of view as a 33-year-old single male preoccupied with mating, was that you got to see everyone naked in the hot tubs every day. If there was someone you were interested in, you could see their body *before* the first date, instead of soon after, and thus avoid a lot of potential disappointment. Call me superficial. Or call me a man. Or really, call me a child. Having grown up in a naked-free environment, the nudity at Esalen was an incredible novelty at first, and those first few days I gaped in innocent wonder at the incredible variety of shapes and sizes of male and female body parts.

But then, miraculously, in a very short time, just as career nudists will tell you, people's naked bodies literally became completely irrelevant . . . except sometimes.

I worked on the farm at Esalen, and as my friend Sarah stood next to me in the muddy potato beds, stark naked except for her rubber work boots, I remember thinking how exciting this scene would look to me if I saw it in a magazine or film. But I remember recognizing that I had to perform those sorts of mental gymnastics in order to eroticize what was otherwise, in fact, just my friend Sarah in her work boots. (Okay, true, but maybe it wasn't quite as banal as that: I found farming with naked women infinitely more interesting than farming without them.)

But again and again I discovered that when the fantasies of my inner teenager became realities, they tended to be disappointing. Because adolescent male fantasy—the only kind there is, as far as I can tell—is largely a story in one's head. Without the necessary narration, the actual facts of the matter are neutral. For example, as Stan Dale sadly revealed in his sex workshops, which I will talk about later, the sexual allure of a "tit" is transformed into a merely functional "sack of fat" when the erotic mental overview is removed. So while I could imagine writing my friends back home about being in a hot tub with five naked women, the actual experience had nothing inherently sexual or exciting about it whatsoever.

For my birthday one year, Gabrielle arranged for five gorgeous young women to simultaneously give me a full-body massage. I would have killed for such an event when I was 16, but what I discovered in actuality was that it was not nearly as relaxing and pleasurable as getting a massage from one person. So the sexual freedom that outsiders might imagine goes on at Esalen, was for me a simple normalizing of the naked human body, a growing up.

❋   ❂   ❀

Esalen was also the place to build an authentic life. To the friends that I had left behind in New York City I appeared to be a great adventurer when I wandered out west without a long-term plan, whereas I soon found out that my story was no big deal out there. As a "work scholar" I was part of a group that met every night, and on the first evening I learned that nearly everyone there had just ended a marriage, left a career, or sold all their possessions. I was surrounded by people in "free fall" who had closed the door on their previous existence and come to Esalen en route to the unknown next chapter of their lives.

The uncertainty of "not knowing" can be nerve-wracking and anxiety-producing, but it can also be very exciting, particularly in contrast with the more predictable lives we had all left behind. Having no fixed future in mind left all possibilities open, and the atmosphere at Esalen was tangibly permeated by that energy of great "human potential." Conversations were charged with the sharing of new discoveries and insights into oneself and wild conjectures about the nature of Being and Reality. The relationships I formed at Esalen, based as they were on more genuine and naked self-revelation, would become the basis for a new circle of close friends that remains with me today, over 20 years later.

Night after night, after our days on the farm, chopping vegetables in the kitchen, or working behind the front desk, we work scholars would flop ourselves down in a circle on oversized floor cushions, and with the guidance of a leader, do "the work" of uncovering our authenticity, expressing our essential selves, and putting our lives together from a new center of gravity. We were learning to be real, and to make choices that were in alignment with who we wanted to be. There were lots of tears and fears, confrontations and confessions, angry outbursts and sobbing breakdowns. Group hugs and laying on of healing hands, experienced for the first time, were powerful events of merging with others, out of the isolation most of us hid within much of the time. This was before such events would become a clichéd parody of themselves.

We were also taught to own our projections on people, and as a way of practicing, it was suggested that we alter our way of speaking (at least in group sessions) so that, for example, instead of saying to someone, "You seem insecure," we were encouraged to say, "In your presence I become aware of my own insecurity." However, this technique would invariably devolve to the point where it became simply a thinly disguised and therapeutically correct way of telling someone what you really thought of them, as in: "In your presence I experience the arrogant, self-centered, and tiresome pompous jerk within me."

All sorts of people turned up at Esalen. One night I was walking through the main lodge at dinnertime, and through the crowd I happened to catch the eyes of an extraordinarily attractive woman with bright eyes, golden hair, and a big smile that was directed right at me from across the room and literally pulled me over to her table. Before I could even say hello, she said, "I know you think you just caught the eyes of a beautiful, strange woman and you came over here to check it out and maybe flirt a bit but I want you to know that first of all, I just got married, and secondly, you have only one chance with me, and that's to be my brother and friend, and if you don't take that chance you're a complete idiot."

You'd think that would be my setup for an interesting story to follow. Actually, it isn't. That *was* the interesting story.

One night a trance medium from Brazil named Luis Gasparito offered a demonstration of his talents. As I watched from a few feet away, Luis, in a frenzy of activity, rapidly picked up paints in both hands, and simultaneously worked on two channeled works of art, moving incredibly fast, eyes closed or open and wild, staring up at the ceiling, paints applied blindly in a mad chaotic fever, until in a matter of moments it was done. Before him, *upside-down*, were two paintings: a Renoir and a Modigliani. Unmistakable styles, and clearly impossible to achieve through any rational explanation.

It only takes one experience of this sort to force one to acknowledge the existence of other dimensions of reality and possibility. Yet the unique karmic disposition of the 99th Monkey is basically to believe everything, while continuing to behave as if none of it is true.

I observed a healer once working on a girlfriend, claiming she was raising the astral antennae on my girlfriend's head so that she could once again be in communication with her home planet. When it was my turn, she removed a bunch of incorporeal snakes from my abdomen, which she handed to an assistant to carry outside, and then she asked everyone to step back so that the Mother Ship that was hovering just overhead in a different dimension could beam information into my brain. You'd be astounded at the number of people who don't think this is funny, how many otherwise sane people believe the most amazing things. In Taos, New Mexico, the local residents complain of a humming sound. A friend informed me that it emanates from an alien society inhabiting the interior of the nearby mountain, where the headquarters are situated. She said they send out agents who install chips—psychic implants—in humans for monitoring purposes. When such *National Enquirer*-ish stuff was starting to come to me in my daily life, it occurred to me that I had definitely wandered off the main road in my quest for deeper meaning.

I went through a "rage process" at an Esalen workshop in which we were encouraged to push through all our resistance to a complete, visceral, and loud expression of total, furious anger. I blacked out. And as someone who has done not only that rage process, but also spent a year and a half in Primal Therapy screaming my head off; beat the stuffing out of countless pillows over the years in one therapeutic encounter or another; danced out my anger with Gabrielle; hit people and tables with "battacas" (a harmless spongy bat designed for such a purpose); had a very large, overweight woman therapist at Esalen literally *sit* on me for a very long time in order for me to re-experience being smothered by my mother; had eight adult men lie on top of me, holding me down, not to mention the three oversized maniacs at Chareeva ripping my shirt off and playing ping-pong with my body, all in the name of "getting your anger out"—I can now report, with confidence: it doesn't work. You can't get rid of anger through "release work." You can temporarily release some energy and lose your voice and perhaps pull a muscle, but the anger remains.

Suppressing it doesn't work either.

Maybe we should take a hint from the Dalai Lama, whose audiotape I have: "Transforming Anger Through Patience." Of course he also mentions in passing that even a single moment of anger can literally destroy all the good karma accumulated from a lifetime of good works. If that's not enough to piss you off, I don't know what is.

I somehow managed to break into Esalen as a workshop leader, through a few fortuitous connections with staff people there, particularly John Soper, who turned over to me the leadership of one of his weekend intensives as a pure act of intuitive faith, since he barely knew me at the time. John was a fascinating man, and years later, when I discovered he was quite a talented sculptor, I asked him, "John, how is it that you've been through about three or four of my creativity workshops and I never learned you were a sculptor?" He replied, "Well, I realized that to do a sculpture the way I liked required me to be alone in a room for hours and hours, and I'd rather be with people, so I gave it up." Later I learned he was also a gifted palm reader, but he said, "I discovered that if I read one person's palm at a party, everyone would want theirs read as well, and I'd end up sitting in the corner reading palms and miss the party. I'd rather be at the party, so I gave it up." He had become what I would later call "an Artist of Being."

I once asked John to help me with a month-long group I was leading that had turned against me. So John came in and said "Everyone who is *for* Elliot stand together over here. If you're against him, stand over there. If you feel neutral toward him, sit here in the middle. And you can change positions at any time." I watched in amazement during the course of the evening as people self-righteously stomped across the floor and switched their allegiance over and over, until nearly everyone had been in all three positions. It was one of the most powerful lessons I had ever received as a group leader: that very little of what the people in a group are feeling about me has anything whatsoever to do with me.

Being in a leadership position brought out a very powerful aspect of myself that did not tend to make an appearance in my day-to-day life. This split would haunt me for years—even now—but back then I believed that if I could only get the part of me that ran workshops to run my life I'd be cured. Now I see that is just how it is: certain situations of service call forth from within us an expression of our fundamental wholeness and love in a way that is tangible and healing for ourselves and others . . . and other situations don't. I was always browbeating myself into believing that each and every moment should be the situation calling forth my highest Self, but it never worked. Full Aliveness has always been a part-time job for me. The point remains, however, that most of us are quite able to rise to the occasion when the very best of ourselves is required.

I had always assumed that the "real" teachers were walking their talk all the time, living in their power from moment to moment and not just turning it on for a weekend. And I'm certain there are those for whom that is more the case. But I needed to make peace with the fact that at one moment I might be at Esalen, sitting in a circle of people around a candle, leading them in a Native American chant, playing conga drums, guiding them through a series of cathartic and powerful exercises, and the next minute, when the event was over, I'd be retiring to my pal Marty's room where we'd get into our pajamas, smoke some dope and watch Abbott and Costello reruns.

Yannawanna ho.

The other powerful lesson John Soper offered me was the time I ate one too many marijuana brownies at a party and wound up hugging the toilet bowl, puking my guts out. When I saw him come into the bathroom out of the corner of my eye, I felt hopeful, thinking he would offer me some comfort or nurturing. Instead, he propped up a mirror against the bathtub opposite me so that I could observe myself puking more clearly, and left me to it. You gotta love a guy like that.

Sadly, John passed away quite suddenly several years ago, at the age of 67. Several days prior to his death, he seemed completely healthy and successfully ran the notoriously difficult Big Sur marathon. A day or two later he was diagnosed with leukemia, and a day or so after that he had a stroke and died. *Thank you for everything John, wherever you are.*

In 1985, there was a catastrophic fire in Big Sur. Esalen was evacuated at five in the morning. I remained behind to help. I got to wear goggles, carry a hose, and say things into a walkie-talkie like: "We have smoke coming up from Burns Creek, do you read me?

Over." We witnessed an entire mountain range going up in flames, giant redwoods exploding, airplanes dropping chemicals on homes, and the sky an unearthly orange for days. Many of us inhaled the fumes of burning poison oak, creating a sense of wanting to turn your body inside out and scratch yourself to death. Miraculously, the fire never jumped across Highway 1 to Esalen.

One day my friend Charles and I, feeling like men, took our axes and climbed down into a steep ravine and spent six or seven hours sweating and vigorously attempting to put out all the smoldering embers, the remains of burnt redwoods. We felt noble, doing our part for the team. We later learned there was no need to do any of that—that there were miles and miles of such embers and they would all die out of their own accord.

In the middle of all this, I was fired from my position at Gazebo, the Esalen preschool, because while I should have been helping to evacuate the children, I was instead helping an Esalen staff person evacuate her record collection. In my defense, I should note that her collection included an original mono recording of the Broadway musical, *The Most Happy Fella*.

❀   ❀   ❀

To live in Big Sur was to truly live on the edge—of the cliff, of emotions and consciousness, of life and death. In my two or three years there, I was personally acquainted with no less than eight people who fell over the edge into the next world. That would be an average number for an elderly person whose friends are passing away, one at a time, from cancer, heart disease, and the rest. But it seemed like a lot to me: two of the eight were traffic fatalities, one was a suicide, one a drug overdose, and the other four were very unique deaths, unique to the edge that is Big Sur.

Dick Price, one of the founders of Esalen, and a well-loved resident therapist, one day took his daily afternoon walk into Hot Springs Canyon and never returned. When they found his body, it appeared that he may have been meditating when a rock, loosened by the fire, came tumbling down from above, hitting him on the head.

Wolfgang, a young German man who had taken my workshop and was temporarily living at Esalen as a work scholar, also went for a hike one day and never returned. His body was found three weeks later in a ravine, with a broken leg.

Steve, the guy who drove down the coast every day to deliver newspapers to Big Sur, one day drove right over the cliff and plummeted to his death.

(And, less tragically, my friend Lois left her brand-new car in neutral while running back into her house for a minute, and returned to find that her car, too, had taken the leap.)

And finally, my friend Lynn, who I worked with as a front desk clerk at Ventana Inn, went for a walk along the beach one morning with her sister and two dogs. A wave washed them all away.

So you learned to watch your step in Big Sur. And the road. The workshops at Esalen created a sense of that same edginess, only it was those places in oneself that one usually shied away from, those inner cliffs of consciousness that one hoped to leap across and arrive unharmed on the other side, in a new land of possibility and vision.

After getting fired, I wound up living down the road from Esalen in a rustic Big Sur cabin overlooking the crashing surf, laughing to myself at how every day at Ventana Inn, where I worked, people paid up to $400 a night to have an "ocean view," which meant you could see the ocean in the far distance if you stood outside your room and squinted through binoculars. And meanwhile, I lay in my glorious bed in the cabin with a window through which I could hear, contemplate, and gaze upon the wondrous and mad Pacific Ocean, almost as if should an unexpectedly large wave slap down against the cliff, the spray would splash my window. And I paid $150 a month for this, provided I took on the daily chore of shoveling horse manure from the stables into buckets and then distributing it in the flowerbeds.

One of the most remarkable things I discovered living in Big Sur was my astounding ability to sometimes fail to notice the ocean. I did all my shopping an hour north in Carmel, and the ride home via coastal Highway 1 is, I believe, one of the most incredible stretches of land in the U.S. Whenever I drove an out-of-town visitor down that same road, I'd have to pull over for scenic views and photo ops every few minutes. And yet there were days when I'd arrive back in Big Sur and suddenly realize that I hadn't seen the ocean that day. I had been lost in thought, an accurate way to describe it: the ocean, as well as who knows how many other sights, sounds, and experiences, had been *lost* to me that day, whilst I was *in thought*.

Doug Madsen, somewhat of a Big Sur legend and contemporary of Henry Miller's, was my eccentric artist-landlord. He was about 70, gay, and lived in the main house with his young lover J., who kept the place going. In addition to the half-dozen horses, there were goats, sheep, chickens, and peacocks. Doug kept his extensive grounds immaculately landscaped as a Zen expression of art-in-nature as it sloped downward toward the Big Sur cliffs, hidden from coastal Highway 1 above. He instructed me to remove individual leaves from the rock pathways that traversed between the seven or eight dwellings on his land, and had a tendency to scream at me if he discovered a single, random leaf on a path somewhere. He saw me as a potential disciple, a pathetic city kid he could whip

into country shape, teaching me the ways of the land. I would prove
to be a huge disappointment to him in that regard.

Shortly after I secured the cabin, I flew back East to retrieve
my car, and while I was gone I agreed to permit a young German
woman from Esalen to stay there, named Anya. When I returned to
move myself in, Anya refused to move out. Period. She had herself
all snuggled into a little alcove and wouldn't budge, wouldn't listen to reason. It was the most amazing phenomenon. My pleas of
"But this is MY house! I rented it!" fell on deaf ears. What I didn't
know at the time, which explained everything, was that while I was
gone she had become the secret lover of Doug's apparently bisexual
partner, and they were enjoying clandestine, literal rolls in the hay
every day, as if out of some turn-of-the-century period film.

Plus, I discovered Anya loved horses, goats, sheep, chickens, and peacocks, and was already well on her way to knowing how
to run the whole place. Given the situation, she knew that if anyone was going to have to leave, it was likely to be *me*. So we struck
a deal: she would shovel and distribute the horseshit as her half of
the rent, while gallivanting all over the property with her lover, and
I would be left alone in peace to dream my Kerouac dreams, be my
own romantic writer hero in the Big Sur cabin on the edge.

Meanwhile, I got involved briefly with another German
woman named M., but ended the relationship when she told me
one day, "I vould like to make little cuts in your body and taste
your blood." I declined. "You vill not feel the cuts, they vill be very
small." I had dinner with her years later and confessed that she had
scared me off with talk of making cuts in my body. She paused and
reflected, then said, "Yes, that vould still be possible."

Soon after, I was once again seeing Susan, a woman I had
fallen in love with at Esalen the previous year, whose name was not
really Susan. (We got together only after I climbed a tree at 2:00 A.M.
one night and failed to convince God to grant me the affections of a

different woman, named Jeanie, whose name wasn't really Jeanie. I later invited Jeanie to room with me at Esalen—coed roommates were common—and she was about to accept when a group leader pointed out what was obvious to everyone in the room except Jeanie: I was assuming that once she moved in with me she'd quickly discover my sheer wonderfulness and we'd wind up making love, as Woody Allen once put it, "in the manner of the flying Wallendas." But alas.)

Whenever Susan and I made love, at the very instant of our climactic moment, Doug Madsen had a bad habit of banging angrily at my door, screaming obscenities, and when I'd go to see what was up, I'd find him standing outside my door, naked except for work boots or sometimes a skimpy pink tutu, enraged that I had not cleared away a few small leaves that lay on the path to my house. Nine months of this was all I could take, and I reluctantly gave up the cabin.

I never quite knew if perhaps I had simply not recognized Doug as a crazy Zen lunatic artist with whom, had I surrendered, I could have learned whatever it is crazy Zen lunatic artists can teach you.

Or if he was just nuts.

Chapter 10

Sex

The exercise in which Warren and I asked people to say "doody" was part of a larger "Taboo Word" exercise, in which people said all sorts of things. I discovered that most women don't like any of the available words for their genitals. This was of course long before the liberating influence of the *Vagina Monologues*. Actually, I wish there was a male version of that show, because it occurs to me that I don't really have a comfortable way to address my private parts either. We're not even on a first name basis. But in 1987, I took a sexuality workshop in which both male and female genitalia were referred to as "the wee-wee."

Stan Dale was the leader, an overweight, 60-ish man whose claim to fame was having been one of the original voices of *The Shadow* on the radio. He was in relationships with Helen, his wife of many years, as well as a young woman half his age, and all three were present at the workshop and apparently congenial.

Many people there were experimenting with what they were calling "inclusive relationships," as distinct from both exclusive and open relationships. Inclusive relationships included everyone involved, whereas an open relationship invariably meant someone eventually got left out and hurt. (The problem that arose with inclusive relationships, however, is that eventually someone got left out and hurt.) I lived for a short time in a household that experimented with this idea: a husband and wife owned the house, and had separate bedrooms. The husband had a lover visit on the weekends, and my friend Steve and I took turns sleeping with the wife. The inclusive part involved hours and hours of "communication" and "sharing our feelings." If you think one relationship takes work, the amount of sheer maintenance required to keep that situation afloat was utterly exhausting, and after three months I not only quit that scene, but also officially went on relationship strike for several years.

Another idea Stan Dale was promulgating at the time was that "the event equals the event." Meaning, if you kissed someone, it merely meant that you kissed someone, and not necessarily that anything more was implied or promised. Similarly, if you had intercourse with someone, it didn't necessarily mean a relationship would result. Hint: next time you make love to someone, try saying "the event equals the event" and see how that works out. (Amazingly, however, I began to realize that there seemed to be a whole different tribe of people for whom this idea *did* seem to work. I had always been from the school where sharing a cup of coffee with someone more or less implied a lifelong commitment to fidelity, and if I had a cup of tea with someone else, I'd feel guilty of betrayal.)

In Stan's workshop, there was one point where he and his three co-leaders stood stark naked in front of the 70 participants, arms around each other, swaying side to side, singing a little children's song:

> *It's only a wee-wee so what's the big deal?*
> *It's only a wee-wee so what's all the fuss?*
> *It's only a wee-wee and everyone's got one . . .*

And I can't remember the last line.

In "About Sex," one of the follow-up 10-week seminars that *est* offered, they showed lots of fascinating films, which were designed to elicit a strong internal response and to dredge up old feelings and beliefs to examine and perhaps revise or discard. One film merely depicted a series of naked bodies, one after the other, men and women of all ages, shapes and sizes. Another showed a man masturbating, then a woman. Then two men making love, two women, and a man and woman. But the film that seemed to trigger the most response from both the men and women was a film of giant vaginas, close-up. Some of them were wet. Some had strings hanging out of them. What did many of the men report feeling? "Nauseated." And the women? "Angry." Put male nausea together with female anger and make a baby!

I don't believe that *Men Are from Mars, Women Are from Venus*. Given even the little I understand about people and sexuality, a more accurate title would be, *Men Are from Mars __and__ Venus, and So Are Women—So Good Luck!*

I received the following information from a medium recently, during a channeled reading:

"A very long time ago, when the Star Beings were first designing human beings, you were on the committee. A dispute developed as to the form humans should take: some insisted there ought to be two distinct genders. You were on the opposing side, pushing for one androgynous human being. Your team lost, and on some level you've been uncomfortable ever since with the division of male and female and anything having to do with sex."

Oh. That would explain a lot, I guess.

In Stan Dale's sexuality course, there was an exercise in which those women who were willing, lined up in front of the room, naked, spread their legs and opened themselves with a speculum, and invited the men in the room to go from one to the next, peering up inside each vaginal exhibit with a flashlight, like a sexual 4-H club. This was a very sobering experience. The mysterious and greatly coveted female cave into which men often devote their lives to gaining entry, was, in this setting, not at all unlike a nostril. Just an opening with soft tissue and fluids. Imagine. And it wasn't at all nauseating.

How would my life have turned out if I had been shown, as a teenager, that the female genitals were little more than an opening with soft tissue and fluids? Or if I had read then what Ramakrishna said to his male devotees: "This female breast that you are obsessed with is nothing more than fatty tissue, muscles, blood, mucous and other vile substances." Or even worse perhaps, was Stan's description of female breasts: "They're basically nothing more than sacks of fat." Try feeling erotic with that phrase running through your brain. I told Stan I appreciated his notion of demystifying sex, but could he possibly restore some of the mystery so I wasn't left with only nostrils and sacks of fat?

Dale offered a whole series of advanced level workshops, each one a weekend long. In each succeeding course the stakes were increased. In Level II, we were divided into groups of four, all naked, and were instructed to hold hands and remain physically connected as a group for several hours. We were two men and two women, and among other things that occurred during this exercise, the two women and I had the dubious privilege of standing naked in the bathroom together, witnessing our fourth group member having a bowel movement, a man who would go on to become a distinguished Harvard scholar. Later, we all showered together, after being reminded by Stan that "the shower is a great place to pee!" (Was I the only one with a silent "Echh!" response? Where is the line between being repressed about bodily functions and having a healthy privacy boundary that I would describe, say, as a BATH-ROOM DOOR! My early family training didn't really prepare me for this sort of thing.) And then we were guided in group massage, each of us taking a turn receiving from the other three. The instructions specifically included touching and kissing the genital region. So yes, I kissed a penis.

But the pièce de résistance: they introduced "The Tush Push" in Level IV. I described this exercise in graphic detail in the first draft of this book, but my brother insisted it was over the top. Suffice it to say, it was a partner exercise involving little rubber finger gloves and Vaseline, and sharing your feelings. I stopped attending the workshops after Level IV, which began to look like outtakes from *Debbie Does Workshops.* I later heard they were up to Level VIII. I just can't imagine what they came up with: The Double-Reverse Oral Sex Combination Special? Hold the lubrication.

But the bottom line is, I am a sexual casualty of a sexually damaged generation of men. My school chum Al Reinhardt mailed me my first torn-out pages from a pornographic magazine when I was 14. Real naked women! I think I threw it away when I was about 30.

In our sexually damaged culture, straight men all over the world, from Bangkok to Detroit, are inexorably drawn to three words, blasted in neon across the earth: "Live Naked Women." (Or its close relative, "Real Nude Girls.") When we were teenagers, that's *all* we cared about. As we've grown up and matured, many of us still have what is fundamentally a teenaged sexual sensibility with an overlay of whatever adult personality we have managed to come up with.

If an alien spacecraft were hovering nearby, the earth would appear as a sphere-like, rotating, Parisian bordello, with those three words flashing on and off all over it: "Live Naked Women." If the aliens in the spacecraft were randy teenaged boys, or men, surely one of them would say: "Let's go to *that* planet!"

One solution to all of the problems in this blessed universe would be to have all women be naked all of the time.

Although this would likely be a problem for the Taliban and other Islamic cultures, who came up with just the opposite idea: make all women be fully clothed and covered and concealed all the time, at the risk of death by stoning. I think naked would work better in the long run.

So there are many men out there who love their wives and families, but on a sexual level still yearn for Hot Naked Cheerleaders, now available any time of any day right at your own personal computer! Personal pornography pouring into your own home!

But I simply cannot begin to imagine who and where those millions and millions of girls are that can be found on the porno web sites and in magazines and movies: I know they're not anyone I know.

Although I *did* have a brush with Destiny, once, so to speak. Destiny was an exotic dancer in San Francisco whom I met at the sexuality workshop. She was a highly entertaining and bright woman whose card indicated she held an M.A. in psychology. I was intrigued by the combination, and we were laughing a lot together, which is always a good thing. So I asked her out and she told me to meet her at work.

This was a very different line of work than any woman I'd known. Destiny's job consisted of coming onto a stage as music played, doing a choreographed strip down to full nudity, then bringing out a long silver vibrator and moving it in and out of herself, with perhaps 40 men or so watching from a shabby, dark theater. (This was my *date.*) Other scantily clad women walked the aisles in the theater during Destiny's performance, and for a small fee would sit on the men's laps and gyrate their buttocks against their groins.

I was too shy to try that part—what would we talk about, I wondered?

I suppose "meet me at work" was considered good first date material in the exotic dancing crowd: "If a guy can't handle seeing me do what I do here, we've got nowhere to go."

As it turned out, we had nowhere to go. I just couldn't handle it. How would I introduce her to my parents? Unfortunately, I didn't realize this until we were back in her apartment, engaged in the preliminaries to sex. She was actually sitting on top of me naked when I had this epiphany, that perhaps we weren't right for each other. I backed off as politely as I could, and we never spoke again.

But that was some brush with Destiny.

It's only a wee-wee, so what's the big deal?
It's only a wee-wee so what's all the fuss?
It's only a wee-wee and everyone's got one
so . . .

What rhymes with "fuss"? Gus?

It's only a wee-wee and everyone's got one,
and the name of my wee-wee is Gus!

No, that wasn't it. I just can't remember that last line.

Woody Allen wrote a short story about the interior split many men experience between the women they love and the women they want.

In one story, he has a mad scientist put Tiffany Shmeederer's head on Olivia Something's body, but she's still not perfect.

If I was Kurt Vonnegut, I would create a subplot at this point about a group of alien men who come to Earth because they are attracted by all the neon signs flashing the message about all the naked women. They would land in all the major cities of the world, and head for the topless bars. The President would appear on national television during the alien invasion, and say: "It appears that the aliens want to see naked women. I am instituting a martial law, effective immediately, mandating all women be naked all the time until the aliens are satisfied and go home." Most of the human men would go off with the aliens in the end, partying and planet-hopping, looking for more naked women. The women on Earth would remain naked and all the little boys would grow up to be men who had no more interest in seeing naked women than in seeing the sky.

Esalen is sort of like that. I bet the children who grow up there don't go out of their way to see naked people.

I took another sexuality course in New York City once, called Men, Sex and Power. There were about 200 men in the room, and the basic message was that, contrary to the feminist-influenced thinking of the average, sensitive, New Age guy, what women truly want and need from their men is that we be real men. And what is a real man? According to the course, a real man behaves more or less like a gorilla, as in the following riddle:

How does an 800-pound gorilla make love to his mate?

The answer: Any way he wants to.

We were encouraged to start throwing our mates around more, and to "take" them, when we wanted, how we wanted. And the women they invited into the room at the end of the course to share with us and answer any questions the men had, confirmed that *was* what they really wanted.

The leader, Justin Sterling, informed us at the beginning

that we could set our own ground rules for the weekend. I watched in amazement as the majority of men voted to "Allow violence." The group did not want an artificially safe workshop environment, since men have to live in a world of fearful, competitive, and violent other men all the time. As a result of this decision, if someone was being a jerk during the course, he ran the risk of getting the shit kicked out of him by large groups of men. And as a result of this, I mainly kept my mouth shut for two days. The course ended with all 200 of us standing naked in a big circle, jumping up and down and grunting like gorillas, followed by a free-for-all naked wrestling match.

And I recently did one more men's sexuality weekend, some 20 years after the above account. I hated it, mostly because I hated seeing how pathetic we all seemed. My cynical 99th Monkey voice was very loud in my head: "We're just a bunch of middle-aged white guys with big bellies and lousy sex lives, sitting naked in a Lakota Sioux sweat lodge ceremony, praying to the spirits of the four directions, and calling each other 'brother.' And then eating tofu salad at lunch."

On the opening night we did a go-around, and it was very sad to hear everyone's stories: J. had been married 40 years but hadn't had sex with his wife for the last 10 and meanwhile was attending Sexaholics Anonymous to deal with his addiction to lust. S. had gotten divorced at age 41 after a 22-year marriage, thinking he'd enjoy playing the field again. Ten years later, at 51, he was still looking for the field, and spending most of his time on the Internet, looking at pornographic websites. R. had been married 14 years and had an eight-year-old son, and when asked if he loved his wife, said with deep resignation, "No, it's mostly obligation." He said he didn't like the monogamous rules of marriage. On and on and on.

When it was my turn I suggested that we file a class action suit against Hugh Hefner for wrecking our sex lives. They all knew what I meant. *Playboy* trained us to find our partners' bodies generally wanting, in comparison to the alluring, glossy, air-brushed photos of young, thin, often blonde nymphets with a staple in their belly that men have secretly masturbated to since age 13, give or take. And worse, *Playboy* trained women to find their own bodies unacceptable as well.

Really, I'm just jealous of Hef, and would drop the class action suit if he'd just invite me to one of those parties at the mansion with all those unbelievably sexy girls everywhere.

But suppose I just stood around at the party the way I usually do at parties, and never even got to meet any of the unbelievably sexy girls? Just my luck. Or worse, I *do* meet them, but they just see me as some pathetic, horny, middle-aged guy that reminds them of their Uncle Louie who comes to family gatherings wearing his pants way too high.

In the workshop, we stood on our "love pillow" to feel into who we are when we are feeling loving. I felt whole, happy, simple, and emanated a basically cheerful and friendly sort of demeanor. For most of us, our girlfriends and wives belonged with us on that pillow. Then we stepped over to our "lust pillow" to see what that felt like. I felt electrical currents of desire and longing course through my body, communicating "I want you" in every cell. On that pillow were various women I know who more closely resemble the young, skinny, sexy girls of *Playboy*. It felt like I had to choose between "I love you" and "I want you."

Naturally, we were told to put our pillows together and step on both at the same time. I have to say, in terms of healing that core sexual split in my psyche, the pillow trick was not all that effective.

A friend was recently bemoaning his lack of passion for his wife of eight years, and I said, "But at least you two had that initial passion for a year or two which lots of people say is important for couples to start out with, as a sort of bonding glue."

This is what he said to that: "No, you're in much better

shape without that. Because if you've had that in the past, then both of you are always comparing that to the present and it's incredibly depressing, the lack of passion is so obvious. You're in much better shape if you skip the middleman and go straight to the state of no passion."

"Still," I told him, "I think I would have liked that middleman."

When the 30 of us stood in a final circle, drumming, watching the co-leaders dance around holding antlers over their heads and a driftwood phallus, a closing song was requested. I jumped into "I'm a Man" by the Spencer Davis Group, playing air guitar:

> *I'm a maaaaan,*
> *yes I am*
> *and I can't*
> *help but love you so*

My conclusions after all these sexuality and men's workshops? Apart from my father and possibly the Dalai Lama, I don't think I've ever met a man that isn't on some level basically a pervert. It's just that some of us can fake normal, mature adulthood around women better than others.

Over the years, I have had a lot of people ask me if I'm gay, and several who simply assumed it and didn't bother asking. When the question came from several women I was casually dating, I got nervous, although I also wondered if perhaps that was the only way they could explain to themselves my lack of sexual interest. I also wondered if maybe it was due to the flamboyant magenta colors I often wore, only because I've never understood why anyone would choose to add more gray to this world. One of my ex-girlfriends had a gray coat, and it figured strongly in our breakup.

Or else it's all the work I've done to open up, contact my emotions, express my feelings, learn how to communicate and to release my "inner feminine." It's as if "gay" is the only model our culture has for men if they aren't closed-up, unfeeling, repressed, macho assholes.

Or maybe it was because I was into Liza Minelli. Or that I liked the Tush Push exercise just a little too much.

For a short time I considered the possibility that perhaps I was a transgender cross-dressing lesbian in a gay male body with a preference for straight women, but it just felt a bit too complicated to sort out. But being suggestible, and given how much difficulty I seemed to have working it out with women, I thought I owed it to myself to allow for the possibility that perhaps I *was* gay but hadn't come out of the closet to *myself* yet. So I befriended a few gay guys from my Men, Sex & Power men's group, and they took me to gay bars, sent me to a gay masseuse who specialized in "release" work, bought me gay porno magazines. I also began seeing a gay therapist who told me he hadn't realized he was gay until he was 44 when his father died, which made me, from that point on, acutely aware of my father's health.

On two occasions I even went home with gay acquaintances, but found I was trying to force myself to have a gay experience and it didn't work. Try as I might, nothing seemed to "take." Finally, I went home with a gay friend one night who had always openly expressed his attraction to me. Once we were settled in his living room, however, he proceeded to tell me how when he was around 21 or so, and attempting to date women, one of them had sat him down and told him, "Peter, maybe you just have to face and accept the fact, once and for all, that you're gay." After a pause, he looked at me somewhat wistfully, and said, "Elliot, I think you might just have to face and accept the fact, once and for all, that you're heterosexual."

Actually I prefer the label Stan Dale came up with: natur-osexual. It means we are naturally sexual, whether it's with men, women, or Scottish terriers. Or monosexual, which is more accurate for me: it means I generally only make love to myself. Thank God I'm one of the best partners I've ever had.

Oh, I remember the last line of the song:

There's better things to discuss.

Chapter 11

Drugs

Neem Karoli Baba once said about LSD, after being unaffected by a huge dose administered by Ram Dass, that "if you are in a place that is cool and peaceful, and you are alone and your mind is turned toward God, then you may take the yogi medicine. LSD allows you to come into the room and *pranam* [bow] to Christ, but after two hours you must leave." The implication, Ram Dass explained, was that "it is better to *become* Christ than to merely visit with Him."

One of the comments often made about the use of psychedelic substances is that they provide an artificial ride to the top of the spiritual mountain and the only way to truly get there is to trudge up on foot, step by step, through traditional spiritual practices and discipline, requiring enormous patience, commitment, and, perhaps, lifetimes.

The late Terence McKenna, who was perhaps the leading contemporary advocate for psychedelic exploration, had a different take on this, for himself: Terence said that he "scoured India" and tried many spiritual approaches and concluded that it was simply very difficult for him to be moved off of his "fundamental baseline of consciousness," and he had therefore turned to psychedelics as being more reliable in terms of actual impact on his consciousness and life. (Perhaps it is easier to become Christ if you visit Him more often.)

Terence McKenna died several years ago from a brain tumor. But don't jump to conclusions: some of my best friends have had brain tumors and never did any psychedelics. And I know many people who have experimented with psychedelics who don't have brain tumors.

Some would rightfully question this very impulse to be "moved off one's fundamental baseline of consciousness." That very desire *is* suffering itself. The very honest, spiritual impulse for the great "Something More" (more than just "this") is paradoxically also the impediment to realizing that what one is craving to change is actually to be free of the craving for change, thus able to exist fully and wholly in one's present condition and circumstance exactly as they are.

And all the mad mystics insist that *this* (here and now) contains Paradise itself, but remains obscured to us because we're too preoccupied with changing ourselves and our lives so that *someday* we might find the very Paradise inside of which we are already conducting the search. "Someday" is the great impediment to a life lived with passion today. If God isn't present here and now, under what conditions do we think that That Which Already Is will suddenly come into being? (For "God," think like the physicists if that's easier: All-Pervasive, Omnipresent Energy/Source of Everything.) The seeker remains committed to finding or creating the right conditions for God to appear, and such conditions don't exist, or more accurately, they *always already* exist.

However, in order to truly and finally rest peacefully and wholeheartedly in appreciation of the present moment exactly as it is, needing nothing whatever to change, most Buddhists insist that one must meditate, or "put one's time in on the cushion," as Dharma teacher Christopher Titmuss puts it. (Paradoxically, "needing nothing whatever to change" does not at all mean that one becomes complacent about the great suffering in our world. It simply means releasing the *demand* for life to be a way that it isn't, which is a sure setup for even more suffering.)

I actually know many people who have put in three months
or more of time on the cushion in a single shot, and have done this
repeatedly over the years. Some practitioners of Tibetan Buddhism
regularly put in three-year periods on the cushion, on solo retreat.
And it appears to work: I've seen friends who are long-time medi-
tators grow visibly more wise and loving, if a bit pale. I've done 21
days here, 16 there, 10, etc., perhaps totaling 100 days.

Small potatoes. I finally realized that despite the benefits I
felt and still feel from practicing sitting meditation, the fact is I just
don't have the time to be Buddhist. At least with psychedelics you
make your own hours.

When I arrived in Big Sur in 1985, there was a new drug in
town, nicknamed "Adam." Its chemical abbreviation was MDMA.
Today it is known as Ecstasy, the popular, illegal, and some believe
dangerous recreational drug that has received lots of press. There
are a plethora of books and research studies on it available now,
some demonstrating remarkable therapeutic benefits, some claiming irreparable depletion of serotonin levels or other physiological
damage. A drug of many faces, it has been used in therapy sessions
to help people deal with post-traumatic stress disorder, and it has
been widely used by kids at all-night "raves." And there has been
the rare death over the years.

But this was before all that, when it was new, and had not
yet been declared illegal by the FDA. Therapists in the Bay Area
were using it with patients, claiming that their clients were gaining
more insight from one session on Adam than in months of ordinary
psychotherapy. The patient was often blindfolded and listened to
music on headphones for the duration of the three- to five-hour experience, and the most common report was one of feeling a healing
sense of great love and empathy for other people, a notable absence
of separation and fear, and an awe-filled sense of appreciation and

connection to the universe.

To go from the underground therapeutic circles of San Francisco to the always-experimental, go-for-it world of Esalen was not a long journey. And so it wasn't hard to find Adam in Big Sur, and for a while nearly every week a group of us spent our Saturdays at a magical spot on the Pacific or in the mountains, incredibly high and in love with each other and with the whole of existence.

Gazing out at the shimmering, Big Sur sunlit surf, the waves would rise and fall in unison with my own breath, as if I myself were the ocean, breathing life itself into being with each exhalation. The subtle knot of fear in the center of my chest that I ordinarily live with, which keeps me perpetually on guard and separate from other people, would miraculously dissolve in a release of love and bliss, and I would find myself spontaneously embracing people, seeing their beauty and perfection, and professing my unconditional love for them. All barriers to authentic communication would likewise disappear, and I would confess my deepest truth to those with whom I'd normally be polite and reserved at best. A lot of "I love yous" would flow back and forth, along with hugs, tears, and joyful proclamations and profound insights.

And once, I took Adam prior to attending an Easter morning church service with the Carmelite monks in the sanctuary at Immaculate Heart Hermitage down the road from Esalen, thinking it would intensify my religious experience. But instead, it caused me to begin to quietly sing and do the hokey pokey during the service, while my friend Warren kept whispering desperately, "Please don't do that here, please don't do the hokey pokey here."

The downside of Adam trips for me was usually the next day. The floodgates of unconditional love and ecstasy would slam shut once again and I'd be returned to my ordinary reserved way of being in the world. The contrast was so profound that it often put me into a serious depression for days. And the people I had heartfully embraced and shared my intimate secrets with usually went back inside their shells as well, leaving our relationships no closer than before.

Those of us who were in couples often used Adam as a short-cut to intimacy—for it easily increased the depth and level of sharing, communication, and sensuality. It isn't a particularly sexual drug for most people, however, because among other things, it makes orgasm nearly impossible (unless you are *very* committed). But in the final analysis, you couldn't drug your way to a happy relationship—"Adam-couples" broke up as much as any others in the end.

Despite the drawbacks and limitations, I confess to having taken MDMA at least 60 times or more. And I also confess that the first five times were profound and sacred heart-opening experiences of unity with all of creation, whereas the next 55 were merely, at $30 a pop, an expensive, recreational, and insignificant rush of passing, pleasurable sensations, with no very obvious lasting value whatsoever. (But as passing, pleasurable sensations go, you still couldn't beat it.) Actually, the experience of Ecstasy, as well as other psychedelics, left me with the maddening certainty that my banal day-to-day existence was an illusion behind which lies a glorious and radiant possibility that I somehow didn't have access to ordinarily. Which is precisely the way Colin Wilson described the agony of the outsider years before: a single glimpse of a higher possibility in consciousness renders our ordinary selves prisoners, mad with the urgency to be released into the grander vista once more. Once Plato's cave dwellers see the light, how can they ever again be content gazing at mere shadows on the wall?

There's a fine line between substance abuse and being a bohemian, consciousness-seeking psychonaut. The latter point of view would put me on the cutting edge of human evolution, alongside pioneering souls like Timothy Leary, Ram Dass, Terence McKenna, and thousands or millions of others. A less fun interpretation is that I have basically wasted a lot of time on drugs, obtaining repeated openings to a place in consciousness that I have been otherwise unable or unwilling to cultivate. In either case, I have certainly indulged in the psychopharmacological agents of my generation: primarily marijuana and Ecstasy, but also, to a greater or lesser extent, hashish, psilocybin mushrooms, LSD, ayahuasca, peyote, mescaline, 2CB, and probably a few others I've forgotten.

Oh yeah, I tried cocaine at a party once and found myself madly attracted to every single woman there except my girlfriend. And once I tried cooking a cactus I bought at Lowe's hardware store, believing it to be the psychoactive San Pedro variety. Nothing happened apart from Shari wondering why half of our cactus was gone and I found myself hesitant to explain that I had eaten it.

I always seemed to be especially prone to more intense reactions to these substances than the people around me. Often they would reduce me to a state of paranoia and utter terror. But, to paraphrase Robin Williams, "anything that makes me paranoid and terrified, give me more of that." Some of my friends got to the point where they would avoid partaking with me, in fear of my fear, and also because I often began accusing them of being the Devil.

Or I'd be in a seemingly harmless, low-key situation in which four or five us were settling in with popcorn to watch a video, and a joint would be passed around the room. Gradually I realized with amazement that the rest of the group was relaxed, laughing, and most astounding to me, actually *watching* the movie, whereas I was experiencing my consciousness to be somewhere on the ceiling, engaged in a final battle between Christ and Hitler for possession of my soul.

The problem with drugs is random reinforcement. Social psychologists have indicated that to punish kids sometimes and not others for the same actions is much more harmful than consistent negative attention. It leaves them with no sense of cause and effect in reality. Drugs are the same way: just when you're convinced that pot is an insidious, disempowering, fear-producing drug to which you're addicted and it's about time you got yourself into a 12-step program, you have an ecstatic and meaningful, profound and pleasurable experience, topped off by an exquisite sexual moment, and you think, "Well, maybe I can handle this stuff after all."

One of the entrance requirements to the counterculture outlaw underground, of course, is to be busted. To truly qualify one should probably spend some time in jail. But as an upper middle-class Jewish outlaw with the equivalent of a trust fund, I managed to get arrested with as few consequences as possible.

I was expecting a few joints in the mail from a friend that seemed to be taking forever to arrive. Our local postmistress informed me that a letter had come with insufficient postage and she had sent it back, but would try to track it for me. I lived in a tiny town where you knew your postmistress by name. And so it wasn't all that strange, then, that she called me at home the next day to say she had retrieved my letter, and I could pick it up at noon.

Then the phone rang again, and it was the hospital. Rania, my 16-year-old female housemate, who had just gotten her driver's license that week, had rolled her car on the way to school and was in the emergency room. Apart from a few stitches, she was physically unharmed, but emotionally shaken up. I was the available adult in our household at that moment, so I went to the hospital to be with her.

Several hours later we were driving home, and Rania seemed to be feeling nearly herself again, so I didn't think it would be a problem if I quickly stopped at the post office to pick up my missing mail. I casually tossed the envelope into the backseat of my Toyota Camry, which, incidentally, had been hand-painted top to bottom by my friend Asha, four 12-year-old girls, me, and Rorian, Asha's three-year-old grandson, sitting on the roof with a paintbrush.

Before I was able to even turn the key in my ignition, two vans appeared out of nowhere, sandwiching me in, and four guys got out, one of them pointing a gun at my head and flashing a badge, ordering me out of the car and up against the wall, where I was frisked and handcuffed. Amid this tumult I realized that they also had poor Rania up against the car, frisking her at gunpoint as well, and I yelled at them that she was an innocent bystander, a kid, on her way home from the hospital after a car wreck, and they let her go. (But that was *some* morning for my friend Rania.)

Apparently my friend really *had* put insufficient postage on the envelope, and it really *had* been returned to the false return address—Wollapalooza Inc.—and there just happened to be a real person living at that address in Philadelphia who, apparently, was not a pot smoker.

So the authorities set up a sting operation using my postmistress, and I wound up getting fingerprinted for the first time in my life. But on the way to the station I realized that the cops were starting to see that I was not a Columbian drug kingpin, but just a little schlepper. I spoke to the driver about his daughter's guitar lessons and, knowing nothing whatsoever about football, discussed the Super Bowl at length, and by the time they were finished with me at the station, I even got one of the arresting officers to drop me off at the private school where I taught music, just in time for a faculty meeting. With a lawyer's help, I avoided getting a conviction on my record (I was told) by agreeing to surrender my driver's license for six months and peeing into a cup every three weeks for a cute girl named Lisa who worked at OAR (Offenders Something Something). And that was the end of it, I thought.

I read a quote recently: "There is nothing more difficult for a writer to overcome than a privileged upbringing." As a bohemian wannabe with money, I couldn't even get myself arrested properly to truly qualify as an outlaw. However, as it turned out, 13 years later I volunteered for a hospice and they ran a background check and discovered a misdemeanor conviction. I tried to set the record straight but discovered that my lawyer, the court, the prosecuting Commonwealth Attorney and the OAR all purge their records after 10 years. So unable to prove otherwise, I remain guilty as charged, and I had peed into the cup for nothing.

There's a more or less accepted point of view within New Age circles of interpreting everything that happens to you to be a lesson or message of some sort from Universal Intelligence, one of the codenames for God. Or that you in fact somehow create or draw into your experience everything that happens for a reason. Sometimes this is a useful and appropriate way to view one's life. Often it isn't. Many people do not make this distinction. I was on the phone with my friend Mary once, for example, and I told her, "I have to call you back, my toilet is overflowing." She said, "Why don't you just take a look at the shit that's been coming up in your life lately." I said, "Yeah, I'll do that . . . after I FIX THE TOILET!!"

It certainly could be argued that having a gun pointed at my head and being arrested and handcuffed could be interpreted as a message from the Universe that it might be time to give up smoking pot. But you have to learn the distinctions: I saw it as a sign that I should give up using the *mail*.

Then there was the time I took LSD in a public campground with a girlfriend and became convinced that I was dead, and that she was working for the "other side," whoever they were. I began screaming at the top of my lungs about Nazis, and threatening to kill her, as she explained to concerned campers outside our cabin that "it's just indigestion." I wound up whimpering in her arms, seeing a desolate, black-and-white vision of the charred remains of civilization—everything gray ash—muttering, "Hitler won."

And once when I was about 28, I took mushrooms in my Greenwich Village apartment. Realizing I was God, I proceeded to empty the contents of my medicine chest into a wastepaper basket, declaring aloud to my bewildered cat, Zorba, "God does not need ointments and creams. God, the All-Powerful, Creator of the very heads which might ache, does not need aspirin."

Later that day my girlfriend Sharon helped me retrieve all the stuff from the garbage and I reluctantly replaced them in the cabinet. From that moment on, however, I silently chastised myself if I so much as applied some Vaseline to a chapped lip. For it meant that I was buying into a vision of myself as merely human, a denial of the God-Realized state that had appeared self-evident on mushrooms. My creams and ointments were blasphemy in the face of the Divine.

There was more to that trip: I turned the radio on and heard a news broadcast about an event occurring in Poland, and there was mention of "men with bayonets."

"Do you mean to tell me," I asked Zorba, "that as I sit around, comfortable in my little apartment, having a psychological crisis about a crummy tube of chapstick, that there are actually men with bayonets in Poland pointing them at other men, without bayonets?"

"That's precisely what I mean," Zorba meowed.

I suddenly understood the meaning of the word "duty," and felt myself called into action. I would travel overseas, become a missionary, sneak up behind the men with bayonets and trip them. Teach naked black people about Christ, impoverished Indian farmers how to make Rice Krispies Marshmallow Treats. I began contemplating a nationwide bake sale to raise funds.

There was no time to lose, and I started dashing around the apartment, frantic, madly throwing clothes around, emptying drawers: what does one take on a mission of that sort, on such short notice? I finally decided to bring nothing at all apart from what I had on, which happened to be turquoise drawstring pants, a purple shirt, a bright green wool hat and plaid scarf, a Mexican poncho, and sneakers.

I left the apartment, headed for India. In all the excitement, I had forgotten about Poland. First I had to say goodbye to Sharon, and I got in my car to head uptown. That was a major error in judgment.

As I drove up Third Avenue, life suddenly began appearing to my consciousness and perception as simply a meaningless collection of noises, pictures, energies, and colors, materializing for no reason in the middle of nowhere. It seemed to me that were I to run over a pedestrian, it would have as little consequence as stepping on a leaf. It wouldn't be killing anyone, it would simply be moving energy around, squeezing it out of the little container and letting it float around in the big one, like wind.

Then it occurred to me that this applied to myself as well and I scared myself with the thought of blowing my own brains out. Fortunately, I was now parked in front of Sharon's apartment, and I managed to buzz her and she came down and sat in the car while I sobbed, telling her, "I killed myself. I'm already dead and I can't come back."

"No," she said wisely, "you're on a drug and you will come down from this experience."

"No," I replied, "I know I'm on a drug and will come down. But I'm also already dead."

Looking back now, I realize I was experiencing the shock that my consciousness was already Spirit, and that this would remain true in life and death, on mushrooms or not. I just didn't have the vocabulary for that experience, which left room for only terror instead of awe.

Sharon escorted me upstairs, spoon-fed me miso soup and insisted I watch an episode of *The Honeymooners*. This was a good move, although I took the show very seriously: "Edward Norton is my living Spiritual Master," I told her. "Ralph Kramden is the Antichrist. Alice and Trixie are angels. I am restored by this visitation."

I was finally cured of my psychedelic curiosity when I had the quintessential bum trip to end bum trips, the ultimate nightmare experience.

I had some mushrooms on hand and since it had been a very long time since my last trip, I spent several weeks re-reading psychedelic literature to prepare myself for what could happen. I took all the advice to heart about the importance of "set and setting" and prepared a cozy, safe space in our meditation room complete with blankets, food, and water, soft Zen music and a candle-lit altar. I was alone, but knew Shari would be returning within two hours or so, and she knew of my plans. Everything seemed ideal for journeying in the solo warrior tradition of Terence McKenna, who often spoke of taking what he called a "heroic dose" in order to catapult him into the other realms.

The trip began gently, and I experienced floating on a magic carpet, as the ceiling of the room opened up to an infinite expanse of space and stars. I lay down with eyes closed and saw dazzling and colorful fractal visions. A while later, I was feeling something incredibly painful digging into my side, and I was wishing it would go away.

Then I realized I was using this powerful electric massager we have—"The Thumper"—and all I had to do was turn the machine off and take it away from my body. The realization that I had been hurting myself and could just stop was hilarious to me. But then there came a complete time gap.

I don't know how or why I left my safe haven, but the next thing I remember, I was lying on our kitchen table downstairs, etching my last, dying words into the wooden top: "I'm dying, I'm sorry, I love everyone, next time I'll try to be a Bodhisattva . . . "

I then calmly walked over to the phone and did something I may never fully understand: instead of taking a Xanax, or a bath, or any number of things that might have helped, I dialed 911 and informed the woman on the line that "I believe I may have overdosed on mushrooms. I can't breathe or swallow, and everything hurts." She put me on hold for a moment and then came back and said, "So what were you saying? You can't breathe?"

This enraged me, and I screamed, "YOU'RE NOT HELP-ING!" and I hung up on her. Unfortunately, or fortunately, though, she had my caller ID and could track me down.

Then things went from bad to worse, and I found myself lying on the living-room floor, screaming at the top of my lungs in our secluded country house, but I soon recognized that it was all for naught. Nobody could hear me, and it wouldn't have mattered anyway, for I had entered what I would later learn is a standard tripper's hell realm, a place of eternal torment and suffering, in which nobody and nothing anywhere or anytime could possibly help me.

Even if someone came, I knew they would merely be part of the problem. I was in hell and would never, ever get out, and there was simply nothing that could be done. If I was feeling cold, it made no sense to get a blanket, because I would still be in hell, only with a blanket. Next thing I knew, my neighbor was sitting over me, with two cops and seven guys from the rescue squad standing behind him. I vaguely heard him explaining to them that I was generally a pretty nice guy, normal and sane. He told me the next day that I asked if someone would massage my feet, and he had asked the cops if they wanted to do that, and they said, "No, sir, we do not."

I was in a state of delirium, wondering if there was such a thing as a "person," and if so, was I a person? I touched one of the rescue guy's cheeks to see if *he* was real, and asked him if he was a person. They carried me out on a stretcher, throwing up on the lawn as I went, and they put me into a helicopter. I have vivid memories of flying in what I perceived to be an open-air plane of some sort, wondering if I had wings, looking through the cockpit window at the night sky, the pilot needing me to be quiet so he could land safely, and the Nazi sitting watch over me being very mean. I was informed the next day that there had been no helicopter; I had been transported in an ambulance.

In the ER they stuck an IV in me, and I was sedated and returned to normal within an hour or two. Shari had returned home just as an ambulance was leaving our premises, and the neighbor's kid told her that I had "od'd," which to her meant that I was dead. By the time I awoke in the hospital, she was next to me, studying for her GREs.

Luckily, the police took my neighbor aside as they carried me away and told him, "We're not going to press charges—he's suffered enough already."

When I wrote this account to my friend Bebe, she responded with, "I think we can agree that the key point in this whole story is, 'He's suffered enough already.'"

So why did I persist in these experiments when the results were often horrific? First, it granted me membership in the '60s hippie outlaw psychedelic club. And secondly, there were all the positive experiences: the blissful Ecstasy trips, feeling waves of speechless pleasure in blissful states of ecstatic union with all of life; the incredible paintings I did on mushrooms, the creative force pouring through me like electricity in channeled, bold brushstrokes, revealing inner dreamscapes in living color; the full-moon solo acid trips in which I danced naked and alone in the desert, saw neon dancing star spirits and touched the enchantment of all existence. Or the accelerated marijuana RPM quotient—revelations per minute—like a psychic waterfall of new, joyful, and inspired ideas, which, unlike most stoners, I always made a point to act on and make real. (If, for example, I suddenly thought it would be cool to give 15 friends a can of spray paint, all different colors, and simultaneously paint my car while listening to the second Bach Brandenburg Concerto, you can bet that a week later my Oldsmobile Cutlass would resemble Ken Kesey's psychedelic Merry Prankster bus.) And finally, most drugs tended to provide me with the most unbelievably intense orgasms. So there was definitely a plus side; I just never knew which way these experiments would go.

I met an extraordinary healer in Brazil named Baixinhe (By-sheen-ya) who told me that every drug has an astral being that presides over it. The entity associated with cocaine wears all white, including a top hat and gloves, and his hands are filled with gold coins. The mushroom being is an ancient, wizened little Oriental man with a twinkle in his eye. For marijuana, there is an androgynous being: if one smokes as part of sacramental use for creativity and prayer, the male side, dressed in green and white, can take you to wonderful heights. If you merely smoke unconsciously, for recreation or out of boredom, the red and black female side will push the male behind her and drive the user mad with paranoia and other mental afflictions.

I have generally found this to be true. Those times I truly reserved my marijuana intake for creative projects, I often had a very pleasurable and enhanced outflow of energy and ideas. When I would gradually succumb to habitual use for everything from watching a movie to taking the garbage to the dump, I would eventually find myself in a psychic pit of either fear or despair. (Although, I have to say, I have had some truly profound and extraordinary connections with the guys who work at the dump.)

Plus, the paradox of marijuana is that, if one has the notion about life, as I do, that "This is it," the very act of smoking is an ontological contradiction—for generally it is an action that emanates from the underlying belief that this *isn't* it and the hope that the substance will get one *to* it, or improve it, which is a painfully impossible situation—like trying to get to Baltimore from Baltimore.

Ironically, therefore, contrary to the New Age party line, it may well be that the use of psychoactive plants are preferable as recreation, rather than as a sacramental religious tool, because recreation's purpose is merely fun, not God-Realization, and therefore God-Realization won't be confused with particular experiences or mind states produced by a chemical. For one thing is certain: God's presence is not dependent on anything. No blissful state brings God forth, and no hellish circumstance denies God's reality. The presence of the Eternal logically pervades all possible experience, and lies beneath and behind and within all experience.

As a Jew, this means you have to confront the fact that God was alive and well at Auschwitz. The common, unexamined belief in God as a personal director capable of intervening in human affairs forces one to conclude that God was/is powerless. The horrific tragedies of human existence, therefore, either argue for atheism or push one deeper inward toward a broader understanding of the Divine that cannot be contradicted (or affirmed) by events. Either one loses faith or expands one's theology to realize the God Which is Present is there even in what looks like the very worst of circumstances.

Thus there are tales told of religious Jews who marched into the gas chambers singing affirmations of the presence of God.

But on the level where we experience having choice and free will, clearly *we* are in charge of whether we strive to practice being kind and harmless to other living beings, or whether we keep on murdering and torturing people and creatures. There is no external God to hold accountable. God lives in us and as us and gets expressed through our choices and actions in an ongoing co-creation of reality.

At the end of the day, Alan Watts was correct:

When you get the message, hang up the phone.

And Ram Dass was correct:

It's about being high, not getting high.

And Neem Karoli Baba was correct:

It's better to become Christ than to merely visit Him.

Not that I got to visit Christ much anyway—a few glimpses here and there, but we never got to share any real quality time.

Chapter 12

From Lama to Jerusalem

Father Theophane,
Rabbi David & Shoshana Cooper,
Rabbi David Zeller
& Rabbi Shlomo Carlebach,
Asha Greer

The Lama Foundation, a residential spiritual community, sits quietly and peacefully 8,600 feet up the Sangre de Cristo Mountains in northern New Mexico, just north of Taos. A central structure—the "Main Dome"—has an octagonal picture window that looks out on the oceanic horizon of the Rio Grande Valley spreading itself below. Otherworldly sunsets in purples and gold join with the orange-clay glow of New Mexico light at dusk.

Originally established as "an instrument for the awakening of consciousness and the unification of the body, heart, and mind," Barbara Durkee (now Asha Greer) formed Lama in 1967 with her husband at the time, Steve (now "Noorudeen") Durkee. They were visionary artists and devotees of Meher Baba and had been traveling around with USCO (The "Us" Company), a multimedia, spiritual theater troupe in the Merry Pranksterish spirit of the times.

Along with their friend and former housemate Richard Alpert, they
helped inspire the first Human Be-In in Golden Gate Park. Then,
as Alpert was going off to India to become Ram Dass, the Durkees,
joined by Zen and tai chi practitioner Jonathan Altman, decided to
form what was at first conceived to be a school, then a spiritual dude
ranch, a family monastery, and finally what it became, an ecumenical spiritual community.

I first wandered up Lama's three-mile mud road in 1980
to attend a Ram Dass retreat, camping on the land with some 200
people. I would return nearly every summer afterwards for many
years. Of all the ashrams, monasteries, and spiritual communities
I have visited or lived in, Lama was the place where the heartful life
of prayer, devotion, and service emerged for me in the most easeful
manner. Unlike other communities, where I usually felt as if I were
a guest in somebody else's house, from that first moment Lama always felt like home to me, even when I was a stranger to it. Perhaps
it was because the mountain belonged to no one; or, perhaps it was
because the community still carried its ancestral links to USCO—
the "company of us." It was as if Lama was a family, and everyone
that wandered up the mountain was a long-lost relative.

In 1987, I was invited to Lama to be the arts instructor at a
month-long, multi-traditional retreat that also included a Christian
monk, a Buddhist teacher, a Sufi sheik, and David Cooper, who was
not yet officially ordained as a rabbi, but functioned as one nevertheless. (Ironically, three of the four "multi-traditional" teachers were
in fact Jewish.) Each instructor offered a week of intensive study and
practice in his own path, and retreatants were asked to select one of
them with whom to spend the week. I would lead the whole group
through my creativity workshop on the weekend.

Each teacher led an early morning practice at 5:00 A.M., and
I likewise instituted a morning arts practice of movement, song,
journaling, and painting. I began to pull some of the others' stu-

dents away from their chosen traditions, and David accused me of trying to start a new religion.

I chose to spend the week studying with the Christian monk—Father Theophane—because he was a mad, mystical character, had been a monk for over 40 years, and seemed to emanate spiritual wisdom, if not enlightenment, through the twinkle in his eye. I opted for the teacher with the biggest twinkle, which I still believe is a very good gauge of spiritual teachers. (Ironically, Theophane spent most of the week teaching not Christian mysticism, as I had hoped, but talking about Buddhism and the three-month vipassana meditation retreat he had participated in the previous year!) We met over dinner the first night and I was enchanted as Theophane mostly quizzed me about *my* life and work, which was always a topic I found endlessly engrossing, but never expected to interest anyone else, least of all a "wise elder."

At some point in our conversation, I remembered that I had agreed to be the after-dinner table-wiper, and it being the first night at Lama, I wanted to be sure to do my job in order to demonstrate I was a reliable team player. Yet here I was engaged in a wonderful conversation with someone I felt to be a true spiritual mentor. I finally forced myself to interrupt our talk to explain I had to wipe down the tables. Theophane's response? "Well let me help you!" and he joined me in the chore, merely so he could continue talking with me about me! I couldn't believe it. It was the opposite of most teachers I had experienced, where I would have to timidly hope for an opportunity or appointment to have a brief moment with *them*.

Theophane really blew me away when he showed up on the weekend to be in my workshop, and he participated fully, painting, dancing, and enchanting us with an old Irish folk ballad. He had an innocence, humility, and delight about him, and in his presence I actually felt like a real person who someone like him would want to know!

Over the years, despite many moments of deep self-recognition of my own core personhood, the truth is, I have rarely felt like a real person in this life, on this planet, with this particular group of people living here at this time. In fact, I realized the other day that I have spent my entire life trying to figure out how to spend my life, in hopes that one day, if I made the right choices and got a few lucky breaks, I might become a real—that is, legitimate—person. When *Wild Heart Dancing* was released, I discovered that publishing a book gives me about two years worth of feeling qualified as a real person, whereas a magazine article is only good for the few weeks it is on the newsstand.

This is how it is for me, despite one of the fundamental lessons of spiritual kindergarten: "Do not look outward to establish your worth." I *do* tend to look outward for my worth, and all I ever find out there is a world filled to capacity with people who are more successful than I am, have achieved more, contributed more, have better sex lives, and are more responsible and more able in a million areas of living. (Particularly in building and carpentry where it seems as if every guy I know suddenly reaches a point in life where overnight they know how to construct houses and use a Sawzall.) Certainly they all make more money than I do, since I basically never seem to make *any* money. Having been given in this life, so far at least, just enough for Shari and me to maintain a fairly moderate and frugal lifestyle, I've always sought out things to do for reasons other than financial, and as it turns out, Shari finally figured out one day that I seem to go out of my way to find work that actually winds up *costing* money, and the more the better.

My encounter with Theophane reinforced something Stewart Emery had said years before: "The way to evaluate a teacher is by how you feel about yourself in their presence." At the very least, one can expect to feel safe, loved and free from judgment in the presence of someone purported to be an evolved soul. (If, on the other hand, you feel attacked, demeaned, and frightened, I would consider switching gurus.) This truth hit home again several years later when I had the opportunity to greet the Dalai Lama face-to-face for just a moment. I left the encounter beaming and radiant, feeling seen and recognized at the most primordial and original place in my own being, a place I was certainly not consciously in touch with ordinarily, or ever. It was like finally getting the ultimate attention we've all been craving. Finally God notices. People like the Dalai Lama are able to see into the soul, and what they see is similar, perhaps, to what you or I would see if we gazed with our hearts open at a flower: something natural, free, and beautiful, infused with divine energy. Or maybe the Dalai Lama just sees an empty mirror, reflecting back the empty mirror that he is. It's all mirrors. (Bottom line? I don't have the foggiest idea what the Dalai Lama sees.)

Sadly, or knowing him, perhaps I should say joyfully, Father Theophane passed away several years ago.

I found that I was envious of all the teachers at Lama who were rooted in the ancient traditions, and so I decided to try to dive into Judaism, or at least to wade in the shallow end of the pool. In the fall of 1988, I arranged to meet David and his wife Shoshana, along with our Buddhist friend Howie Cohn, under the Eiffel Tower at 5:00 P.M. on a day about three months from then, and with no further confirmation of our plans, we all showed up on time and flew from Paris to Israel together, where the Coopers had their home in the Old City of Jerusalem, and where I would stay for three months.

When I was a kid, I used to think Times Square was the center of the universe. But it is really the Old City of Jerusalem. It certainly seemed to be the center of the action for *this* planet, anyway. The Old City is divided into four quarters: Jewish, Arab, Christian, and Armenian. The Coopers' balcony literally formed the border between the Jewish and Arab quarters, so in some ways it felt like we lived in the center of the center of the action on the planet.

Of course, the real center of the center for Jews is the "Holy of Holies," an inner sanctuary in the Holy Temple that was destroyed twice, the last time in 70 C.E. (C.E. means the Common Era, and is the Jewish version of A.D., but we refuse to measure time in terms of Jesus's death. Can you blame us?) The famous Western, or "Wailing," Wall is the only part still standing, just beneath what's called the Temple Mount, where the temple proper once stood. It is also the spot where Abraham is said to have nearly sacrificed his son Isaac, as per God's instructions, had not an angel showed up just in the nick of time saying essentially that God was only kidding. (A real practical joker.) The Temple Mount is also said to be the site of the Prophet Mohammed's Ascension, on which the Islamic people have erected their holy, golden Dome of the Rock, where only Moslems are permitted to pray, and which is off-limits to Jews.

So that's some heavy-duty spot. Heavier still, given the biblically based notion held by many fundamentalist Jews that the Messiah will not return to usher in the Messianic Times until the Third Holy Temple is constructed on that same site. We're talking prime apocalyptic real estate.

This, obviously, is a problem, because to construct the new temple would entail blowing the Dome of the Rock to smithereens, an option certain radical Jews believe to be sane, despite the fact that it would more than likely precipitate a war that would blow the rest of the world to smithereens as well.

Interestingly, some fundamentalist Christians share this story line, believing the Third Temple is one of the preliminary events leading to the return of Jesus Christ, the well-known young Jewish man from Nazareth.

Do you know what Jesus would probably say if he got wind

of all the explosive trouble brewing in the Old City of Jerusalem in the name of bringing him back? He would say, "Jesus Christ, are you people out of your fucking minds?" Or perhaps, "That's a very pretty dome. What do you say you Jewish guys build the Third Temple just down the road a ways?"

Speaking of Jesus, right around the corner from the Wailing Wall and the Dome of the Rock is the Church of the Holy Sepulchre, said to be the site of the crucifixion, and where there is a tomb said to contain Jesus. And not far from the Church of the Holy Sepulchre, just outside the Old City, is a garden, which is also said to be the site of the crucifixion and tomb. I considered setting up shop on the other end of town, kind of the Ray's Pizza of Jesus sites.

The people who are fanatically devoted to re-creating the Temple have already constructed architectural models and blueprints, designed the proper ornaments, and have begun to breed the unusual red heifers needed to perform the sacrifices as described in the Old Testament.

As if God never rethinks anything. As if God is just waiting around for us to start butchering red heifers on the altar of the Holy Temple before He'll kick things into gear, get this World-to-Come business under way. No bleeding cows, no Paradise—take it or leave it. For some inexplicable reason, God is non-negotiable on the animal sacrifice bit. Nobody has ever figured it out.

The innermost sanctuary in the center of the Holy Temple was called the "Holy of Holies." Only one man, the high priest, was allowed inside, and only once a year, on Yom Kippur, the Day of Atonement. He would prepare himself with extensive purification rituals because it was known that if he entered the Holy of Holies and was the least bit impure, he would die on the spot. And despite all his efforts to purify first, a precautionary measure was taken nonetheless: a rope would be tied to him before entering the Holy of Holies, so that if he in fact did not survive, he could be dragged out.

That's some job.

Once inside, the high priest would intone a secret, sacred 72-letter name of God, for which "God" is merely a nickname. It was never said at any other time. I have no idea what the high priest did the rest of the year. Being a high priest was definitely seasonal work.

At a retreat with Reb David and Shoshana in California, we re-enacted this, each participant getting to spend a few minutes inside a small cave with a 10-foot red thread tied to their finger. David sat outside and when his watch timer went off, he'd tug on the thread to pull people out. It inexplicably reminded me of that old recipe on the back of the Ritz Crackers box for "Mock Apple Pie," which didn't actually use any apples.

I went on a tour through the underground tunnel system adjacent to the Wailing Wall that winds underneath the Temple Mount. There is one spot under there where our guide informed us that we were directly beneath the spot that had been calculated to be the site of the Holy of Holies. If the Holy of Holies had had a basement, we were in it. I conceived of the idea that if the Holy of Holies had possessed a trap door leading down to the tunnel we were in, the high priest could have pulled a Houdini disappearing trick, and left the people of Israel mystified and awestruck, holding an empty rope. But I also closed my eyes to meditate and pray, trying to cover my bases.

I visited many such "power spots" in Israel to meditate and pray, including the Cave of Machpelah, where the First Family of Judaism is said to be buried—Abraham, Sarah, Isaac and Rebecca, Jacob and Leah. Although typically I am not particularly sensitive to spiritual vibrations, and often don't feel the power of power spots, I have to say, sitting alongside what I presumed to be Abraham and Sarah's tomb, I *did* feel something. I wept. I felt the same way I felt as a child in my grandmother's kitchen when there was a chicken cooking and there was nothing to fear. The Cave of Machpelah, in my imagination, was the very essence, the very taste and smell, of Ultimate Safety and Love. The Primordial Jewish Kitchen.

On the other hand, just outside the cave in the town of Hebron were lots of Israeli soldiers and lots of unhappy Arabs, and it was perhaps among the least safe places in the world, the scene of many killings over the years, including the massacre of a bunch of Islamic people at prayer by a Jewish revolutionary mad-man with a gun.

The Cave of Machpelah, by the way, is also said to be the place where Adam and Eve are buried, but I don't buy it. That's about as real to me as saying Popeye and Olive Oyl are buried there. (The serpent was Bluto.)

But I figured the most powerful of the power spots had to be the top of Mt. Sinai, God's Fortress of Solitude, where He ap-peared to Moses and gave him the stone tablets inscribed with the Ten Commandments. If God resided in the Holy of Holies most of the year, then surely the top of Sinai was his summer place, like a Hamptons of the Divine.

Using sign language, I got a Bedouin to lend me a blanket for my overnight pilgrimage up the mountain, leaving him my suit-case as collateral. I hired a camel and a camel guy, and they walked me up until the path ended, and I went the rest of the way on foot, the whole trip taking three or four hours. When the sacred moment finally came, and I set foot atop Mt. Sinai, I almost tripped on a teen-aged Bedouin kid who was lying next to a plastic cooler. He scram-bled to his feet and greeted me with those prophetic words that were perhaps second only to the Word with which God greeted Moses in similar circumstances. He said: "Coca-Cola? You buy Coke?"

So I bought a Coke and, wanting solitude, climbed down a bit, crossed over a valley and went back up a neighboring peak, ad-jacent to Mount Sinai; couldn't God swing over to His right a little if He needed to touch base? I laid out my blanket and proceeded to spend the coldest and longest shivering night of my life, hoping God was appreciating the suffering I was putting myself through just to be in His neighborhood.

I talked nonstop to God the whole night, confessing to the whole catastrophe of my soul. He said nothing, like a psychoanalyst, without even the "uh-huh, go on" part. Just that immense night sky silence. Surely the Jews in the camps were not only talking nonstop, but screaming out from the pit of their souls to be delivered from the evil at hand. Clearly, Whoever we were screaming out to was not big on intervention. You'd think that if He could part the Red Sea, how difficult could a few Nazis be? Who needs a good listener at that point? Our God is a good listener. Just don't expect anything whatever to actually *happen* as a result of your pleading. I'm angry with God for being the kind of God that He is: the kind who doesn't necessarily save your ass when the bad guys are about to get you. We're on our own with the bad guys down here, and Thy rod and Thy staff are not comforting me. I am living in the valley of the shadow of death, and I *do* fear evil. (Memo to God: upgrade rod and staff.)

Dawn in the desert was something else. Miles of desolate rock in all directions, and a silence that was staggering. I had the feeling that if I could only figure out a way to live there for about a year, I would come to understand everything there was to understand. But as I only had about a half-gallon of water with me, my fantasy of prolonged and utter solitude was not to be fulfilled in the Sinai. I climbed back down the mountain, retrieved my suitcase, took the bus back to the resort town of Eilat on the southern tip of Israel, glanced one more time at the topless Israeli girls on the beach (real, partially-naked, *Jewish* girls, what a startling concept), and made my way back to the Coopers' house in Jerusalem.

There is a beautiful, tender song sung by the late Rabbi David Zeller, whose delicate and haunting falsetto was sometimes mistaken for a woman's voice:

> *Return again, return again*
> *Return to the land of your soul.*
>
> *Return to who you are,*
> *Return to what you are,*
> *Return to where you are born and reborn again.*

Rabbi Zeller was often a fellow dinner guest at the Coopers' festive table in Jerusalem. There were three continuous weeks of celebration and prayer during the *hagim* (the High Holy Days of Rosh Hoshanah and Yom Kippur, followed by Sukkot, the Festival of the Hut), and the Coopers' long table was usually filled with 20 or more guests. A huge percentage of them were rabbis, Torah scholars, and yeshiva students. Most were American, and were living in Jerusalem as *ba'al teshuvim* (people who had returned to Judaism later in life). They were all living a Jewish lifestyle, which meant observing as many of the *mitzvot* or commandments as possible, certainly honoring the Sabbath and keeping kosher, praying the daily prayers and adhering to all sorts of other daily rituals, and all were learning and/or teaching Torah with a passionate intensity.

Ordinarily, associating passionate intensity with religious study is potentially a dangerous, volatile, and often lethal combination. But the *ba'al teshuvim*, unlike radical fundamentalist Orthodox Jews (or radical fundamentalist orthodox *anything*) seemed to have the passionate intensity for Judaism one might have for a lover, as one would have for anything that had the ability to restore one's connection with the Divine, minus the absolutism of fundamentalists.

So when this group in its many permutations sat at the Coopers' beautifully set holiday table and sang "Return again, return to the land of your soul" along with Rabbi Zeller, it seemed clear that the "land of your soul" was not Israel, but rather a hidden terrain within, barely retrievable yet thankfully not entirely lost, and approachable only through song. It was a place that Reb Shlomo Carlebach used to call the "the deepest depths" of one's heart and soul, an inner landscape where one feels utterly and finally at home in oneself and in the cosmos. And I wept at the table to hear of that place, and to feel it.

Reb Shlomo, who passed on several years ago, was David Zeller's rebbe, and famous throughout the world as an emissary of good will, ecstatic joy, and unbearable sorrow through his poignant melodies and stories. He was a wandering *maggid*, a minstrel storyteller, with a huge heart who never failed to make me cry within minutes of being around him. I met him at least seven or eight times, and each time he greeted me like his closest, long-lost friend, and I also knew that on a personal level, he never remembered me and believed he was meeting me for the first time each time. But somehow he managed to combine a first meeting with the emotional connection of a final meeting. And he did this with everyone in his audience. Shlomo was notorious for arriving two hours late for a scheduled concert, entering from the rear and greeting and hugging each person in the audience individually—"My brother, so good to see you, you're the very best"—which would take another two hours, and his concerts would finally begin at midnight and go throughout most of the night, much to everyone's utter delight.

To sit with Shlomo in a crowded apartment in Jerusalem at two in the morning as he wove one of his heart-wrenching stories through melody and song, one had the impression that if you listened carefully enough to every word and sang every note from the "inside of the inside" of your heart, it was possible you'd enter the center of the world itself where all of God's secrets live.

Elie Wiesel once said of Hasidic singing that it will "drive your soul out of yourself in order that it may rejoin its Source and become one with it in the *Heichal Hanegina*, the 'sanctuary of melody'—it's there I await you in a secret promise."

The "sanctuary of melody" has always intrigued me. What is the secret promise waiting for us in this hidden realm of music, this sacred sphere of sound? Is there a mystical message of melody that can transport the soul to places in consciousness that can never be approached through mere words? Which never-before-heard combination of intervals and tones will unlock the inner doors to the divine realms simply when sounded by one's own voice or another's?

In certain Native American tribes, it is the custom for a pregnant woman to regularly sing a song of comfort to the fetus, repeating it when the baby comes into the world, and again throughout the child's early life. The melody becomes virtually embedded in the child's DNA, such that in later years the very hearing of it becomes an instant, reliable source of comfort, like a hard-wired lullaby, more effective than Xanax. Eventually the person can sing it to themselves as well, with equally self-soothing results. It is the aural equivalent of comfort food.

What if, I've always wondered, God Herself whispered such a song to *us* before the before, when we were merely a glimmer in the Divine "I"? Like the proverbial pilgrimage to sacred sites in search of mystical revelation, one could embark on a musical journey inward, entering the realm of possible melodies, silently listening with a great yearning for that one deeply familiar series of notes, the original healing song of our soul. And once we identified it, we would sing it with all of our hearts, riding the contours of the personally tailored tune until we were restored to our original wholeness.

Spiritual romantic fantasy? Perhaps. Yet it is not by accident that the ecstatic Hasidic tradition has developed the practice of singing melodies without words, using only sounds and meaning-less syllables to articulate the notes. For all words, even the holiest of prayers, cannot help but register in the mind's linguistic mean-ing center, activating the realm of ideas and discursive thought. And even the loftiest sacred thought by definition resides merely on the level of the conceptual, which is several steps removed—or worlds away—from that which utterly transcends intellect.

It is only the purity of melody itself that can transport one's soul "out of itself"; and not just any melody, but those holy melo-dies that the great Hasidic rebbes and masters of music are said to "bring down." It is not accurate to speak of the rebbes as *composers* of the songs they give over, but rather, it is as if they have access to the very sanctuary of melody itself, and merely *find* their melodies, already whole and waiting for the right person to give them voice. Similar, perhaps, to how Mozart described hearing his symphonies already complete, and said that his job was merely to jot them down, as if taking dictation.

In the contemporary world of New Age psychics and chan-nels, none of this is big news. Rosemary Brown, who died in 2001, for one example, was considered by many to be a genuine spirit medium who seemingly "composed" new works dictated to her by dead composers, among them Bach, Chopin, Beethoven, and many others. Given that she had little or no musical instruction and only beginner's piano lessons, it was difficult to explain the complexity of her music (which purportedly included Beethoven's Tenth and Eleventh Symphonies!) in any reasonable scientific manner. The pieces each bore the unmistakable signature style of the composer she claimed had paid her a visit.

In my own firsthand experience, I've already recounted my witnessing of Brazilian spiritualist Luis Gasparito produc-ing paintings in the style of Modigliani and Renoir right before my eyes. But as intriguing as it is to contemplate the possibility of deceased artists still actively working through willing recipients (John Lennon, I'm ready when you are), it is even more mysterious to consider this exploration of wordless melodies, which involve no personalities at all, alive or dead. For to approach even the outermost chamber of the *heichel hanegina*, one must humbly leave one's ego at the door and enter with only a naked heart in search of its original song. The songs themselves, secret sequences of sound, exist unauthored, except, perhaps, by Divine Mystery or a hidden aspect of our own soul.

Being a musician, while in Jerusalem, I made a point of learning as many of Shlomo's melodies as I could, mostly from David Zeller around the dinner table, including one in particular that was fated to embark on a great spiritual pilgrimage—to the sanctuary of melody and back again.

Several years after my stay in Jerusalem, I was traveling in India visiting various ashrams and monasteries. Toward the end of my journey, I took a typically wearisome 27-hour bus ride in order to visit the community of one of India's most widely known gurus, Sathya Sai Baba. I described my experience there earlier, but I left out this unusual sequence of events. Recall that his ashram is huge, and had just hosted *two million* people from all over the world to celebrate "Baba's" 65th birthday. When I arrived, the numbers had dwindled to a mere 20,000.

Exhausted from my trip, I was anxious to get some sleep, and I was assigned to bed #312 in building 24A, one of the men's dorms. I found my way there, and discovered an enormous structure much like an airplane hanger, jam-packed with hundreds of beds. I crawled under my mosquito net and closed my eyes. Within minutes of my head hitting the pillow, I began to hear the angelic sounds of a choir right outside my window, singing "Hine Ma Tov." This can't be, I thought to myself, and rolled over. Then the strains of "Shema Yisrael" began. I was much too tired to get up and check it out, and I drifted off to sleep with the assumption that I was probably hallucinating.

The next day, as I wandered the grounds, I came upon a bearded man wearing a yarmulke and tallis. I approached him, and learned that he and his wife had in fact been celebrating the Sabbath the previous evening, as they had been for several weeks, with a group of about 100 German Sai Baba devotees, in a goodwill effort to bring healing to the German and Jewish circles.

And where had this Sabbath service taken place? Of the thousands of possible locations, they had set up an altar literally beneath the window, right outside bed #312 in building 24A!

The time was early December and Chanukah was fast approaching. This couple—Chedva and Shimshon—were preparing to return to the States, and the mantel of "Rebbe of the Week" somehow fell to me. I puzzled over where I would find a menorah in Puttaparthi, India, and my question was answered in a dream: I saw myself building a huge menorah out of stones, laid flat on the ground, with the candles placed right into the earth.

The next morning I gathered a pile of rocks, found an open dirt field, and constructed the menorah. Before long, I was presiding over a nightly Chanukah gathering of perhaps a hundred Germans and half a dozen Jews, sharing songs and candle-lighting. The spokesperson and musical leader of the German contingent was a lovely woman named Gesine, who was very interested in Judaism, and was eager to learn whatever Jewish music I could share with her. Her favorite was the Shlomo melody I had learned from David Zeller in Jerusalem. ("Sing the 'yai deedai song,'" she would say, since it was a melody without words and I sang it with the traditional Hasidic sing-along syllables.)

Chedva and Shimshon were living in Ashland, Oregon, at the time, and told Gesine and me about their wonderful local rabbi, Aryeh Hirshfeld, also a musician and singer. Several years after that trip to India, and seven years after I first sat at the Coopers' table in Jerusalem, I was passing through Ashland and contacted Aryeh, who graciously invited me over for dinner with his family. When I introduced myself, he said, "Oh yes, I've heard of you."

"What do you mean?" I asked, incredulous.

"Several years ago I was performing in Germany, and a woman named Gesine taught me a wonderful melody. When I asked her where she learned it, she said 'from Eliezer Sobel in India.'"

The following summer I attended a Jewish conference in Ft. Collins, Colorado, and one evening there was a tribute to Shlomo, who had sadly passed away the previous year. He had suffered a heart attack on an airplane in the midst of a concert tour. As I sat there in the audience with eyes closed, I heard the familiar strains of the magical traveling melody as Aryeh played it for all assembled. And so a single enchanting melody had come through Shlomo in New York, traveled via David Zeller to me in Jerusalem, over to Gesine in India, on to Aryeh in Germany, and was now returning to Shlomo after circling the globe and transporting people all over the world to the sanctuary of melody, fulfilling a secret promise.

Such was the magic of Shlomo and his music.

I once served as organist in a small Episcopal church, accompanying the hymns each Sunday. During the time of taking collection, I was asked to play background music, and I would always play a Shlomo melody. Every week, without fail, someone in the congregation would approach me afterward and ask, "What was that beautiful music you played during the collection? It was so haunting and moving."

Nothing personal, I would think, but those are probably the two least likely words that would come to mind if one were trying to describe the Episcopalian hymns I had to learn every week. Not haunting, not moving. Perhaps *stately*, or vaguely patriotic, with Christ as the country.

And in my capacity as a hospital chaplain one year, I was responsible for leading Sunday morning services in the chapel periodically, and there, too, while sidestepping the job of drumming up business for Jesus in favor of a generic ecumenical spiritual offering, I nevertheless got the Southern Baptist Sunday morning hospital churchgoers singing Shlomo's Hasidic melodies and David Zeller's songs.

The fact that Shlomo was also rumored to be a womanizer never erupted into scandal during his lifetime, and I believed for a while that perhaps rebbes of his magnitude received special dispensation from God to fool around, which for a while was an added incentive in my thoughts of becoming a rabbi. Then it all came out a few years after his death, in a flurry of disturbing reports from women with whom he had been sexually inappropriate, including teenaged girls. Similar stories have been revealed about nearly every spiritual leader of our times, from Swami Muktananda to Jimmy Swaggart: I have no original insight to contribute regarding this phenomenon, but the frequent juxtaposition of seeming holiness with depravity among male spiritual teachers does make me wonder if perhaps they are all simply chips off the old block; that perhaps God, too, mixes the divine work of creating and blessing the world with the occasional obscene phone call to fourteen-year-olds.

It's amazing the kinds of things you can get used to in Israel: Getting on a bus and sitting next to young girls with Uzis; going on a tour of famous sites and being escorted by an armed guard with a machine gun; being detained on the street every day while police cleared away possible bombs, sometimes using robots to retrieve suspicious packages that had been left unattended in public places.

I once returned home to the Coopers' apartment and discovered a paper bag sitting in front of their entrance. Being bomb savvy, I knew to be cautious, so I picked it up and shook it. It wasn't a bomb.

When I got back from Israel, I experimented with being Jewish in America, by driving cross-country wearing a yarmulke on my head. I got as far as Denny's outside Kansas City. I pulled into the lot and froze with fear: I realized that there was no chance in hell I was going to enter Denny's in Middle America wearing a yarmulke. The internal visceral response of terror within me was inherited from the German side of my family, some of whom lived and died through the Holocaust. Sitting there in the Denny's parking lot, it hit me over the head: all my life I had believed that my perpetual feeling of being unsafe was a psychological problem, paranoia or neurosis. It had never occurred to me that there was real evidence and justification for it, that it truly *isn't safe* to be Jewish in this world. Not that it is particularly safe to be human in this world. A psychiatrist recently told me I have PTSD—post-traumatic stress disorder. I asked him, "Uh, which trauma in particular do you think I'm post of?" and he said, "Familial, generational, and cultural, and it's still going on because there are people who want to wipe you off the face of the earth."

Explains a lot.

I took an intensive six-week course on Judaism in Jerusalem, which met nearly all day every day, and covered such topics as prayer, Torah, Hebrew, ethics, the oral tradition, the holidays. It was a crash course, taught with great passion and enthusiasm by *ba'al teshuva* rabbis anxious to bring wayward Jewish souls back into the fold. Their main communication to me was that I ought to become a rabbi myself, something I would consider for several years afterward, but finally reject because it demanded being religious and living a Jewish life and while I liked the idea of that in theory, in practice I could never truly buy the Covenant thing, never truly believe that God cared about religion in the slightest.

I'm certain God is an atheist.

Or perhaps a shaman.

But not a powerful punishing force watching to see if the Children of Israel are sneaking off to eat shellfish.

The Coopers made living the Jewish life not seem like a burden at all, but something exquisitely beautiful and sacred. And their generosity and kindness toward me knew no bounds. If anyone were going to bring me back to Judaism, it would be them. And though I was touched deeply, and moved in the deepest depths of my being, the 99th Monkey is ruthless. I'm writing this 19 years later, and not only am I not a rabbi, but having been a nondenominational, interfaith chaplain for a year and talked with countless people about God, many of whom were very sick or dying, I came away feeling less inclined toward things religious than ever before.

Because when push comes to shove, and people are lying on their deathbeds, it's not religion they truly want, it's *you*: human love, connection, and presence. And while being more loving and present is clearly a religious aspiration, too many people forget that, and start to believe the purpose of religion is to be more *religious*.

So I bounce in and out of performing Jewish rituals at home. My weekly Sabbath celebration gradually devolves from what it should be—white tablecloth and ironed cloth napkins, white clothes and festive songs, wine, challah, the Hebrew blessings—to an abbreviated version: I start doing the short form of the prayers, and next I start skipping the tablecloth. Eventually I'm just taking a slug of Manischewitz from the bottle and calling it a day.

Good Shabbes.

There was a constant tension in Jerusalem in the fall of '88. Apart from the bomb scares, the intifada had started, and when I said goodbye to the Coopers after three months, I commented, "I feel as if I'm getting out of here just in time, before the whole place explodes."

Shoshana replied, "Oh, it always feels that way."

Back during the Esalen years, I went through my "inner Nazi" period. To my utter horror, I discovered "the Hitler within," and scared myself to death. Usually fueled by drugs, I came directly into contact with my own potential for evil and a sense of terror and dark foreboding that came with it.

I was leading a workshop at Esalen and a German man named Conrad offered some feedback to me as I stood in front of the group: "You have given us such a vunderful experience of love und light, El-yot, but ven I look into your eyes I see there is also a dark side."

Thank you for sharing, Conrad.

His words cut right through to that shadow place I had been exploring and was so frightened of, so I had us break for lunch and I went off to eat, feeling pretty shaky.

I carried my lunch tray to the sunny outdoor eating deck and spotted a table that was empty except for one extremely attractive blonde woman I had never seen before. I approached and asked f I could join her, and I swear, this complete stranger looked up at me and said: "This fear you've been experiencing lately of your shadow has to do with the fact that in your last life you went way out on the dark side." My mouth dropped open in astonishment. Her name was Samantha, and she was a psychic. A very good one, I thought.

So I began to wonder if I had been a Nazi in a past life. Even though most mainstream American Jews never hear anything about it, there actually *is* a belief in reincarnation built into traditional Judaism, usually referred to as transmigration. But unlike the Buddhist doctrine of reincarnation, which implies literally countless rebirths in all different forms, including animals, the Jewish idea, from what I can gather, seems to limit one's chances to a finite number of lives, and all of them as a Jew. I asked the rabbi I was studying with in Israel if it was at all possible I could have been a Nazi in a previous life.

This is what he said: "No, but maybe you were a *Sonderkommando*."

Sonderkommandos were those Jews who tried to increase their chances of survival by working for the Nazis, doing odd jobs, like depositing the bodies of their fellow Jews in the crematorium using a pitchfork. It was a temp job, since they would eventually suffer the same fate.

In hopes of coming to some peace about all this, on my way home from Israel I stopped in Munich, in order to pay a visit to Dachau. While there, I stood before one of the memorials and put on a yarmulke and recited the Mourner's Kaddish in honor of all who died in the Holocaust. It felt like a dramatic and courageous act for me to be publicly, visibly Jewish, a Jew at prayer, in Dachau.

Still, Dachau was a breeze compared to Denny's outside of Kansas City. (Years later I repeated the Denny's experiment and followed through with it. And as far as I could tell, people were a lot more interested in their eggs over easy than they were in the guy with the yarmulke; I seemed to go completely unnoticed.)

In the Dachau museum there is a huge wall-sized photograph of a pile of dead bodies. As I watched in horror, two young Aryan-looking, rosy-cheeked fellows took turns posing in front of the photograph for snapshots, smiling and flaunting a thumbs-up proudly in the air.

I saw them sign the guestbook as they were leaving the museum, and went over to read what they wrote: "S.O.G.: The Sons of God."

✻ ❋ ✵

I was sitting in the Coopers' apartment in the Old City of Jerusalem one afternoon when there was a knock on the door. David opened it, and a wild wind of a woman in a bright orange parka whirled into the room, and into my life forever. This was one of Asha Greer's last stops on a solo trip around the world. She was an artist, a nurse, and the co-founder of the Lama Foundation. At 53, she was close to the age I am now, and I sometimes marvel that while I still seem to be waiting to one day grow up and figure out who I really am, she was somehow already Asha, and probably always had been: a force of nature, a fearless lover of God, and most of all, simply herself, for better or worse. That quality of striving to *become* somebody or something, so prevalent particularly among spiritual seekers, was conspicuously absent in her.

We spent the next three weeks together exploring Jerusalem and its surroundings, walking miles in the hot sun through the wadis (dry riverbeds that run through the desert gorges) escorted by an armed guard, wandering the maze-like narrow back alleys of the Arab suk (market), finding hidden, dark cafes down broken old stone steps beneath the street, places where I would have been unlikely to venture on my own. But she seemed to fearlessly follow her nose wherever it led, and I was along for the ride. And as anyone who knows Asha will attest, to hang out with her is a ride like no other, sprinkled with her unique observations on all topics mystical and mundane, bound to include at least half a dozen meaningful encounters with complete strangers, generally involving one or two new schemes to save either the world or an individual, and likely to contain several outbursts of pure, unadulterated mirth and laughter.

In meeting her, I felt like I was catching up with my generation, finally entering a piece of American counterculture history, already in progress. Clearly, her life was part of the story of America's great spiritual underground of the '60s, and in becoming her friend, my life seemed to become at least a minor subplot in my own mythical imagination if nowhere else. But she has that quality about her, of seeming to be connected to the center of things, and it draws people to her in a continuous stream.

Her house in Virginia, where I was soon to land, is a place, like Lama, where tired wanderers can kick off their shoes and take a deep breath. I was one such wanderer, and I showed up at her door to visit about two years after we met in Israel. I kicked off my shoes, put my feet up in front of the fire, and stayed for four years. But I am getting ahead of myself.

Chapter 13

Forty-Day Solo Retreat & Paxil

The summer after I returned from Israel, I spent four months living in a tent as a "summer staff" person at the Lama Foundation. My girlfriend at the time, Darsi, lived just across the clearing in her own tent. I got us walkie-talkies at Wal-Mart: her handle was "Deva Darsi" and I was "Shiva Lingam." If there was too much static to understand what she was saying, I had the option of simply calling out from my tent, without the walkie-talkie, which provided a much clearer connection.

At the end of our summer at Lama I had to make a choice: move to Santa Cruz with Darsi and live a block from the beach with her and two of my closest friends, or go back to Jerusalem alone to pursue the rabbi idea. It should have been a no-brainer, but I decided to do a 40-day solo retreat to contemplate my next move. (My brother has a theory that I've actually been retreating since childhood, when I would surround my place at the breakfast table with three cereal boxes, arranged in such a way as to create a little private retreat space for myself at the table. Of course, given that he was the only other person at the breakfast table with me, I must have been retreating from *him*.)

Forty-day solo retreats were in vogue with my "spiritual" friends at that time: there was a mystical rumor going around that it took 40 days to accomplish a true transformation in consciousness, and there were the biblical references to back it up: Moses on Mt. Sinai for 40 days, Jesus in the desert for 40 days, Noah coming in out of the rain after 40 days. Asha had told me of a retreat cabin atop a mountain opposite her land in Batesville, Virginia, and I went up there in October of 1989, intending to come down 40 days later on Thanksgiving Day.

The cabin was a simple 12′ × 12′ wooden structure that took about an hour to get to, a fairly strenuous uphill hike, and I was lugging a backpack, guitar, and food. I asked Asha if there were any animals I needed to know about in the woods there, such as bears or snakes, and she said, "I've lived here over 15 years and I have yet to see a snake." When I arrived at the cabin, sweating and exhausted, I opened the front door and dangling from the top of the doorjamb, in my face, was a five-foot-long, two-inch-thick black snake.

Being of a shamanic bent, I considered this a good omen: "To cross the threshold into the inner chamber, one must get past the snake of desire at the door." Later that first night when I sat down in the cabin's little window seat to eat my first of many rice dinners cooked over one small propane burner, an owl landed on a branch about two feet from my face and we had a 10-minute staring contest.

Being of a shamanic bent, I considered this a good omen: "Once having passed the snake of desire and entered the inner chamber, the owl of wisdom will make its appearance and serve as guide." So far, this was a damn good retreat!

The cabin had a single mattress on the floor, a wood stove, and a little writing table. I dug a latrine in the woods, and collected rainwater in a barrel. I reread my Thoreau quote that I brought along in my journal: "I went to the woods because I wished to live deliberately, to front only the essential facts of life, and see if I could not learn what it had to teach, and not, when I came to die, discover that I had not lived." Nevertheless, 40 days can be a very long time.

Unlike the true spiritual warriors who, in a situation like that, would spend all their time in meditation, I created a retreat more in keeping with my nature: singing and chanting, painting, reading and writing. And meditating, walking, and swinging in the hammock outside the cabin, staring up at the treetops and the Virginia autumn colors. And thinking a lot. I also created a series of one-day workshops for myself on various topics: I devoted a full day each to my mother, father, brother, God, death, sexuality, and life mission.

This was clearly long before I grew weary of self-help. I was still in the fix-it business. Much later I would realize that either things are irreparable or that they have never been broken in the first place, both of which are much easier to deal with than trying to get oneself to be better or different than one *is*.

By Day 23, I was going bonkers, and reminding myself that, "You don't have to stay up here for 40 days just because you said you would. You don't have to prove anything to yourself or anyone else."

Or, "I GOTTA GET OUT OF THIS CABIN BEFORE I BLOW MY FUCKING HEAD OFF!"

Fortunately, however, Asha was very tuned in. We had an arrangement whereby every third day I walked halfway back down the mountain to an agreed-upon spot to leave a note in a bucket with my needs: "more peanut butter, an onion, batteries for the flashlight," and so on. On the very day I was about to give it all up, Asha spontaneously decided to leave for me, along with the peanut butter, onion, and batteries, the 40 cartoons she had drawn, one per day, while she was on *her* 40-day retreat in that same cabin the previous year. Most of them featured a meditating figure with word bubbles emanating from its head, presumably broadcasting all the thoughts Asha had experienced on retreat. I saw myself in each drawing and realized why they say there is only one mind, and my sense of humor was restored. On the strength of laughter and human connection, I lasted it out.

The home stretch was extremely productive: I began writing what would eventually be published as *Wild Heart Dancing*, as well as the start of my novel, *Minyan*. This is what I wrote in my journal on the fortieth day of my retreat:

> *No stone tablets—if anything, I am carrying down this*
> *mountain a host of new Thou Shalts, and leave the*
> *Nots for the religious and fearful—mine is the "Way*
> *of Zorba," the path of the minstrel-lover, of the Heart-*
> *bursting Lover seizing God and Devil by the shirttails*
> *and tossing them aside: "Out of my way, fellas, I've got*
> *some living to do and there isn't much time. Go peddle*
> *your heavens and hells to the suckers who will buy, I've*
> *taken myself out from the Holy Marketplace, I've spent*
> *my last cent investing in the Sacred Promise. I'm a Free*
> *Man, my pockets are empty, my Spirit is barefoot, my*
> *Soul is naked, and I'll be on my way!"*

It was my post-retreat high, a poetic outpouring of spiritual romanticism. In fact, in the actual story of *Zorba the Greek*, I am forever Nikos, the uptight one.

One of the games I played while on retreat was to explore the question, "What would you do if you only had a year to live?" I discovered that I had always wanted to perform in musical comedies but never had. So that year in California I was in *Pippin* and *Camelot*. And several years later in Virginia, I played Judas in *Godspell* and a generic Nazi in *Cabaret*.

These theater experiences helped me develop a theory I called "Finale Energy" that I incorporated into my workshops. I noticed that no matter how I was feeling, no matter how my day had gone or what was going on in my life, no matter my mood, when the curtain opened and it was time for an all-out upbeat production number, the song and dance had to go on! And you couldn't fake "cheerful and enthusiastic" if that's what was called for. It had to be *total*, 100 percent energetic and real if the piece was to succeed.

There was a vital lesson in that: although our tendency is to allow the circumstances of our lives to determine our moods and feelings, and then to allow our moods and feelings to determine our actions, the plain truth of the matter is that we have it exactly backward. We can choose to take actions that will determine our moods, which will create our circumstances. We have the innate ability to flip an inner switch and turn on "finale energy" anytime we want to, on the stage of life as well as the theater. And it is a transformational choice: no matter what my mood before a show, the performance would demand I turn on this authentically positive life force and I would inevitably leave the theater in a radically different mind state.

So if I find myself moping around feeling like the victim of a bad mood or depression, the problem isn't existential despair, it's simply laziness, and the solution isn't self-help, meditation, therapy, or prayer: the answer is basically vaudeville—the old song and dance, the old one-two. Woody Allen came to much the same conclusion in *Hannah and Her Sisters* when he cured himself of suicidal desperation by watching a Marx Brothers movie. If your God is not a Laughing God, change religions, for Christ's sake. Stewart Emery believed one of the first signs indicating that a person has wandered from their authentic self is the loss of their sense of humor. (I used to have a fantasy of being in a New York subway accident and suing the city, claiming that the incident had resulted in the loss of my sense of humor. In the trial, the defense would put me on the witness stand and bring Myron Cohen and Milton Berle into the courtroom to try and make me laugh, as I sat there trying to keep a straight face but eventually losing the case.) As novelist Tom Robbins has said, "We live in hell because we take ourselves too seriously." And as Wavy Gravy put it, "If you don't have a sense of humor, it's just not funny."

And if it's not funny, we're all in big trouble.

(And God Commanded: Thou Shalt Squirt Thyself with a Seltzer Bottle.)

On the other hand, it could also be true that the depression and anxiety I have suffered and struggled with my entire life is nothing more than a defect in my neurological composition, a mix-up at the plant: too much of this, not enough of that, a serotonin uptake inhibitor nightmare. So over the years I've also tried Synaquan, Prozac, Zoloft, Effexor, Serzone, Wellbutrin, and Paxil for depression, with Xanax in my pocket at all times for high-anxiety emergency situations like first dates and job interviews. With the exception of Zoloft and Effexor, which gave me the heebie-jeebies after two days, I usually stayed on the anti-depressants for about eight months at a time. And they generally worked, more or less, in the sense that they would bring me from a sheer hellish gray place of hopeless despair in my psyche up to where I was merely miserable; from there I was on my own. Although, actually, the first time I tried Prozac it lifted even the misery and I noticed with awe what it was like to simply walk down the street feeling ordinary. "So *this* is what people do when they go for walks," I thought. I had never understood the concept before. A walk for me had always been simply depression-in-motion.

Numerous articles began appearing in the spiritual literature with titles like "Meditating on Prozac," arguing that the drugs

at least put depressive types on a level playing field with everyone else, and would enable them to emerge from the dark mental
shadows long enough to meditate properly, and to benefit from the
practice as well. I remember seeing clearly, in the midst of a 16-day
vipassana retreat in which I spent a great deal of time sobbing, the
simple fact that I was not about to meditate my way out of or through
depression, and I got myself back on the meds as soon as I got out
of retreat.

I rarely did any of this under a doctor's supervision; I always managed to get prescriptions from doctor friends who trusted
me to monitor myself. And after eight months of feeling just sort
of ordinary and relatively normal, I would invariably be convinced
that I didn't need the pills anymore and go off them, never sus-
pecting that feeling ordinary was actually proof that the drugs were
working, and not an indication that I no longer needed them. But
I'm a slow learner, and I was also always thinking I needed to give
my body and mind a rest from the foreign substances. I'd substitute
natural products like St. John's Wort, SAM-e, 5-HTP, and others, all
of which proved to be completely useless in my case. And within a
month or two, I'd again crash into a deep despair and depression,
and would choose to go back on medication.

I repeated this cycle for about 12 years. Shari provided me
with a wake-up call soon after we met when she casually mentioned
one day, "Oh, by the way? The next time you decide to go off antidepressants, could you give me two weeks' notice so I can move out?"
Apparently I was a lot less fun to be around when I was submerged
in a stormy black sea of suffering than when I was basically cheerful. Go figure. Eventually, with the support of a naturopath, changes
in diet, and the introduction of exercise—actually moving my body
once in a while—I learned how to sustain my sanity and mood without the meds for over three years recently, before another cosmic
crash came calling.

This time I used a psychiatrist, and he put me back on Paxil and Wellbutrin, after unsuccessfully trying Lexapro, Lamictal, Seroquel, Neurontin, and Buspar, all of which made me completely nutty, and in one case, caused me to smash my head into a lamp in the middle of the night as I stepped on and broke the cat's food bowl. He later told me that he meant to warn me that one of the side effects of Seroquel is that people often smash their heads, but usually it's on the bathroom floor. I placed an emergency call to him when Shari and I moved from Batesville to Richmond a couple of years ago. After 15 years in a place I loved, we had moved to a place I didn't, and the change was freaking me out. Not to mention that as a first-time homeowner, I was making seven trips to Home Depot a day, usually to purchase little metal items the existence of which I had been previously unaware. I also, to my utter dismay, bought not only a sprinkler for the lawn, but a sprinkler timer as well. I had been hoping to get through life without ever owning a sprinkler, and I caved at 54. When my psychiatrist returned my call, I was in fact actually standing in Aisle 10 of Home Depot, staring at the aforementioned assortment of little metal things, trying to distinguish which one would be most likely to fix my house. He said, "What you're going through is WAY beyond a medication solution."

Great, I thought.

When next I saw him, he said, "Don't give up on drugs, we haven't tried Zyprexa, Cymbalta, or lithium yet."

"But you said on the phone the other day that I was way beyond a medication solution?" I replied.

"I did?" he said. "Hmm. I must have been in a different mood that day."

He's the perfect therapist for me: completely inconsistent, impossible to pin down, and always impishly looking at me as if he actually knows I'm here.

But given the foods we eat; the exercise we do or don't do;

the high voltage power lines we live under; the radiation from our microwaves and cell phones; the impact of sugar, caffeine, alcohol, preservatives, and processed foods; the pesticides in our water; airborne pollutants; the information and visual imagery attacking our senses through TV, radio, billboards, the Internet, e-mail, telephones, and other media; the daily news of approaching apocalypse (if global warming, terrorism, or bird flu doesn't get us first) . . . it's amazing *anyone* manages to be a relatively normal, somewhat-balanced human being. We're all a walking science experiment about to blow, as far as I can tell. Picture a lab with test tubes and Bunsen burners and vials of exotic chemicals, everything bubbling and smoking and steaming: that's us. It reduces one to the two p's—Paxil and Prayer:

Dear God:

HELP!!!!!!

P.S. Please monitor my serotonin levels.

Chapter 14

India, the Burning Ghats, Nepal & the Dalai Lama

What I liked best about living in Santa Cruz was that one got the uncanny feeling that nobody there had a job. At any time of day, people were out walking their dogs, rollerblading along West Cliff Drive, strolling on the beach, or throwing frisbees. It was a good environment for a guy like me. Nevertheless, the following August, of 1990, Darsi and I decided to leave Santa Cruz and do what every bona fide spiritual seeker needed to have on their resume: the pilgrimage to India.

We arrived in New Delhi at two in the morning, and changed money at the airport bank. When I informed the bank teller that he owed me a 100-rupee note, he promptly placed the pile of bills down on the missing one where he had set it aside, scooped them all back up, recounted, and gave them to me. I watched him try the same scam with every single arriving foreigner, most of whom were oblivious. At the water fountain, I discovered a single tin cup, and I watched in astonishment as person after person came up and used it. To their credit, though, they had a technique of spilling the water into their mouths without actually touching their lips to the cup.

Still.

We had been told not to bring many clothes, but rather to

purchase local apparel upon arriving. The streets of the Paharganj district were a maze of alleys and shops, every other one containing floor to ceiling piles of thousands of fabrics, silk, and embroideries, and usually about three or four men sitting around. (The streets, for the most part, were jam-packed with thousands of men, many of whom, apparently, thought it was okay to pinch the young American blonde woman's ass as they passed her in the crowded streets. Needless to say, Darsi was not fond of New Delhi.) The Hindu women seemed to stay home, out of sight, for the most part. Young boys constantly hounded us, asking if we wanted to change money, buy silk or hashish, and we finally allowed one of them to lead us to his family's silk shop.

All I really wanted at that point was a single pair of loose cotton drawstring pants, which they called pajamas. After the boy's father, despite my protestations, had unraveled perhaps 36 rolls of fabric, I finally convinced him I only wanted a simple pair of pajamas and I chose some purple cloth. He then had me follow his son on a long and seemingly circuitous route through tiny labyrinthine alleyways and alcoves, in order to be "fitted." We finally arrived at his home, where his mother and sister took the most comprehensive measurements I've ever experienced—waist, ankles, calf length, thigh length and width, knee circumference; I was imagining this would be the most custom-tailored article of clothing I had ever owned.

I picked them up the next day: they were, as far as I could tell, a "one-size fits all" giant pair of pants. The waist was roughly triple my waist size, and could be tightened with the drawstring to fit virtually any human being of any size or shape I could imagine. Little moments like that occur daily in India, and are what make it a most hilariously perplexing country.

Since my original introduction to Eastern traditions had been through Ram Dass, I wanted our first stop to be at Neem Karoli

Baba's ashram in Kainchi, just outside the hill station of Nainital. Getting there required a harrowing 10-hour bus ride up a narrow mountain road. The Indian driving style is to speed around blind, one-lane curves with one hand on the horn and hope for the best. The sight of numerous overturned vehicles on the road and the sheer drops on either side just added to the sense of utter madness and peril. At one point I interrupted my unceasing prayers and opened my eyes to see that there were no less than 12 passengers with their heads out the window, simultaneously throwing up. I know this sounds like I'm exaggerating to make a point, but I'm not. Twelve bona fide vomiters. And I realized that to them it was a non-event, just an expected part of the ride, the same way that users of peyote expect to throw up as part of their journey.

Guided by the indispensable Lonely Planet guide, we stayed at the Hotel Evelyn, which turned out to be the hotel of choice for all the American devotees of Neem Karoli Baba who passed through. In fact, the proprietor was an old friend of Ram Dass's, and informed us that we were staying in the very room that was always reserved for Ram Dass, who was expected in a few weeks. This was all quite exciting to me: it was the New Age equivalent of "Washington slept here."

Our visit to the ashram the next day was disappointing. It was being run by one of Neem Karoli's oldest living devotees, a woman named Siddhi Ma, who was gradually coming into her own as an object of devotion and adoration among the devotees. So getting a private audience with her was considered a special honor. Our experience with her was uneventful, however—just another in a long list of spiritual masters I have encountered in my life, and would continue to encounter, around whom I felt essentially nothing. This is part of my 99th Monkey qualifications: "He has personally met with dozens of Self-Realized Masters and has missed the point." In speaking of the magical qualities and events surrounding his guru, Ram Dass would also say that there were always those people who came to meet Neem Karoli Baba out of mere curiosity and saw only an old man in a blanket, and went on their way. Had I been there at the time, I'm sure I would have been one of those guys.

So while everyone around the ashram was busy saying "Siddhi Ma this" and "Siddhi Ma that" all day long, Darsi and I were not moved by the meeting, and apparently neither was Siddhi Ma, because rather than inviting us to stay for a few days or weeks, as she was known to suggest to visitors, she came up with a different idea for us: "Why don't you see more of India?"

So off we went, vomiting our way down the mountain and wound up several days later in the famous holy city of Benares, known as Varanasi in India. Every spiritual pilgrim worth his salt knows that the thing to do in Varanasi is meditate on the burning bodies at the funeral ghats. So I did.

Varanasi is considered an auspicious and holy place to die, and aging pilgrims from all over India hobble their way to Varanasi in hopes of dying there. The ones who can afford it receive a traditional Hindu funeral: every day you see a procession of people, some playing drums or horns, others holding aloft a corpse that has been ceremonially prepared for cremation at the burning ghats, draped in fabrics and adorned with strings of flowers and spices. The less well-to-do have to forego the pyre and simply have their bodies tossed into the Ganges River—the "Ganga"—and one was always seeing mummy-like apparitions floating by in the water. But in the Hindu world, even having one's unburned body tossed into the Ganga in Varanasi is considered auspicious as well.

I befriended a young boy named Kamla—he was probably around 15 but seemed much older because of the amount of responsibility he had already taken on, both in helping his mother care for all his little baby brothers and sisters, but also in single-handedly operating the family business. Kamla ran a concession stand right near the burning ghats where families of the dead could purchase all the paraphernalia and accoutrements necessary for properly prepping their loved one for the funeral pyre. Kamla showed me his store, which resembled a transient carnival snack stand only much older, dark and ancient. Or maybe it was the surroundings—all the stuff of death, the bodies floating by in the river, the unspeakable smell of burning, smoked flesh forever in the air, the atmosphere of mourning alongside the sense of business as usual for the Indians who lived and worked and hung out in the area.

Kamla walked me through death's antechamber: a damp, dark stone building just adjacent to the burning ghats, where the old and decrepit lay in amorphous lumps on the cold hard floor, crumpled under blankets, waiting for their turn to burn. Were I more in touch with the Mother Teresa within me, or even the chaplain, I would perhaps actually have made some human contact with those people. For all I knew, despite the wretched horror of their end-of-life condition to my eyes, some of them might have been spiritually elated simply to have made it to Varanasi on time. But I missed that possible lesson because I was only able to experience an inner horror and revulsion that made me move through those rooms and out the back as quickly as possible. And thus arrived at the burning ghats themselves.

Three or four individual pyres were in process. From one, a leg could be seen protruding through the flames. Little children— not more than three or four years old—ran about from one fire to the next, picking around the ground, looking for coal debris to add to their buckets. This would become their family's fuel supply, Kamla explained. I noticed a dog munching on the remains of a human skull that had rolled off one of the pyres. And all the while I kept thinking of those gurus whose stories I had read, whose masters instructed them to sit by the burning ghats and meditate on the inherently transient nature of existence. My inner seeker kept repeating, "Make sure you're getting all this. Pay attention! Take it all in. This is the place to get the Big Insight." Needless to say, that sort of lust for breakthroughs never works. One simply cannot will "Aha" moments.

The smell, the bodies, the children, the dog, the skull, the glorious Ganga, the glow of the flames and murky white smoke against the hot night sky, the dark and glistening faces, the people huddled in the waiting chamber: in the midst of this overload of sensory input, Kamla encouraged me to actually step more directly into the ghats themselves, to approach more closely. Experience-junkie that I am, of course I went. Being horribly American—that is to say, oblivious of my surroundings and anything apart from my inner "I'm having the intense burning ghat experience which is supposed to be good for my spiritual growth" voice—I approached one of the lit fires and as I stared at the various body parts being consumed, a man tapped me on the shoulder.

I looked up and he pointed to another man who was squatting by the head of the corpse. And he said, "This was that man's mother." I looked into the mourner's eyes, and suddenly the living reality of the situation came flooding into my thick consciousness. I realized in a flash of recognition that this was *not*, in fact, a spiritual tourist attraction, but was actually the funeral of a real man's mother, a man sitting not two feet away, watching his mother burn, feeling his grief and saying his goodbyes. What was I doing there? A strange foreign intruder gawking at another man's burning mother. I immediately withdrew, putting my hands in the common prayer position, backing away saying, "I'm so sorry."

Which I was. And ashamed and embarrassed at how I could be so unaware of what was happening and what I was doing. So that was my lesson, my "Aha," at the burning ghats, and I think it was a good one.

❁   ❁   ❁

I got very sick in Varanasi. In America I would have called it flu
symptoms: fever, shakes, aches, etc. In India, I was afraid it was
malaria, so I went to the local hospital, which didn't look anything
like a hospital. If you had just dropped me there and didn't tell me
where I was, I might have guessed I was in some sort of depot. No
white coats, no information desk, nothing remotely medical-look-
ing or familiar. I was surprised when I asked someone where the
doctor was and they pointed me to a room, where in fact, a man in
casual street clothes sat behind a desk. I told him my symptoms.
Without any examination whatsoever, he told me to go back to the
lobby to purchase a blank prescription form from the vendor there.
Which I did. There was a man with a pad who tore off a small sheet of
paper in exchange for two rupees, roughly six cents. I took it back to
the doctor, he wrote me a prescription, and I went to have it filled.

There were four "chemists"—drugstores—in the immediate vicinity of the hospital. At each and every one of them, when I
handed the proprietor the prescription, he took it from my hand,
held it quizzically in front of his eyes, held it up to the light, squint-
ed at it for awhile, then returned it to me, shrugging his shoulders
and saying simply, "No." If I wasn't feverish and ill, I would have
found this to be one of those hilarious events that can only happen
in India. But the hilarity was lost on me, and so rather than risk dying of malaria, Darsi and I decided to get out of India and hopped
the next plane to Kathmandu.

Nepal was such a relief. From the moment we stepped off
the plane, everything seemed cleaner, friendlier, safer, and easier.
We secured a great penthouse room for about six dollars a night
with a beautiful view of the city and the mountains beyond, and ate
what to us was "real" food for the first time in weeks. Just outside
Kathmandu, a couple hours hike up a mountain, sat Kopan Monas-

tery, and we wound up going there to participate in a 10-day Tibetan Buddhist retreat.

One of the basic Buddhist tenets is that in one of our zillions of incarnations over eons of "beginningless time," as they would put it, each and every one of us, including critters, have at one time been everyone else's mother. As a figurative construct, this is a useful notion in that it assumes that one loves one's mother and would treat her with the utmost of kindness, love, care, and generosity. And since any- and everyone with whom we come in contact was once our mother, it is incumbent upon us to treat every living being with that same unconditional respect and love.

As a literal belief, however, it could be taken to extremes. I learned the following story about Lama Zopa, co-founder of Kopan, from one of the Western monks, an Australian named Max the Monk. Max had been accompanying Lama Zopa on one of his journeys, and they were sharing a room. One night Max happened to wake up and glance over at the other bed, and Lama Zopa had removed his mosquito net, had lifted up his shirt, and was crouched over, his back host to hundreds of mosquitoes. "What are you doing Lama Zopa?" Max had inquired, incredulous. "For the kindness they did for me when they were my mother," the Lama replied, "the least I can do is feed them a little of my blood."

The other co-founder of Kopan Monastery was the late Lama Yeshe. And as is the Tibetan custom, his reincarnation had already been located, and was at that time a boy of about four or five. Max the Monk had a good story about him, too: Just prior to his death, Lama Yeshe had walked Max over to the monastery's jeep, which was Max's job to maintain. He pointed to the front tire and the door handle, wagged his finger and scolded Max for not replacing or repairing them. Several years later, when the toddler-Lama was introduced to everyone, the child walked right up to Max, grabbed him by the finger, and pulled him over to the jeep, where he pointed at the tire and door handle, still in disrepair, and wagged his finger with that same scolding attitude.

Max informed me that nearly all of Lama Yeshe's students had experienced something similar, in which the child had done something that only an individual person would understand, as his way of making contact and saying to them, "Yes, it's me. I'm back."

We had a wonderful retreat at Kopan, the highlight of which occurred on the final day, when the abbot of the monastery came in to speak with all of us. This was pretty much all he said, in broken English: "So, you have been meditating for 10 days. So now, you are more enlightened than me!" At this, he cracked himself up, laughing so uproariously at his own little joke, that the rest of us couldn't help but join in, and we all laughed uncontrollably, and deeply, for about 10 minutes. None of us quite knew what was so funny, which made it even funnier. As far as I am concerned, that abbot's laughter was the clearest transmission of enlightenment I have ever experienced. Hearing it, and joining him in it, was more valuable by far than any of the esoteric information we had heard during the course of the retreat, and had more impact than any of the meditation sessions.

After doing an exquisite four-day trek to the breathtaking, snow-covered tippy-top of the world—well, not exactly Everest, but close enough for us—Darsi and I booked ourselves on a 72-hour bus ride back to New Delhi.

Huge mistake.

When we got to the Indian border, we learned that due to student strikes and violence in Varanasi and elsewhere, the border was closed. For a fee, our driver arranged for the border guy to stamp all our passports as if we had entered India, and then drove us 12 hours further north in Nepal to make the crossing somewhere in the very middle of nowhere.

Not good.

It was 3:00 A.M., in a dense, dark forested area, just over
the border into India. We heard four loud gunshots and the bus
came screeching and skidding to a halt. Darsi and I were in the very
first row of seats. From our window we saw four dacoits—bandits—
wearing white masks and loincloths, and wielding what looked like
civil war muskets. Long round-barreled rifles. They had shot out
the tires. We frantically began stuffing money into our socks, hiding our passports under the seat, and then I heroically lay down on
top of Darsi as the door of the bus opened and a bright light shone
in. There was a lot of shouting going on in foreign tongues—most of
the other passengers were Nepalese—and as Darsi and I slowly got
up, one of the bandits grabbed her by the crotch and dragged her off
the bus, ripping her thin cotton Indian pants in the process. I followed, descending the steps right into a gun pointed at my head. I
bowed and said "*Namaste*," the Hindu greeting that means "I honor
the light within you, so please don't blow my head off."

So yes: an upper-middle-class, suburban Jewish guy has
twice had major firearms pointed at his head. I get some outlaw
points for that.

All of us were ordered to huddle on the ground, held there
at gunpoint as the others ransacked the bus. There had been many
stories in the Indian papers every day about random violence, particularly on trains and buses. Tales of killings. These guys were
moving fast, screaming maniacally, hitting some of the passengers
with the butt of their rifles, and I realized there was a good chance
we would all be shot. My heart was pounding and I was saying the
central prayer of the Jewish tradition, which one is supposed to say
at the time of death: the "Shema," praising the One God. This was
my Jewish equivalent of Gandhi saying "Ram" as he went down.
I said the Shema internally, over and over again, like a mantra:
"Shema Yisrael, Adonai Elohenu, Adonai Echad."

I turned to Darsi in the midst of my terror, and she said,

"It's a good day to die." Which was a Native American phrase that I had originally heard in the movie *Little Big Man*, and a very hip and enlightened idea. I found it hard to believe that she meant it, but she did seem a lot less visibly perturbed than me.

The good news was they didn't shoot us. They merely stuffed everyone's money, cameras, and other loot into canvas bags, grabbed my guitar, and ran off into the woods. They over- looked our money, which was in Darsi's shoes and in a wallet I wore under my shirt around my neck, which they luckily missed when I was frisked. We found our traveler's checks and plane tickets in the morning, scattered about on the ground. The dawn also began to rouse the 10 or so passengers on the roof of the bus who had man- aged to sleep through the whole event. A few things became clear the following morning.

The Nepalese travelers pointed out that in fact we were not quite as isolated in the middle of nowhere as it had seemed; we were, in fact, only about a half a mile from a police checkpoint. They explained that the dacoits were in cahoots with the police, who would get a kickback from the take, in exchange for taking ap- proximately four hours to make the half-mile journey to help us. The Indian equivalent of Inspector Clousseau was on the case. For his comprehensive report, he carefully measured the distance from the place on the road where we first heard the shots, to the place where the bus eventually had come to a stop, counting it off in steps. He also measured the length of the skid marks.

Meanwhile, another person told us that this was a common occurrence on this particular route, and that we were lucky, because the last time it happened, along with money and cameras, the da- coits also took one of the Western women with them. What would I have done, I wondered, if four crazy men with guns ran off scream- ing into the woods, dragging Darsi along with them?

I was very grateful that we were both alive and that Darsi

was not abducted. So was she. And she'd had it, she was done with India. And, apparently, with me. When we arrived in Delhi the next day, she booked the first available plane to Paris, thus ending not only our pilgrimage to the East together, but, as it would turn out, our relationship as well.

It was a very vivid moment, when she left: we were in a hovel of a room somewhere in Delhi, and she left for the airport at four in the morning. I found myself suddenly alone, feeling abandoned and bereft in a dreary room in India in the middle of the night, still in shock from being accosted at gunpoint hours before. To be fair, Darsi invited me to go with her, but I wasn't finished with India. Instead, I decided to go directly to Dharamsala, a 12-hour journey north, where the Dalai Lama and many Tibetans had settled as refugees after escaping from Tibet.

It was a good choice. Still somewhat traumatized by the events of the previous two days, I stumbled onto the grounds of Tushita, the "sister" monastery to Kopan in Nepal, and was thankfully greeted by the gracious Thubten Chodron, who happened to be an American Jewish woman, and after I spilled out my harrowing tale, she and the other Western monks there fed me, assigned me a room, and invited me to stay as long as I wished. I felt safe and at home again, and stayed three weeks, the last 10 days of which I participated in a retreat along with 30 Westerners. At the conclusion of the retreat, the monks arranged for us to have an informal audience with His Holiness, the Dalai Lama, in his own living room! We filed in, and His Holiness engaged us in a 90-minute informal question and answer session that was filled with laughter and delight. Afterward, we each approached him individually to have a "moment" and presented him with the traditional white "kata" scarf that he ceremonially placed around our necks.

It was perhaps one of the most profound and wonderful seven seconds of my life. It's as if the Dalai Lama's gaze instantly melted everything within me that wasn't radiantly free and happy. And the sensation wasn't so much that I was looking *into* the vast empty eyes of a living Buddha, it was the spontaneous awareness that I was looking *out through* the vast empty eyes of a Living Buddha: my own. It takes One to know One. And that's why he's who he is: he has the capacity to look right into the living Buddha essence within each person that crosses his field of vision. I left the encounter beaming and grinning from ear to ear. After we had all greeted him in this manner and had begun to depart, His Holiness stood on his front porch laughing and waving goodbye, just like my grandmother used to do, until every last one of us was completely out of sight.

I like that in a living Buddha.

I was reminded of a story: a man has been searching all his life for God. After years and years of seeking and struggle, someone finally points him toward God's house, saying, "Just go and knock." The man hesitantly creeps toward the house, walks slowly up the stairs, reaches up for the knocker, and gives it a solid rap or two. Then, just as God is opening the door from the inside, the man turns around, leaps down the stairs, and runs as fast as he can in the opposite direction, never looks back, and has been running ever since.

After meeting His Holiness the Dalai Lama, I would have been kidding myself to pretend to still be searching for the "real thing"—a Self-Realized human being, the pinnacle of possibility for each of our own evolution. It manifested in His Holiness as a sense of boundless compassion and loving-kindness to all other sentient beings. Thus the entertaining search for more and better gurus suddenly lost its urgency and allure. God had answered the door, and now there was nowhere else to go.

I have met the Guru and he is Us.

The lesson is always the same: the answer to every spiritual question is always related to giving, rather than getting. The St.

Francis prayer spells this out clearly:

> *Lord let me not so much seek to be loved, as to love. Let*
> *me not so much seek to be understood, as to under-*
> *stand.*

The ultimate resolution to the seeker's quest is never some sort of personal victory or a bells-and-whistles Great Event. Recall Werner Erhard's way of putting it: "The angels are not going to blow in your ears!" Rather, genuine realization is a humble relinquishment of the search itself in order to begin the true spiritual work, which is the practice of loving-kindness and compassion, a giving to others of the very thing one has been seeking all along.

There was also a sense in which my meeting with the Dalai Lama was profoundly ordinary. I didn't become his disciple or a student of Tibetan Buddhism. (Although when I returned to the States, I *did* get a "Free Tibet" bumper sticker for my car.) But it brought me face to face with a much harder problem to solve than the search for God or enlightenment: How does one live when the search is no longer one's primary underlying driving force? When the question is no longer "How can I find it?" but rather, "How do I give it away?" There is both a freedom and a responsibility in that, and I have been struggling to deal with it ever since that day. Fortunately, as the 99th Monkey, my commitment to seeking would ultimately remain stronger than any experience of finding, thus enabling me to continue on my merry way.

For I was still on my once-in-a-lifetime trip to India—which, as it turned out, it wasn't—and there were still a few key spiritual hot spots to visit: I flew to Bombay, took a train to Pune to visit the ashram of the late Bhagwan Rajneesh, then worked my way south to Puttaparthi to visit Sai Baba, both of which I've covered earlier.

When I left Baba's, I had the liberating sensation of having been "sprung from the joint." To celebrate the freedom I felt,

I managed to score some local pot through a kid I met on line at the post office, and I headed down to Kovalam Beach on the southern tip of India. The fact that there *was* a line at the post office was in and of itself a new experience, unheard of in the north of India, where the only way to purchase stamps in a post office had been to scream and shout and physically shove everyone else out of the way, literally hurling money at the guy behind the counter while holding other people at bay. If the queue concept ever emerges in northern India, the entire texture of the subcontinental culture will shift in such a dramatic way that world peace might well result. It's what Buckminster Fuller called the "trim tab effect." To steer the great ship of state, you make small adjustments to the trim tab, which is what moves the rudder that steers the ship. To make the incremental shift the current world paradigm needs in order to move up to a new and sane human level, the post office in Lucknow has got to get its act together.

Darsi and I had spent a few days in Lucknow on our way to Varanasi, in order to visit H.L. Poonja, affectionately know to his followers as Poonjaji. About 75 at the time, he was one of the few living disciples of Ramana Maharshi, and was just beginning to rise from obscurity to worldwide fame, due to a young American seeker named Andrew Cohen who experienced an irreversible transformation within 20 minutes of meeting Poonjaji. Andrew would go on to become a spiritual teacher in his own right, and before long, Westerners were flocking to Lucknow, an unusual percentage of which reported having huge and powerful life-changing events in the presence of Poonjaji. I'm always a sucker for huge and powerful life-changing events. We were lucky to get there in the period just before Poonjaji began attracting huge crowds, and so we got to sit daily in a small room with him and perhaps only a dozen other visitors, one of whom was a young American woman named Toni, who seemed to be glowing, radiant, and blissed out a lot. She was apparently becoming enlightened before our eyes, for she was to emerge soon after our visit as the world-renowned teacher, Gangaji. We were *there*!

Needless to say, neither Darsi nor I felt a thing in Poonjaji's presence, and after three uneventful sessions with him, we took off, completely unenlightened once again. It's really annoying when that happens.

On the way to Kovalam Beach, I stopped overnight in Cochin, the former site of one of the only Jewish communities on the Indian subcontinent. It was quite an experience to walk down Govinda Lane, hang a right on Krishna Road, pass the Narayana market and Ganesha Shoe Repairs, and arrive on Cohen Street, in what is locally referred to as "Jewtown." I passed some Hindu shopkeepers, proprietors of Goldberg's Fabrics, and came to an overgrown cemetery where the ruins of tombstones had Hebrew lettering on them. And finally, I reached the main landmark of Jewtown, the original synagogue of Cochin, but alas, it was the Sabbath and the synagogue was "Closed on Saturdays."

I spent New Year's Eve sitting in cafes on Kovalam Beach with some folks I had met back in Dharamsala. As big as India is, it seemed that there were very specific spots that most Western backpackers went to eventually, so you kept running into the same people all over the country. I enjoyed walking along the beach wearing my Rajneesh outfit—the one-piece, long white robe that I had purchased in Pune—and getting mistaken for a holy man on more than one occasion. I also enjoyed politely noticing, out of the corner of my eye, the topless Western women sunning themselves on the beach, a fact that did not escape the local Hindu men either. Only they were far less discreet than I was, and walked in groups of 10 or so, all wearing polyester suits and ties and leather shoes on the beach, in the scorching sun, and literally would stop directly in front of a topless Western woman's blanket, and just stand there and stare.

Not that I blamed them. I'm certain it was the equivalent for them of how it would be for us if a flying saucer landed in our backyard and two aliens got out and started singing "My Yiddishe Mama." We would stare too.

Around then—this would be January of '91—the Persian Gulf War was brewing, and warnings were issued to traveling Americans to come home if possible. I felt done with India anyway, so I took a 48-hour train ride to Bombay, in which I did not have a berth and had to sleep squeezed in on the floor amid 12 people, using my trusty *shmatte* to protect my face from the grimy surface. *Shmatte* is Yiddish for "rag" and usually refers to a particularly ugly or ratty-looking women's garment, as in "This old *shmatte?* I only wear it to clean the house."

Before I left for India I had asked my buddy Shivaya, who was a seasoned veteran of many India trips, to tell me anything special I needed to know. He only told me one thing: "Get yourself a *shmatte* the first day you're there—it'll come in handy a million different ways." He was so right. You could buy these rag-type cloths for less than 10 rupees (30 cents), and you wore it like a scarf at all times, to wipe the sweat off your brow, to wipe the silverware in a restaurant, to sleep on the train floor, and on and on. Everyone had a *shmatte*.

I actually enjoyed being on my own in India. When you're on the road and you're not part of a couple, there's a tendency to more eas-ily meet and hook up with other solo pilgrims, which I did. And in the back of my mind, I more or less assumed that Darsi's abrupt departure had been a shock reaction to getting mugged on the bus by the maniac dacoits, and I figured we'd probably pick up where we left off when I returned.

Not how it turned out. I got back to the States, phoned Darsi, and discovered that our relationship really *was* over, from her point of view, and she had already moved on to a new life for herself without me. So I belatedly did what people often do when a love affair ends: I completely fell apart, contemplated suicide . . . and moved in with Asha Greer in Batesville, Virginia, one of the best moves I've ever made, for her home was one of the sanest places I'd ever been.

Sane in the sense that Asha is fundamentally a joyful person, and freely opens her home to an ever-changing group of housemates, visitors, and people in crisis, who are inevitably seduced out of their personal dramas and begin to share in Asha's zest for life and her appreciation of the pastoral beauty that surrounds her home.

For the four years I lived at Asha's, with various other housemates coming and going, I don't remember a single argument or raised voice. The worst it ever got, perhaps, was minor irritation that say, a favorite book I might have lent Asha had wound up in her giveaway pile—she didn't like accumulating stuff—and I ultimately found myself at the local used book store having to buy my own book back, at more than I originally paid!

I remember a conversation we had in her beautiful, Japanese-style tea hut, situated on her property down a wooded hillside along a stream, in which, as an example of something, Asha off-handedly inquired of me, "You know, the way you feel when you feel really, really deep down fine?" And then she continued speaking but I stopped listening because all I heard was a voice inside me responding, "No! I don't know what it's like to feel really, really deep down fine!" And the recognition of that difference in our interior experience was somewhat shocking and revelatory to me. But it explained why so often people on the verge of spiritual collapse would stagger into her household, broken, and stride back out days or months later put back together.

And it is not through anything she *does*—in fact, apart from the random cup of tea together on the porch, she is more apt to go about her business and ignore you! It's one reason everyone feels so at home in her house—it's clear that one's presence is not imposing on her or inhibiting her activities or altering her day in any way whatsoever, unless she chooses to stop what she's doing.

I remember when my first novel came out, after nearly 20 years of writing, revising, wishing, hoping, having multiple agents and multiple rejections—it was a significant milestone in my life, to say the least. I was cheered and praised by friends and family, acknowledging my achievement. Asha's first response was to simply state, "You know, it doesn't make me love you more," instantly cutting through my whole drive for success, approval, acknowledgement, praise and, yes, love, all of which were certainly tied into this publishing event. She couldn't offer me any of those things in response to my book coming out, because she already showered me with all of them *just for being.* There was nothing I could do to increase or diminish that gift. I knew her love and appreciation of me was already total and I could rest inside it.

When I would be endlessly struggling to figure out who to be and what to do with my life, she would comment, "You just need to find something to do between breakfast and dinner." Another time her solution to my life dilemma was to suggest, "Well, you could mow my lawn." Which I did.

She once confessed that given how much she enjoyed her days and her independence, her ideal relationship would be someone with whom she could "spend midnight to 6:00 A.M." But having survived two marriages that both ended unhappily, and having raised four extraordinary and beautiful daughters, she would often proudly announce to anyone listening, "I'm so happy my ovaries have dried up and I'm done with all that! It gives me more time and energy to paint. It's all just a trick anyway, to keep the species reproducing."

A striking beauty in her youth, I've seen her now, at 73, glance into the mirror, somewhat shocked by her own aging, largish body, and just declare the obvious: "Somehow the image I see looking back at me doesn't match my own aesthetic sense of beauty," which is her way of simply acknowledging and summarizing—and letting go of—what would obsess and depress many women for years.

And her house is also a sane place in that for the 20 or more years Asha has lived there, she has never had a lock on her door, nor did I in the 11 years that I subsequently lived in my own place down the road. I would go away for up to six weeks at a time, leaving my front door, which was actually only a screen door, unlocked. Car keys stay in the cars in Batesville. The kids and dogs roam free. People still dance around the Maypole. Seldom is heard a discouraging word.

The best place to meet Asha is on her porch. There, on the beat-up old Salvation Army couch, gazing out at her rugged land and flowers and the majestic mountains across the way (the wild growth obscures her "shoe garden," a natural depository for abandoned footwear), she will make you a cup of tea and talk about anything and everything. Should the phone interrupt, she will answer it, but within a minute or so you will hear her say, "Hey listen, there's a real live person here with me, and I feel that humans have priority over machines," and thus excusing herself, will return to you as if there has never been a guest more important than you.

And as she puts the portable phone down, you'll notice it is smeared with red paint, or blue or green, as are her hands, and probably her face. Asha is a painter, and her life rhythm and style is primarily the wild, unkempt spirit of the artist. Although she is also a teacher and practitioner of the Japanese Tea Ceremony, with a great appreciation for the aesthetics of simplicity and order that surround that discipline, her wild artist-spirit tends to override that side of her, and so it's quite possible that you might reach into her kitchen cabinet for a clean tea cup and discover an old used teabag still clinging to the side of it. And if you glance over by the phone, you will see phone numbers scribbled directly onto the white walls, along with perhaps a quote she found memorable, possibly uttered by the five-year-old who lives down the block. Or perhaps Byron. And you'll see the pencil scratches on the wall marking everyone's height, not only her grandkids, but the adults in the family as well.

So this was a good place to be when falling apart. And not only did my pain and depression fail to be a "downer," Asha claimed that my company was a continuous delight, no matter how I was feeling. It almost seemed that the worse I felt, the more she insisted I was the life of the party.

After four years in Asha's house, it eventually dawned on me that all the new friends I made who were always coming over and visiting were actually visiting *her*, and I decided to get my own place, and Shari moved in with me a few years later. Our home was a one-room converted barn, situated on 10 acres of Virginia hills and streams with an awesome night sky, shared with one other couple across the yard, as well as free-range dogs, domestic and feral cats, deer and hummingbirds everywhere, very loud frog choirs, and the occasional escaped cow who would wander nonchalantly past our front window. Up to five strange dogs would gather in our yard in the early mornings, huddle up to discuss the business of the day, and then wander off as a group to their next destination.

It was a rustic life and we loved it, despite the winters when we had to wear our down parkas first thing in the morning until we got a fire going, and despite the freezing pipes and the cold out-house, and in summers the infestation of wasps, wolf spiders, and about 17,000 ladybugs in our living room like some sort of Hitch-cock special effect. Not to mention stumbling on the occasional decapitated bunny or bird in the bathroom that our cats brought in. But apart from all the creatures, which also included mice that pilfered the cats' food pellets and stored them in our oven mitt, and a snake that crawled across my lap as I sat inside meditating one morning, I could go days on end without seeing anyone besides Shari, and often did. Therefore it made sense that I would become fast friends with Daniel the Woodsman, whom I called Daniel the Hermit. In actuality he was neither a woodsman nor a hermit, but you would never know that at first glance.

Daniel is about 70 years old, and for the last several decades has lived in what some people would probably describe as a shack. There is no running water or bathroom. Daniel pumps water from a well outside and keeps a bucketful in the house for washing and drinking. In the warm months he leaves his door open and birds fly in and nest in his kitchen. Flying squirrels and raccoons often invade his larder at night. In winter he warms the hut with a small wood-burning stove, and his latrine is a hole in the ground with two boards over it for squatting, located a short way down a path through the woods. Year-round, Daniel sleeps outside, beneath a three-sided wood structure, open on the fourth side to sky, elements, and critters of the night.

He is known by everyone in the local community for his generosity, quirky sense of humor, inscrutability, and his exquisite garden with its fish-filled ponds flowing artfully down, Zen-like, one into the next, surrounded by lush plants and wildflowers. Up to a hundred or so friends and neighbors gather there every Thanksgiving to share a moment together of thanks, and to enjoy the warmth of Daniel's bonfire and hot soup or cider before going off to their own family celebrations. At some point everyone forms a circle and Daniel stands in the middle and spins around like a whirling dervish, blessing everyone present. There is a similar event every Easter, with the additional element of an Easter egg hunt for the kids.

The kids in the preschool down the road actually gave him the title Daniel the Woodsman. Or really it was their teacher, who would bring all the kids over to Daniel's every year on Halloween morning to meet this mysterious man of the woods. She painted such a mystical and exotic portrait of him beforehand that when the kids arrived Daniel didn't have to do a thing but be there, which was one of his favorite things to do. The kids were already enthralled, and would join Daniel on blankets placed on the ground around the fire to share sweets and listen to him improvise on his silver flute

Despite that back-to-the-land and off-the-grid look of his, he would be the first one to point out that not only is he *on* the grid, but because of my terrible influence, he now has a little combination TV-VCR unit, and though he has no television service, he has already watched every title in Blockbuster twice over. Sometimes I think I put him on the road to media ruin and can only take solace from the fact that I've been unable to convince him to get a computer or cell phone.

Daniel and I are old smoking buddies, and when the Blue Ridge foliage turns in October each year, we take a drive down to Coal Mountain and hike to the top where we take a toke and he will invariably stand on his head and then stand up ecstatically, arms outstretched to the sun, emitting loud sounds of release and joy. Beaming with love and some sort of glimpse of Paradise, Daniel is living evidence that for some, marijuana is a legitimate spiritual path. Meanwhile, I sit nearby, scribbling all the things I want to remember into my note-to-self pad. (The problem is, I generally forget to check the pad until weeks later, at which time I'll discover such unlikely entries as: "Willfulness: 543 is not the answer" and "Find out birthplace of Rudy Darmstatter," both of which remain a complete mystery to me to this day, but I am still too afraid to tear the pages out of my book.) At the end of our day on the mountain, we have a tradition of driving to a local tavern and throwing back several straight shots of whiskey and pretending we're real men.

And then there was the time Daniel saved my life, or tried to. We were in Colorado hiking on the Continental Divide and we had reached the top of a mountain of ice with a menacing group of spiked boulders at the bottom. There seemed to be no way down. I put one foot out tentatively to see how slippery it was, and off I went. Instantly, without thought, Daniel leaped off the mountain after me, grabbing my leg, and the two of us went careening down, head over heels, wrapped around each other, speeding towards a certain death, smashed against the rocks below. As it turned out, we landed gently in a cushion of snow, got up, brushed ourselves off, and went on our way.

But he is perhaps best known as the guy to call on when you need *anything*. He will take you to the airport, babysit for your elderly mother, cut down your cedar tree, help you chop firewood, make you breakfast, help you load your clawfoot bathtub onto the back of the pickup—those kinds of things. So while at first glance he may look like some old hermit living in seclusion in a rustic old woodsman's hut, in reality he is well known and treasured by many, many people as a local angel. In fact, over the years I have come to think of him as a "lamed-vav tzaddik," which, in the Jewish mystical tradition, is one of the "hidden ones" of which there are thought to be 36 alive at any given moment. Their presence on Earth is said to hold up the world. In the old country, it was always the poor, old, bent-over water-carrier, or the poor, old, bent-over tailor. Of course, this is just my romantic notion of Daniel, although truth be told, he *is* a bit bent over. But if you asked him, he would tell it to you the way it is:

"It's all a pack of lies."

And he'd mean it.

Chapter 15

Brazil
& "The Vine of the Soul"

once did nine months of therapy with a guy named Dr. Seider in Berkeley, and he freaked out when I told him I was terminating our sessions. He upped the ante by telling me I was making a huge mistake, and that he believed I had a personality disorder. That got me to come back, because I figured I should at least know what he was talking about. He played hard to get for another session, but finally at our last meeting, he pulled out his diagnosis, like a trump card: I was a "borderline." And if I didn't stay in therapy with him and deal with it head-on, I would never get past it, and despite all my brains and potential, I would join the ranks of all the other borderlines he knew who were still working at menial jobs years later.

I got the hell out of there, and wandered the streets of Berkeley feeling like a borderline: I really felt like it wouldn't take much for me to lose my last vestige of self-will and just sit down on a curb somewhere and join the ranks of the street people. It wasn't a real possibility, but I somehow knew what it would feel like to be that way. I often have those kinds of moments, when I literally feel what it's like to be someone else, or to be me making different choices. Once, on LSD, I freaked out because I believed I had become my Uncle Irving.

My Uncle Irving was a harmless and beloved relative, but I'm certain Dr. Seider would have called him a borderline, too. He never married or even dated anyone; lived with his mother, my Grandma Becky, until she died at 97; worked as a cashier and stock boy in a supermarket; never ventured out of Paterson, New Jersey; watched cartoons on TV; wore the same clothes for years—and he was overweight. At the end of his life, in the hospital, one of his last communications to my father was to let him know that there was 35 cents in one of his pants pockets back home. As for his last meal, my father asked him if he wanted some Jell-O. My beloved uncle, near death, responded, "Does it have whipped cream?" My father said no. Irving made a face and replied, "Nah." He died soon after. Some time later my brother and I helped clean out his apartment and we found something stashed away in one of his dresser drawers, carefully wrapped in a cloth: a nearly used up bar of hotel soap, circa 1947.

When I believed that I was becoming Uncle Irving, I had the sensation of collapsing backward onto a couch, turning the cartoons on, and never getting up again. It felt like an utter lack of will to either live or die. It was terrifying to deeply feel that state as one of my possible destinies. In a panic, I called my friend, a wacky psychiatrist—wacky, because he used to masturbate his dog during therapy sessions with me, and several times had offered to spank me during our work together, but was otherwise a rather brilliant, amusing, and eccentric man who I knew had done his share of psychedelic journeys. He told me that each of us has a full cast of characters living inside our psyches. If we looked we would find our mother in our head, our father, brother, and in this case, Uncle Irving. Not to worry, he said, because "you're not the cast, you're the director."

I found myself wishing I could go back to Dr. Seider and tell him, "You're mistaken; I'm not a borderline, I'm Uncle Irving." But instead, I took a weekend workshop at Esalen to learn more about borderline personality disorders and was relieved to discover that with the exception of perhaps a handful of people living in the bush in Borneo, the entire planet is crawling with borderlines. In fact, there is a very good chance that *you're* a borderline. (A psychiatrist told me recently that "borderlines are so '80s"; he said that it was merely the popular diagnosis of the day, later to give way to Attention Deficit Disorder, and lately to Bipolar Disorder. These fads in psychiatric diagnoses are mysteriously linked to the funding needs of the various psychopharmacological companies.)

I began teaching music at a local alternative school, and experienced a recurrence of something I'd suffered from on and off in certain situations for most of my life: early morning dread. I woke up with knots in my belly every morning and needed to take a Xanax just to get myself to show up for work, even though I was good with the kids and all was going well at the school. So I decided to try and get a handle on it once and for all and began seeing a therapist twice a week to look into it, at 90 bucks a pop, no insurance. Progress was negligible, and a few months into the therapy, my therapist informed me he was going to Brazil for a few weeks.

He came back transformed. At least one of us was getting better. Unbeknownst to me, he had been pretty much burnt out when I was seeing him, not only from his work, but in all ways. And apparently he experienced something in Brazil that had restored his energy, vitality, and enthusiasm for life and work in a rather remarkable and visible way.

It was the Daime, a form of ayahuasca, an ancient shamanic brew cooked up from vines in the Amazon. In other words, my therapist had found a drug he liked.

So, naturally, being who I am, I asked to go to Brazil with him the next time and see for myself. Here's what happened.

It is 4:00 A.M. I am standing in a line of men, all of us dressed entirely in white, in a hexagonal wooden church in a remote area of Brazil. At the head of the line, I will be handed a cup filled with a foul-tasting beverage that in all likelihood will make me—and most of the other Americans—violently ill. But it also brings the promise of visions, insights, and guidance from what our Brazilian hosts believe to be a divine realm.

I reach the serving bar and choke down the rank, reddish-brown liquid. Before long, I feel a wave of nausea rise in my throat, and I can't help but ask myself: Why have I come here?

Flash back two weeks: I was flat on my back in Brooklyn with a feverish illness. In just a few days, I was supposed to fly to Brazil to participate in what promised to be an intense and physically demanding three-week workshop with members of an indigenous religious group known as the Santo Daime. Bedridden and miserable, I was in a state of extreme fear about placing myself in the hands of strangers somewhere in Brazil for the express purpose of ingesting a powerful, mind-altering substance, the Daime.

I decided to see a physician. As I neared his office, I found myself asking for a sign. Should I go or not? I was willing to forfeit the five grand I'd invested if my intuition and physical health suggested I should stay home. In the doctor's waiting room I noticed that there was only one magazine, a current issue of *Omni*. I flipped it open to the first article: "Drug Tourism in the Amazon." In it, an anthropology professor stated that a host of "so-called shamans" in South America were charging naive "drug tourists" thousands of dollars to sample various herbal psychedelic brews, including the Daime. Such experiences, the author claimed, often catapulted users into psychotic depressions and "even make it impossible to read or write for an entire year." For someone looking for a sign, this was a pretty direct communication.

Three days later, I was fastening my seat belt on Varig Flight Number 860 from New York to Rio. I had called Gabrielle Roth for advice, and she said, "You don't have to drink the drink when you're down there. You'll still be able make your own informed choices. If nothing else, you'll get to have a three-week vacation in Brazil." So I ignored the ominous *Omni* warning and the advice of the doctor and went south.

The Daime is a variation of what is generally referred to as yagé or ayahuasca (meaning "vine of the soul"), a substance used for centuries by the native peoples of Brazil for healing, divination, and religious rituals. To the members of the many Daime groups in Brazil (and others around the world), the drink, brewed from two psychoactive rainforest plants, is a sacred potion believed to help users directly experience the Divine. The Brazilian government, finding no evidence of abuse or ill effects, legally sanctioned the beverage's use as a religious sacrament, finding that the ritual use of ayahuasca among native peoples appeared to promote social stability and actually reduced the abuse of alcohol and other drugs.

The Santo Daime community I visited was located in Visconde de Maua, a lush, green mountainous region approximately five hours inland from Rio by bus. The members of our group—twelve Americans, average age about 50, mostly therapists and "helpers" of one sort or another—had all come at the invitation of Brett, my therapist, who said that the time he had spent there was "the most powerful, intense, and meaningful month of my life."

Our group was put up in the lovely Casa Bonita, a warm and welcoming tourist inn about an hour's ride from the community. The plan was for us to travel to the community every three days for a Daime "work" and then return to the inn to recover and prepare for the next session. Back at the inn we'd discuss our experiences as a group and rejuvenate with healing exercises, massage, regular saunas, immersion in cold mountain streams, and gourmet vegetarian meals.

At 9:00 A.M., the day after we arrived, we boarded the van for our first work, an all-day affair that would end near midnight. In accordance with the ways of the church, we dressed completely

in white. The bumpy dirt road took us through several small villages before we came upon a patch of woods and farmland in which
sat the community's primitive structures. Their central house of
worship was a wooden hexagonal church. Most notable among the
building's features were its floor (concrete, painted blue, covered
with 6″ × 12″ squares outlined in yellow) and its many windows, the
important function of which would soon become clear.

   In the center of the church was an altar: a large table in
the shape of a six-pointed Star of David, from the middle of which
rose the church's principal symbol—a Christian cross—but with two
crossbeams. One beam represented the coming of Jesus, the other
the rebirth of Christ Consciousness within each person. Twist-
ing and growing around the cross and up to the ceiling was a thick
vine—*Banisteriopsis caapi*—whose woody stem is one half of the
ingredients of the Daime (the other being the leaves of the bushy
plant *Psychotria viridis*).

   A Daime work is a highly structured ritual. Each of us was
assigned to one of the little squares on the floor, where we would
stand during the event, women on one side and men on the other.
Musicians sat on chairs in the center, surrounding the star table.
In the rear of the church was a "serving bar." When it was time to
receive the Daime, we formed separate lines, slugged down a cup of
the nastiest-tasting stuff imaginable, and returned to our squares,
where for the next six to twelve hours we sang hymns to God in Portuguese while doing a simple two-step dance movement in perfect
unison. Roughly every two hours another drink of Daime was offered.

   The hymns contained the theology and doctrine of the
church, a mixed bag of Christian and African imagery. References
to Jesus and Mary were common, alongside prayers to Master Ju-
ramidam, Mother Oxum ("o-shoom") of the waters, and the Holy
Daime itself. This eclecticism dates back to the church's origins

in the '20s, when a simple Brazilian rubber worker of African descent—Raimundo Irineu Serra—drank ayahuasca and received the vision and guidance to establish the religion. It is said that the Virgin Mary herself commanded him to sing, and that he subsequently received from an astral plane the hymns that are still sung by Daime groups around the world.

My initiation to the Daime faith was not so revelatory: I spent a good deal of the day either about to vomit, vomiting, or recovering from vomiting. I began to consider the church windows my friends: when the time arose, I made a mad dash from my spot in the men's dance line to the windows, where a "guardian" of the ritual politely waited and offered me wads of toilet tissue with a friendly smile.

As the Brazilians proceeded through the day, however, they were visibly unaffected by the Daime—they remained glued to their spots, often smiling, and singing and dancing with seemingly boundless energy.

I was astounded and relieved to see three-year-old children, elderly women, and even pregnant women receiving the Daime and participating in the ritual. This eased my mind somewhat, for they all seemed fine. I learned later that women are given the Daime during childbirth, and that when a baby is born a drop of Daime is placed on the infant's tongue as his or her first welcome to the world.

As the Brazilians continued to dance and sing, I watched my fellow gringos drop like flies—most of the people from our group were flat on their backs for at least part of the day. And there was much activity at the windows, with lots of toilet tissue being offered. Several people in our group also suffered the humiliation of defecating in their pants, right there in the church. I couldn't help but think to myself, as I heard these reports later, that this was madness. What kind of path to God required bringing along a change of underwear?

To the true believers, the Daime is neither drink nor drug nor substance of any sort. It is nothing less than a divine being, a living spiritual intelligence that teaches and interacts with people through the medium of ingestion. The drink is also said to bring one into direct communion with the presence of, among others, Christ, the Virgin Mother, and God; an experience that can heal whatever ails you—spiritually, physically, emotionally. Miraculous healing stories abound, but perhaps the most significant was that of José A. Rosa, M.D., head of the community and leader of our workshop.

José, as we called him (or Padrinho to the community, which means "Godfather"), was a psychiatrist-turned-spiritual teacher who practiced in both Rio and later the United States for many years. In 1984, during a visit to Rio, several friends and ex-clients strongly urged José to try the Daime. His initial experiences were intense and scary, and he vowed "never again." But several years later, at the urging of an inner voice, he took the Daime again. This time, José recounted, "the Daime got me powerfully. I was shown the spiritual realm. From then on, I was on the religious path of the Daime."

Then, in December 1988, he was diagnosed with pancreatic cancer—a particularly virulent form of the disease. The following week he traveled to Brazil and officially became a "Star Person," or initiate of the church, and began his quest for healing. Only a month later, José received a vision during a work stating that "the spiritual aspect of your healing is complete, but the body will take longer." By the following summer, an ultrasound and CAT scan revealed that José's cancer was completely gone, and any doubts about his relationship to the Daime or its power vanished.

My doubts about the Daime, however, were just beginning to flourish—into outright paranoia. It was our second work, and all my worst fears began to arise as I felt myself slipping into a state of abject terror and utter horror. Any attempt at prayer or positive thinking had given way to a nightmare of racing thoughts: I'm trapped in the jungle with some weird Christian drug cult; everyone looks like a zombie, lining up to take this drink that makes you sick; José is Jim Jones and we're all going to get the Kool-Aid next; they want to steal my soul and convert me to Christianity; my father's going to die when he finds out his son has had a psychotic breakdown. . . .

I asked Brett to help me. My exact words, when I tapped him on the shoulder, were, "I'm freaking out." Brett pulled himself back from whatever realm his own Daime-influenced psyche was traversing to put his hands on me and help me breathe through the experience. I calmed down, but I was reaching deep inside myself for a way out of this hellish mental state. Then I remembered Gabrielle's advice: "You don't have to drink the drink. You have a choice." I grabbed onto this notion for dear life, relieved that there was something I could do—I could "just say no" to the Daime. And I did, for the rest of that work.

Both Brett and José were suspicious of my decision. From where they stood—a place of utter faith—there was rarely a justifiable reason to refuse a drink of Daime. Such refusals could only be a symptom of fear and resistance. To the devoted initiate, the Daime is a divine intelligence. So the best thing you could do when freaking out is . . . take more Daime. José was confident that such an approach would see a person through to the other side of virtually anything. In fact, his oft-repeated bromide for any problem, fear, or complaint was: "Daime and time." And because José had his own life—saved from cancer—to prove this, it was difficult to argue with him.

But I did argue. I had no such faith or confidence in the Daime. What I did have confidence in was my ability to say no, which was providing me with a hold on reality.

During the next few days, as I pondered whether I would attend any of the five works still to come, I began doing intensive prayer sessions of my own at night. I had brought with me my Jew-

ish religious tools as a backup—a tallis, *siddur* (prayer book), yarmulke, and tefillin

I prayed deeply for guidance and protection and reached
into the core of my heart for strength. I decided to wear my yarmulke to all future works, kind of like a Jewish good luck charm to
ward off the possibly evil gods of other nations that might be lurking in the area. And before receiving the sacramental drink, I would
recite—when everyone else genuflected—the traditional Hebrew
blessing over the "fruit of the vine." I figured that would cover me,
plus maybe I could somehow tone down the Jesus hymns a bit. (I
could always resort to the lip-synching technique that I developed
in elementary school when the class was singing Christmas carols
about Jesus and there was nothing more wrong or alien to my soul
than that. In families with Holocaust backgrounds, there tended
to be a total conflation of Jesus and Christianity with Hitler and
Nazism, inspired, obviously, by having had personal contact with
Christian Nazis. All this just to say that singing to and about Jesus
doesn't come easily to me.)

Meanwhile, the rest of our group was pretty much divided: At least half reported very positive experiences and remained
consistently enthusiastic. "For me," one woman said, "taking
Daime is like picking up a telephone and getting God on the other
line . . . the connection is that clear and that awesome." The rest
of us continued to do battle with fear, skepticism, ambivalence,
vomiting, defecating, and terror. When I told of my use of Jewish
practices to help me survive in this seemingly threatening Christian context, one woman of Baptist upbringing whose experience
of the Daime had been particularly frightening, confided, "There
isn't anything Christian about this stuff except the picture of Jesus
on the wall."

Another woman, suffering from lupus, was knocked out
every time she took the Daime. One night several of us had to carry

her home as she emitted random bubbling sounds in what seemed
to be a state of permanent psychosis that scared the hell out of me,
as I imagined having to explain to her loved ones back home that
she had accidentally been reduced to a babbling idiot. Yet the next
day she showed up singing the praises of the Daime, ready for more,
feeling that a deep healing was under way.

The Daime experience differed radically from person to
person as well as from work to work. Some people reported very
clear visual material similar to the effects of other hallucinogens:
"There were snakes swarming around my feet, and I felt the floor
was liquid." Others spoke of a more religious experience: "Mary
came and embraced me, and I felt my heart soften with her love."
Still others reported experiences that sounded shamanic: "The
Daime came and showed me something all wrapped up in a bundle
and said, 'This is what I took from you.' I unwrapped it and found
a dead rat. I knew this was my self-hate." Yet others had little to
report: "It was almost as if I drank water."

In my case, after several works, my most cogent summary
remained "I was nauseated all day."

How did José account for this huge inconsistency of effects?
Again, the Daime was not considered to be a drug, a substance whose
effects can be counted on to be reliable and consistent. Rather, as
a living intelligence, the Daime was said to interact with each participant according to his or her state of consciousness, which varied
from work to work. Feeling cocky and arrogant? The Daime might
just knock you on your ass or send you reeling to the windows for
cleansing. Open-hearted with a reverent mindset? The Daime
might pave the way for Christ to lift you to the heavens.

The language people used to tell of their experiences most
commonly referred to the Daime as a tangible external presence, as
in: "Then the Daime told me to lie down," or "I was guided by the
Daime to breathe more deeply." I, on the other hand, seemed to hear

only one voice clearly, and it wasn't the Daime. It was my mother. "What are you, *meshuga*? It's four in the morning and you're vomiting in a church in the middle of Brazil, and you're going back for more? What is this *mishegas*?"

For our third work I wore my yarmulke, and as added protection I meditated on a photo of the Dalai Lama. Invoking his gentle presence, I repeated a Buddhist phrase used for generating a spirit of loving-kindness: "May all beings be happy." I repeated this statement nearly nonstop during the entire eight-hour session, with surprising results. No fear assailed me. I remained calm and centered throughout the event. And I experienced a deep emotional stirring, a sense of both profound love and unbearable grief.

Our next work was another 12-hour affair, ending at dawn. Again I spent the entire night nauseated and vomiting and experienced no other alteration in consciousness. I decided that this was a positive sign: I was being shown, in the spirit of Zen, that ordinary mind was sufficient; just who I am was enough. Or so I told myself.

When I presented this insight to the group, Brett confronted me. "First of all," he said, "being nauseated and vomiting all day is not 'ordinary mind.' And, secondly, it seems you're failing to grasp the very first lesson of the Daime: If nothing is happening the question to be asking yourself is, where am *I* that the Daime isn't showing me anything today?" (Months later, Brett told me that he believed my consistent nausea may have been due to the mix of ayahuasca with the antidepressants still in my system, even though I had discontinued their use a month prior. The combination is not recommended.)

The sixth work, our next to last, was a departure from the Daime tradition. It was a *gira*, which derives from Umbanda, an African religion that is practiced throughout Brazil. Mercifully, it was held outdoors on a beautiful day; we were free of the incense-rid-den, claustrophobic confines of our little yellow-lined squares in the church. The *gira* was conducted by Baixinhe, or, more precisely, by various *caboclos*—Indian spirit guides—that inhabited her body and ran the show. We were free to stand, sit, lie down, or dance and were encouraged to let ourselves be "possessed" if, literally, the spirit moved us.

There was much drumming and singing, grunting and howling, writhing and shaking. At some point Baixinhe grabbed my hands, pulled me into the circle, and (as José declared "total surrender!") spun me off into an ecstatic drunken dance that continued for 10 minutes or more. As I danced I recalled a dream from the night before—my publisher had changed the title of my book from *Wild Heart Dancing* to *Wild Spirit Dancing* and now as I whirled about the circle in total abandon and freedom I knew I *was* the wild spirit dancing and that my dance was a gift of liberation, an offering to others. I was totally blissed out.

I spent the rest of the day in ecstasy, feeling as if I was being granted a glimpse of Paradise. The women in particular seemed exquisite angels of mercy in their flowing white clothes, gently moving about and laying their hands on those people lying prostrate. Everything around me had transformed. The hymns, which at previous works had struck me as musically banal and repetitive, now sounded like sacred, inspired melodies. Certain accompanying hand movements I had previously refused to perform—seeing them through the eyes of fear as something cultish and weird—I now recognized as being roughly akin to those of "I'm a Little Teapot." In fact, I later learned, the words they illustrated were quite innocent: "I am the shine of sun, I am the shine of moon," and so forth. I was amazed to notice how the world transformed itself when I shifted my perception from fear to love.

The work concluded with the group singing and clapping for a solitary bird fluttering above us, clearly dancing to our beat.

All of us enjoyed a profound moment of communion. Then the Brazilians broke into spontaneous circle dances that resembled the hora; indeed, the atmosphere was like that of a joyous Jewish wedding celebration. I left feeling that there is just one universal prayer of the human heart reaching for the Divine, with different cultures simply using different names, words, and forms. And though it sounds simplistic, the purpose of life also seemed quite apparent to me: to learn to love ever more fully and deeply, removing any impediment or fears that obscure the heart.

At our discussion the next day, my usual "story" was short and to the point: "I'm happy," I said, and nothing more. What the group did not know was that I hadn't uttered those two words together as a simple declarative statement for as long as I could remember.

At our final gathering at least half of our group seemed to have embraced the Daime as a path to God. "I know, with a deep certainty," one woman said, "that I am being healed of fear. I pray with respect and gratitude for having been given the opportunity to take this divine drink that I might be transformed." She and several others, I later learned, would return to the United States inspired: They would begin studying Portuguese; erect altars in their homes, centered around the double-beamed cross; and join others in the States working to establish Daime churches legally in North America, meanwhile conducting Daime works underground.

As for me, well it goes without saying: it was going to take a bit more than throwing up in Brazil with a little ecstasy and a few insights to move the 99th Monkey to make a significant breakthrough on the path, not to mention the Jesus factor. But I did feel that I received a subtle but important healing of the heart: a remembrance of love as a source of comfort and a common denominator among seemingly disparate religious traditions and peoples. And for that I was grateful.

Sadly, Padrinho José would die several years later when his cancer returned.

My visit to Brazil ended with a 24-hour stop in Rio, during which time I arranged for a ride with a local hang glider. After driving up to a cliff high above the beach, I was strapped in beside my pilot, Vachin, and on the count of "*um, dois, três*" we ran down an inclined launching platform that ended in mid-air—in space—and leaped, trusting, off the edge into glorious, weightless flight, soaring like eagles over the houses, trees, ocean, and sands of Ipanema.

What better way to conclude my trip? For if I learned nothing else, it was that the life worth living would occasionally require leaping into the unknown, trusting that we will soar freely, see the wider view, and then be put down gently on solid ground.

Chapter 16

McChaplain

Tired of looking for myself, in 1997 I decided to do something more directly of service to others, and signed on for a one-year chaplaincy training residency at a major university hospital. An unbearably horrible thing happened one night while I was working the overnight shift.

I was paged at 1:30 in the morning by Pediatrics. I answered the phone in the on-call room where I was sleeping and was informed by a nurse that the parents of a brain-dead infant wished to have me baptize their child. The parents claimed their baby had fallen off a couch while being diapered, but the doctors had discovered such massive internal injuries that the parents were under investigation by the police for child abuse. My response to the nurse, from within my sleepy stupor, was, "You mean now?"

She did, so I dressed, put on my white chaplain's coat, frantically searched the chaplaincy office for the manual that guides one through various rituals and ceremonies, retrieved my aluminum cup to serve as the Holy Chalice (which I had purchased from a street vendor in Bodh Gaya, India, for six cents), and up I went. The suspected mom was hysterical and sobbing, the suspected dad was silent and morose, and the baby had tubes and wires and respirators and IVs coming in and out of all parts of its tiny body. As suggested by the manual, I read a verse from the New Testament about becoming as children in order to come unto the Lord. And as

I sprinkled water on the baby's forehead, I blessed him in the name of the Father, the Son, and the Holy Spirit, and offered his soul up to Jesus for safekeeping.

And I really meant it.

(There are no atheists in neonatal intensive care units.)

And yet part of me was standing way back inside myself watching this performance with awe. If a Christian chaplain was needed, I could do it. I was the Zelig of religions. I was also a bit alarmed that I could move so casually in and out of such a devastating scene and not feel more disturbed by it. I think the shock of being close to such utter horror rendered me numb; perhaps I knew on some level that to open myself emotionally to what I was witnessing would have left me as shattered as everyone else in the room, and thus unable to offer pastoral support. So I went back to bed. (Eventually I would learn that it was both permissible and at times preferable for the chaplain to be shattered along with everyone else.)

The Chaplain's Koan

All is Well in God's Universe
...AND...
Horrible Things Happen All the Time.

The day after I baptized the brain-dead infant, my colleagues in the chaplaincy department listened to my account, and then suggested I was out of touch with my feelings.

I really hate when people say that. Too bad I wasn't baptizing babies while I was in Primal Therapy: *then* they would have seen some feelings.

✸   ✸   ✸

In my early 20s, I worked one summer as a security guard at Alexander's Department Store in Paramus, New Jersey, and I learned the power of uniforms. (Most amazing, though, was being trained to basically "just stand there," as the guy who was training me put it, a 30-year man, a career security guard, one of the old-timers. He knew his stuff: "You just stand there.")

On the day prior to beginning work, I got locked out of my car in the Alexander's parking lot and went to get the security guard to help me break into my car with a coat hanger. The next day, my first day on the job, a distraught woman approached *me*, locked out of *her* car. I was now the one in uniform, and it somehow magically conveyed skills I lacked only a day before. I confidently went out and broke into her car with a coat hanger. (Once, many years later, even without a uniform, the following occurred: a friend at a retreat center was struggling to unlock and open the front door in the early morning from the inside of the building. She called her husband over to help, and they were both stymied. I walked over and said: "Let me try it from the outside." I effortlessly pushed the door open and closed it behind me.)

But the guard uniform *really* had power when I had to frisk a kid who was about my age, brought in by the plainclothes detectives for shoplifting. I thought it was a game, like the guys on TV, until I noticed the utter terror in his face, and I realized he didn't know I was just some other kid—he was seeing a *cop*. So I quit.

And if you think *that* uniform had power, you should put on a white chaplain's coat someday and wander through a hospital ward, in the south particularly. It's as if there is Jesus, and then there's you. You're presumed to have a direct hookup to God Central. And, just as the security guard uniform really *did* empower me to actually *be* a security guard, and do the things that security guards do, the chaplain's jacket likewise enabled me to contact that part of me that *is* in touch with God.

My last patient one Friday was a 43-year-old guy who came into his house with a sore shoulder from weed whacking, and had a heart attack in his wife's arms. A neighbor did CPR and the rescue squad came soon after and his heart was actually revived and restored and he was otherwise a healthy man. The only catch was that he hadn't been getting oxygen to his brain during this event, and so wound up brain dead with "zero chance of recovery" according to neurology.

The doctor explained to me that withdrawing him from various forms of support would not necessarily cause death, and that he could actually live for years as a brain-dead vegetable. He also said that since it was illegal to kill him, the only option left was to withhold all feeding so he would eventually starve to death, which was somehow distinct from killing him.

It was my job to help loved ones receive information like that, and affirm their faith in God simultaneously.

That's some trick.

I performed the Catholic prayers for the dead on a 62-year-old alcoholic homeless guy with no family except his godson, who was there, crying and upset that he missed the final moment by about 20 minutes. I encouraged him to speak to the deceased anyway, explaining gently that some people believe the spirit can linger around the body awhile after death and still hear people's words. He nodded with understanding, and then asked me, as we stood by the body, "How do we lift him up?"

"You still sense him here?" I asked, incredulous, since I never sensed anything one way or the other. (I am incredibly dense when it comes to perceiving subtle energy forms floating about in space.)

"He's hesitating," he replied, to which I offered some instant theology about how God and the patient's soul would work out the exact timing of the journey, with no need of assistance from us, apart from letting go and saying goodbye—and the funny part was, all of that was probably true.

I moved on to the next room where I had to tell a woman coming out of surgery that she had no feet, while her grown sons, one of them a real preacher, secretly listened in from behind a curtain, grateful that they didn't have to do it.

I met a patient waiting for a heart transplant, a 60-ish Southern Baptist who had worked for the National Security Service for 33 years. Although still politically conservative, he was now married to a New Age psychic healer who had transformed his life, turning him back toward his Cherokee roots. She had him drumming, making walking sticks, meeting in dreamtime, and praying to Grandfather Spirit and the Four Directions. He insisted on shaking his surgeon's hand before the operation, to "feel his energy" and also to determine if the surgeon knew the secret Masonic handshake. I prayed with him and offered up an eclectic prayer with at least some Native American flavor and I realized again that I'm the Crazy Eddie of chaplains: "You want it, I got it. You need to pray in Jesus's name, I'm your man. Grandfather Spirit, no problem. Nobody beats our prayers." When I informed my brother that I had literally become a chaplain overnight, he labeled the phenomenon "McChaplain."

One night, Delilah, a 40-ish African-American woman with cancer, called me in for a visit, and at first I was literally dripping with nervous sweat because I had a sense as we spoke that I was somehow failing to meet her needs as a chaplain and would get "found out" by her as a fraud. She asked me which scripture she should read for healing, a subject about which I was shamefully ignorant. I fumbled around and finally managed to come up with Lazarus and read it to her out of Gideon's Bible with all its "speaketh thises" and "thouest thats." Then there was a moment's silence and she demanded, "What *you* got to say? Speak to me about da Lord. You da *chaplain*!" and again I panicked and tried to get away with "Maybe I'm a different kind of chaplain."

"What you mean?"

"I sort of pray silently, trying to tune in to your soul."

She bought it, and by the time I left she was asking me to come back and smiling with her one gold tooth. She would always ask for me after that. ("The cute one," she would say.) The nurses informed me that she was terminal, but that she wouldn't hear of it. Her faith was strong and was focused on getting well. How does one determine the distinction between denial of one's condition and faith in the possible? If she believed Lazarus was raised, what was the big deal about cancer? Had ye but faith ye could move mountains. But as Ram Dass once pointed out, if you had that kind of faith, you'd be one with That which put the mountain there in the first place and you wouldn't choose to move it. And if cancer is the mountain, you can see how that logic turns out: Delilah was gone in a few months. Just before the end she seduced me into sneaking her a Hershey Bar, a Kit-Kat, and a Baby Ruth.

I spent some time with a man handcuffed to his bed, attended by two armed guards. He was a convict from a nearby correctional facility, in the hospital for the day to get a test, but who had been in prison for 10 years without parole for breaking and entering, assault, larceny, and drug charges. He told me that his main problem had been substance abuse, that he didn't actually do any breaking or entering, and was spending much of his time trying to get a court hearing.

He described himself as "worthless" several times, which I challenged, and he finally said "I'm not a worthless person, but I'm in a worthless situation." In his file, he said, a psychologist had labeled him "an inadequate sociopath" after a 15-minute interview. When he read that, he told me, he said to himself, "God, I can't even do *that* right." His wife was also in prison, for murder—she sliced her boyfriend's throat.

"Quite the family," I said.

ECMO girl. I was paged to the Cardiac floor to visit with a 35-year-old woman named Nancy, awaiting bypass surgery. She was a former financial officer, and had developed Hodgkin's lymphoma in her chest 10 years earlier. In the process of curing her cancer with radiation treatments, her heart had been damaged beyond repair. She was in dire need of a heart transplant, and the bypass surgery was only to sustain her until a new heart showed up, because she could no longer get out of bed and cross the room without collapsing, out of breath.

I actually met with many people awaiting new hearts. They were in a strange situation: they had to hope someone with the right kind of heart would die, because in the meantime, if no one else died for them, they would have to die for themselves. Some of them did.

I entered Nancy's room and discovered a drop-dead gorgeous woman sitting up in bed wearing not the usual striped hospital gown, but a red nightie you might purchase at Victoria's Secret. It was very revealing of her ample bosom. And I was the chaplain.

Thank God her mother was beside her. I averted my eyes as best I could, and after chatting a few moments, the three of us held hands and I offered a prayer. Prior to becoming a chaplain overnight, I was not the praying type. Certainly not aloud. But I actually had gotten pretty good at it—everyone seemed to like my prayers, and I never even mentioned Jesus. I usually said something like this: "Dear God, Divine Source of our very being, infinite well of all healing and love, please bless and be with Your beloved child Nancy at this time, helping her release all fear, trusting in Your presence that she may know and feel You near in the very heart of her heart and soul of her soul. May You guide the work of the doctor's hands, for we know You are the real surgeon . . ." and so on.

People were usually very touched. The whole time I prayed with Nancy, she cried and her mother kept chiming in, "Yes, Jesus, thank you, Jesus."

The fact that I was not Christian never came up. The fact that I really didn't believe in a personal God that responds to petitionary prayers was irrelevant. I had a job to do, and it seemed to help people.

Later Nancy's mother told me that after I left the room, Nancy said: "He didn't have a ring on his finger, Momma." I felt somewhat relieved to hear this, because it indicated that I was not just some lecherous, perverted chaplain leering at a dying woman's breasts, but rather, I was a lecherous, perverted chaplain who was in fact sensing the energy she herself was also putting out towards me.

And then another chaplain told me he also visited Nancy

once, and had experienced something similar, only on that day her teddy had been a black lace number.

On the day of the surgery, I accompanied Nancy to the operating room, and I was the last person to wish her well as they wheeled her in. Some five or six hours later, the operation was complete, but she never regained consciousness, and was kept alive through extreme measures for one week before the doctors gave up and pulled the plug.

The most extreme measure of all was the ECMO machine ("extracorporeal membrane oxygenation"), which essentially took over all bodily functions and performed them externally: pumping the heart, circulating the blood, breathing the lungs, and so forth. The doctors explained everything very carefully to Nancy's family, filling them with hope. Privately, I learned that no adult patient who had ever been put on ECMO in that hospital had come out alive. Doctors don't give out those kinds of statistics to families. Meanwhile, I had to share in the family's hopes and prayers all week, all the while knowing that the situation was utterly hopeless.

(For a chaplain, you might think I lacked faith. It's not true. Faith, for me, can never be about events that do or don't happen, as in, "Dear God, please allow my daughter to live." We've all seen enough bad stuff happen to enough wonderful people near and far to recognize that the Glorious Living Presence of the Divine, Here and Now and Always, clearly must have no visible correlation whatsoever to the actual events occurring in this existence. And I have faith in That.)

Meanwhile, I suffered the additional horror of witnessing the young, sexy woman I had secretly lusted for swell up and become bloated beyond recognition. On the day they disconnected the ECMO machine and allowed Nancy to die, her family set up a tape recorder near her head, playing her favorite LeAnn Rimes tape. It was a country-western death. Some weeks later I received a copy of her obituary in the mail, in which I was acknowledged. The photo in the paper showed Nancy, a former finance officer, dressed like a Las Vegas showgirl.

May her soul dance free in God's chorus line.

I told my colleagues in the chaplaincy department about the whole experience, fearing that they would say I was out of touch with my feelings again. But this time they said that my experience of lust *was* a feeling: a *sexual* feeling, and that chaplains had sexual feelings just like anyone else. Boy was I relieved. Thank you, Jesus.

There was often a discrepancy between what I observed and heard from doctors behind closed doors and what they presented to the families of patients. The most dramatic example occurred in my first week on the job: I was sitting with a tearful woman in the waiting lounge while her husband, in critical condition, was being worked on in the intensive care unit next door. The mood among her gathered family members was extremely tender, fragile, fearful, and full of sorrow. We spoke and prayed together gently, and then I offered to go into the ICU to check on their loved one's condition.

The scene I came upon was this: About 15 young male doctors were surrounding the patient's bed, most of whom were barely out of middle school. The team leader was speaking loudly: "Well, we could try to bronchilate him but I wouldn't fuck with his lung, 'cause he won't self-ventilate. . . . Nah, forget it, this guy's a dead man, someone tell his family."

That someone would be me, so I took that information and translated it for the wife and family: "I'm afraid the doctors are not being overly optimistic right now."

I actually grew to dislike many of the doctors, particularly heart surgeons, who seemed to be extremely skilled at heart surgery, but not very accomplished in their people skills. I guess if a guy is cutting open your chest and messing with your heart, you're not so worried about him being a nice guy so much as a crackerjack mechanic.

Still.

I never told patients I was Jewish unless they directly asked me. One man with a heart condition was preaching the Bible to me and must have been suspicious because he kept asking me if I was Christian, and I kept evading the question with replies like "Well, not in the way I think you mean it"; this was before I grew brave enough to simply declare my Judaism to patients with no apology. He finally got exasperated, and let me know he could show me how to become a Christian: it simply involved getting down on my knees and asking Jesus to be my lord and savior and come into my heart. It was as simple as that, and if I didn't, "You have no business being in the ministry." It was not a successful pastoral visit.

Had I told him I was Jewish, it might have made the situation better, or quite possibly, worse. One of the two. But I didn't tell him.

The response I usually got after I did start saying I was Jewish to those patients who asked was: "That's nothing to be ashamed of."

Being a heathen in a Southern Christian world had an impact on me. I'm very impressionable, and Shari informed me that within a week of becoming a chaplain, when she would ask me how my day had gone, I was suddenly saying stuff like this: "Praise the Lord, Shari! Hallelujah. God is good."

I was actually very good at relating to the sick and the dying in a way they seemed to find genuinely comforting, and I received lots of appreciation and gratitude from families. I'd probably still be working there had I not let one extremely politically incorrect remark slip from my mouth early one morning when speaking to an African-American female colleague on the phone. It was 7:00 A.M. and I had apparently awakened her.

"Are you still sleeping?" I asked.

"Yes," she replied sleepily. And then I blew it, and uttered the sentence that would more or less cost me my reputation and eventually my job. This is what I said:

"Well get your big black ass out of bed."

I had no idea this would be construed as racist, sexist, or disrespectful. I actually liked and respected this colleague a great deal. Had the situation been reversed, and she had called *me* early in the morning and said, "Well get your skinny little Jewish tush out of bed," I think I would have laughed and considered it an expression of love. Then again, had she said, "Get your cheap Jew-boy nose out of my face" I might have taken offense. It was an important revelation of my ability to completely misread a relationship, and I was very sorry it happened.

Shari and I attended a Yom Kippur retreat following that fall from grace, and we sang a song of atonement in which the previous year's sins were enumerated in verses like: "We've been cruel, we've betrayed, we've gossiped" and so on. Shari, in a moment of profound insight into my individual atonement needs, altered the last verse, and together we sang: "We said big black ass."

Chaplaincy granted one a rather instant yet powerful intimacy with people whose physical condition had left them extremely open and vulnerable, particularly with a person of the cloth, and I must say it was an incredible privilege to be allowed into people's lives on a very deep level, without earning that right through an extended, trusting relationship over time. When people are staring into the face of imminent death, after a lifetime of facades and personas and politeness and putting out a passable front to the world, suddenly they are simply themselves, simply real, on the most core fundamental level.

I wonder what *I* might say after a lifetime of facades and personas and politeness and putting out a passable front to the world, if *I* was suddenly simply myself, simply real, on the most core fundamental level, on my deathbed?

The poet David Whyte asks a similar question, wondering how any of us would feel if, at the end of our lives, on our tombstones all it said was, "She made her car payments."

(Naturally, given the crackpot crowd I hang out with, a friend took offense at Whyte's demeaning reference to car payments as being somehow less important than anything else, and she made quite a good case, weaving an elaborate tale in which someone making their car payments actually resulted in saving thousands of lives.)

But somewhere between "He made his car payments" and "He was fully and fabulously alive" is where I have lived.

Lean over me on my deathbed, up close, near enough to hear me whisper:

"Who knows?"

That was the principal lesson of being a chaplain to the dying: I wouldn't say that to *them*, but somehow when I myself was able to truly relax into the "who knows?" great mystery of being and existence, of life and death, I was somehow able to be present for them in a way that would lessen their own fears.

But really, who knows? Rabbi Cooper would say this as a declarative statement, with "Who" being a name of God and therefore the subject in the sentence, as in:

Who knows.

(Meaning, when all is said and done, Who really *is* on first.)

Chapter 17

Singing at Auschwitz

When my grandmother lay on her sick bed, near the end of her 94 years, she used to randomly say these words: "The Hitler, the Hitler."

She had never recovered from the tragic moment in 1939 when she and her three young children, one of which was my mother, received visas and tickets of passage on the *Bremen*, the last passenger ship that Hitler permitted to leave for America. There was no visa for my grandmother's mother, Elise Grumbacher, who lived with them. Naturally, the elderly woman insisted that her daughter get out with the children as soon as possible, to join my grandfather, who had departed a year earlier to make arrangements for the family in Paterson, New Jersey. They promised to send for Elise as soon as a visa could be obtained.

A short time later, Elise was taken away in a cattle car and died in Gurs, a labor camp near Pao, France.

Nobody gets over such a thing, and it haunted my grandmother's soul until the very end.

Although the Holocaust was never discussed in my family when my brother and I were children, I noticed something peculiar: every once in a while an old black-and-white newsreel would appear briefly on the television screen as our family was gathered around, and my mother would suddenly turn her face away in horror, and say very loudly and abruptly, "I don't want to see that," and my father would quickly turn the channel. Over time I figured it out.

My mother kept an axe under her bed whenever my father was away. I felt utterly unsafe in our house in Fair Lawn, New Jersey, as if we were in imminent danger of the bad guys breaking down our doors. It was a very terrifying way to live, and I developed a unique way to communicate my fear. When lying in bed at night after being put to bed, I would at some point begin screaming one word very loudly and abruptly, in a clipped yelp:

"SCARED!"

I'd wait about 30 seconds, and shout again:

"SCARED!"

I would continue this, infuriating my brother in the bed next to mine, until my mother would virtually sleepwalk into the room and get into bed with me, at which point she'd promptly turn away and fall back asleep. I would remain terrified with no further options.

And then I heard the story, from my Uncle Norbert, my mother's younger brother. Some time ago I mentioned the axe to him and he said: "Oh, you know what that was about, don't you?" I didn't. On Kristallnacht, the "night of the shattering glass," the night the Nazis went on a rampage, setting fire to synagogues across Europe, a couple of them broke down the front door of my mother's house—with an axe—in the little pristine village of Rheinbischofsheim, Germany. The axe fell at my grandmother's feet, and she picked it up and handed it back, saying, "Is this yours?" Thank God, at that point a group of non-Jewish neighbors and friends appeared and chased the two thugs away. My mother wasn't even home when this happened, but that axe somehow traveled through time and space and landed under her bed in New Jersey.

My grandmother went into the burnt synagogue in the village to rescue the Sefer Torah, which she brought to America with her.

Before leaving Germany, my mother, one of only two Jews in her class, was asked to stand up in her classroom and read aloud from *Der Sturmer* magazine, which contained articles that ridiculed the Jews and depicted them as rats and vermin, while the rest of the class laughed and laughed. Her teacher was a Nazi who once asked her an arithmetic question and when she took a moment too long to reply, smacked her hard across the face.

Being directly exposed to terror and evil at such a young age was to forever damage my mother's trust in life and the world. Forever after, life would be a matter of being safe at all costs from "them," with "them" being virtually anyone outside of our immediate family and perhaps a few close friends. "Them" were the Christians, all potential anti-Semites and Nazis, and they were everywhere. We lived in a Christian world and had to lay low. Even now, the sight of a policeman in uniform can evoke in my mother the heart-stopping terror of the Gestapo, coming to take her away.

My brother and I fought her on this. We insisted that her worldview of "us vs. them" didn't apply to us as kids in America. I had only run into anti-Semitism twice growing up, so naturally my personal experience didn't match that of my mother. The first instance was learning that several of my seventh grade classmates lived in communities where Jews were prohibited through an unspoken agreement in the neighborhood. The second had occurred when I was younger, playing down the block in the schoolyard. What I called a "big kid" confronted me and asked me if I was Jewish, and I instinctively replied, "No, I'm Catholic" and he said, "Good, because I beat up Jewish kids." I ran home and told my family the story—all the relatives were over—and everyone laughed and said I did the right thing. But I couldn't help thinking that the right thing would have been to proudly say, "Yes, I'm Jewish" and get the shit kicked out of me.

But apart from that, it appeared to me as if I lived in a world that was largely safe from the things from which my mother was busy protecting me. It took me well into my 30s to truly understand the logic of her position towards life, and then at age 50, at times to share it. For years I worked on my fear as if it was a psychological problem, paranoia and neurosis that had been handed down. Now there is glaring evidence in the real world for it. I am terrified by news of neo-Nazis and the rise of anti-Semitism. I live in a world where people who don't even know me want me dead. When I sink into thoughts like that, even an axe under the bed cannot save me.

Nobody warned me that this was the world I was being born into, a terrifying and dangerous place filled with evil shadows lurking in dark corners. I inherited "fear of Nazis" like a gene. The first breath I took was of the same atmosphere that Hitler had poisoned. The world he ruined for my great-grandmother and my grandmother and my mother remained ruined when I showed up, and I felt it in every cell of my body.

In a sense, my entire life of seeking spiritual enlightenment, of seeking integration in therapies, of trying to find myself, has all been just this one thing: an attempt to cure myself of terror. Now, of course, we have every reason to be terrified. There are actually people whose job it is to keep us terrified. They're called terror-*ists*.

When I was in Israel I met a man, an Orthodox Jew with long sidelocks and a long beard, who lived in Mea Shearim, the ultra-Orthodox neighborhood of Jerusalem. He told me that if we are sad, if we can't be joyful, if we can't sing, then Hitler won. And conversely, the way to prove Hitler lost is to rejoice. It was with this injunction in the back of my mind that I set off for what I imagined could well be one of the most shattering events of my life: a Bearing Witness retreat at the Auschwitz-Birkenau death camps in Poland, under the guidance of the Jewish Zen master, Bernie Glassman.

I brought my guitar, thinking that if I could sing—and sing joyfully—at Auschwitz, then perhaps getting out of bed in the more ordinary world of daily horrors might become more manageable. I would go into the heart of terror, and I would sing. First, I imagined, I would be shattered and broken; I would shudder with fear and trembling, and break down in unspeakable horror and sorrow; and then, I would sing.

The Coopers would be there, and I also asked Asha to join me on the trip, telling her I might need her to take care of me when I fell apart. We took off for Krakow on a cold November morning and some 19 hours later settled into our room at the Hotel Saski. Jet lag got us up at 4:00 A.M., and Asha suggested a walk. It was not something that would have occurred to me, ordinarily, so I said sure, and we wandered in the dark and silent streets of Krakow, walking along the Vistula River, beneath the Wawel Castle. It took me a few minutes to recognize that it actually was safe. Safe in a way you don't feel in American cities at night. It was misty out, and the mist, coupled with the overnight jump from Charlottesville, Virginia, to Krakow, made it all feel very dreamlike at 4:00 A.M. We ended our walk at dawn, attending six o'clock mass in the huge cathedral in the central Market Square. There were figures and designs carved into every inch of the cathedral—the railings, the stairwells, the towering ceiling. Jesus was suspended in mid-air, bleeding.

I didn't take communion.

I did *feel* communion, though. A little.

There were about a hundred of us at the retreat, representing 12 countries. Perhaps 20% or less were Jewish. We gathered that first morning to tour Kazimierz, the Old Jewish Quarter. There were a few synagogues, a Jewish cemetery, a Jewish bookstore . . . and no Jews. Of the 70,000 Jewish people who once brought life to this village, there were perhaps one or two hundred still in Krakow. The rest had been hoarded together into a walled ghetto and later transported to their deaths.

We ate lunch in a Jewish-style restaurant with Jewish-style waiters. I ordered potato pancakes.

In order to board the buses that would take us to Oswiecim (the town of Auschwitz), we were asked to walk about a mile or more through the streets with our baggage. It was intended to give us a sense of what being a refugee might have felt like . . . it didn't. (Similarly, lunch every day at the camp would consist of soup and bread, and we were issued a single bowl and spoon to keep track of all week.)

We stayed at an International Youth Hostel about two miles from the camp, where we would meet each morning in small group "councils" to "speak from the heart and listen from the heart." Some had lost parents and other relations at Auschwitz. Some of the Germans had the "Nazi shadow" in their families. We discovered that our experience as children was the same on both sides: mostly nobody talked about it.

Auschwitz is divided into several camps, including Auschwitz I and Birkenau; eventually Birkenau became the principal extermination center. In the morning we walked the two miles to Auschwitz I to spend the first of many days outdoors in extreme cold. Of my seven layers, two were thermal. Yet somehow, when contemplating the stories of prisoners being made to stand naked outside in the snow all night, the experience of being cold became very easy to bear.

At the camp, we were shown a short, gruesome film made by the Russians at the time of liberation, depicting German civilians carrying truckloads of corpses over to a mass grave. There was a bucket of heads, and a bulldozer moving dirt and body parts as one.

Auschwitz is surrounded by a wall and barbed wire, and contains row after row of large brick structures—the cellblocks— which now house museum exhibits. There was a very large room piled floor to ceiling with a mountain of gray female hair, as well as

an example of the textile that was created from it. There was a similar mountain of dusty black shoes, then thousands of eyeglasses.
Another entire room just for shaving brushes and hair brushes, another for pots and pans, and one for suitcases. The Jews were told to
bring 25 kilos (about 55 pounds) of personal belongings with them,
and they brought their necessities and valuables, all of which were
promptly surrendered when they arrived and sorted through for
use by German civilians.

Death Block 11 featured a basement of cells, including the
"Stand-up Cell"—a tiny bricked-in space in which four or five prisoners were made to spend up to two weeks. They had to crawl in
through a tiny opening at the bottom and stand the whole time,
squeezed together in the dark, relieving themselves in their clothing when necessary. Three of us crawled in to get the sense of it . . .
we didn't.

There were also hooks high up on posts where prisoners
were strung up by the wrists behind and above their heads, as well
as whipping racks, gallows, and an execution wall where thousands
stood and were shot in the back of the head—babies were often shot
first, in front of their mothers.

We were guided into the gas chamber and saw the ovens
where the corpses were burned. A woman cried in there. I didn't
feel anything apart from morbid fascination and a growing inability
to truly comprehend what happened back then. I kept trying to create pictures in my mind, but it was unimaginable. Or rather, whatever I imagined couldn't possibly be anything like the experience of
someone who went through it. We could only bear witness.

We walked another two miles to Birkenau, where we would
spend most of the remaining days. It is huge—about three square
miles, containing the ruins of five gas chamber/crematorium com-
plexes, rows and rows of barracks, some whole, some gone. The
Nazis attempted to blow up the camp near the end of the war and

were only partially successful. The guard towers were still intact and barbed wire was everywhere. We saw the latrine: four rows of thirty holes each, side by side, and we were told that prisoners were allowed only thirty seconds to do their duty or risked whipping.

Day after day, 10,000 or more Jews, gypsies, homosexuals, the mentally challenged, criminals, and others were transported to Birkenau in overcrowded cattle cars, many of them already dead from lack of air and food and toilets. In the early years, there would be a "selection" in which Dr. Josef Mengele would personally decide each person's fate by pointing to the left or right—either directly to death or to the camp for a slow death, or to be the subject of one of his medical experiments. His favorite was twin children. He wanted to figure out the reproductive secret to making twins so that German women could more quickly double the Aryan race. It is said he especially appreciated the opportunity to kill both twins at once, with an injection to the heart at precisely the same moment, and then immediately dissected both bodies for comparative study.

Eventually there were too many prisoners for this "selection" and the people were simply herded off as soon as they staggered off the trains, directly to the "undressing room," then entered the "shower" where they would be gassed and burned in ovens. We read many accounts while there: one man reported what it was like to see thousands of men, women, and children, day after day, marching by his window, and only hours later seeing a truck piled high with ash driving away.

The gas pellets were dropped through the ceiling and broke open when they hit the floor, so people would climb over each other to get higher up and keep breathing as the gas rose, and when the doors were opened there would be a huge pile, often with men on top. Sometimes the gas failed to kill everyone and the living corpses were put into the oven alive. If there were fewer than 500 people, it was not economical to use the gas, and they were shot instead, then burned.

Many people pointed out that Auschwitz never truly ended and still goes on today in horror stories and ethnic cleansings and torture worldwide, as we all well know. However, the scientific efficiency of the methods of genocide used in Nazi Germany remains uniquely evil.

The structure of the retreat was to sit in a meditation circle near the selection site, and from the four directions at once we took turns reading names aloud of those who died there, followed by reciting the Mourner's Kaddish in six languages and attending religious services in either Christianity, Buddhism, Judaism, or Islam/ Sufi. Asha was the instant Sufi teacher there, and one day she and David Cooper combined the Jewish and Sufi services for a simultaneous chanting of the Shema and "La illaha il Allah," which both essentially affirm that there is one God.

But we were free to participate in all that or not, and I often just wandered alone or with someone else through the grounds. One day I went off alone to lie in the middle claustrophobic tier of one of the men's "beds" in the barracks. These were three parallel boards, like bunk beds, that once held up to six men on each level, squeezed like sardines onto the platform, with barely any headroom or air.

Lying there I noticed that on a purely Zen level, clearly, the barrack was nothing more than an old shed, some wood hammered together, a feeling of hardness underneath my body. For it to "mean" anything more, one had to mentally and intentionally add on the story and history of the Holocaust. Or else one had to believe that the subtle energy of a physical place retains a memory of sorts that can be felt by those more intuitive and sensitive than the likes of me. But it was appropriately dark and oppressive.

I fearfully approached the crematorium ruins, where a sign said, "It is forbidden to climb on the ruins." As I nervously considered breaking this rule, it occurred to me that the worst that could happen would be that the local headlines would read: "Jew Arrested for Breaking into Gas Chamber." So I walked slowly through the undressing room, into the gas chamber, and on through to the end where the final flame of the ovens once roared. At the moment of arriving there, I suddenly was able to drop that whole horrible story for a moment, and saw that I was merely standing on some old rubble—rocks and dirt.

A big controversy arose when a German man requested that in addition to reading the names of the victims who died there, that we also read the names of the Nazi SS men who died. As you can imagine, there was much heated discussion. Not all the Germans agreed with him, and not all Jews opposed the idea. Each person had a very personal response. Someone suggested that after we finished reading the 11 million names of the victims, we could then decide about moving on to the tormentors. Others understood the psyche's need to acknowledge the lives and existence of the perpetrators as a step towards wholeness, but objected to doing it in the same manner with which we were honoring the victims. In any event, it was left up to individuals to do it if they wanted to, but it was not agreed to as a community event.

So did I sing at Auschwitz? Yes, I sang the Shema at the execution wall with the group, arms around each other, and I sang a slow "Shalom" chant as we walked along the train tracks, and I sang the Sufi *zhikr* in the snow at Birkenau. But I was unmoved by religion in that place. I didn't think any of it mattered. I didn't believe, as some did, that there were "souls stuck at Auschwitz" who got released through our prayers and songs. I didn't know what was accomplished by our reciting the names. I didn't light a candle when the opportunity was offered. I just plain didn't know if anything made any difference. Bernie had said at the beginning of the retreat that "Don't know" would be one of the themes of the week, so I guess I was right on target. (Apart from a few remarks here and there, Bernie kept a low profile; Auschwitz itself was considered to be the principal teacher at the retreat.)

Then, on one of my last cold gray mornings there, I was walking alone, traversing several miles diagonally across Birkenau, and I began to sing:

> *Blue skies, smiling at me . . .*
> *nothing but blue skies, do I see.*
> *Blue days, all of them gone,*
> *nothing but blue skies, from now on.*
> *I never saw the sun shining so bright. . . .*

It was the closest I would get to fulfilling my intention to sing with joy at Auschwitz. Was I joyous? Not really. But I was definitely on the plus side of numb, and that was all I could muster. It was a start.

So why did I do it? Did I benefit from a 10-day immersion in such a gruesome reality and psychic bombardment of impossible images? I don't know. Perhaps it defused some of my not-so-subconscious terror about being Jewish, through looking at the horror square in the face, making it very real, and possibly incorporating it into my psyche more intentionally instead of through the back door, the way it originally entered. Yet it was impossible to integrate what I saw in any sane way so I was left trying to integrate the fact that some things cannot be integrated.

Or perhaps I did it for Elise Grumbacher, after whom I was named, who was left behind to die. Or for my grandmother, muttering about "the Hitler" in her last days. For my mother, with her axe. For me. For my children's children. And for you.

Chapter 18

Return to India

Christopher Titmuss & Andrew Cohen

O ver the years I would periodically buckle down, if only for a week or two, and attend formal and rigorous Buddhist vipassana retreats, which were always conducted in silence, and involved full days of sitting and walking meditation practice. Generally, I find that two or three days into a silent retreat, I begin to feel restored to a gentle sense of equanimity, without frills. Simple, mindful awareness is a profound quality when one attends to it. When you place one foot in front of the other in slow motion, mindful walking from the meditation hall to the dining room, there can be an enormous spaciousness and presence that one senses, as if one's whole being and entire history is culminating in the present moment of lifting and placing one's foot on the ground. Of course to outsiders it looks like outtakes from *The Night of the Living Meditator*. Nevertheless, this ordinary, present moment is recognized as sufficient and complete, and the habitual movement of the mind toward "something better or different" is eventually silenced.

So I always found vipassana meditation to be a useful and centering practice. But I never found it to be spectacularly liberating or enlightening in any dramatic sense. Yet all the teachers were continually speaking of such matters; enlightenment and "liberation from the wheel of life and death" are the ultimate aim of Buddhist practice, and these always seemed to me to be something way beyond my experience of simply feeling a bit more calm and present. So I asked dharma teacher Christopher Titmuss about it in the midst of an eight-day silent retreat, during a public inquiry session.

"In listening to you speak of liberation," I began, "I became aware that it is not at all the reason I came here. I gave up believing that liberation, or enlightenment, was possible for us ordinary folks years ago. I decided that liberation was only for the extremely rare individual, and I wrote off my quest for enlightenment as mere youthful naiveté; and in fact, I consider my new position healthier and more mature."

"And how would you describe your new position?" Christopher asked.

"That I only came here to slow down, get a bit more centered, perhaps feel a little better. And I've watched hundreds of other people over the past 20 years, and what I see is that we're all just trudging along, opening and growing in very small and slow ways. I don't see anybody getting liberated."

"Would you consider for a moment," he replied, "the possibility of completely letting go of all your mind's beliefs and viewpoints about what liberation is and what it isn't, and all your notions and comparisons about where other people are, and simply be receptive to the very ordinary liberation that is always available in the here and now when you step aside from the voice of 'I'?"

It sounds so simple, yet the power of that statement, coming as it did after some days of silence and sitting, was such that my mind simply stopped, and for the next two hours or so, I found myself in a thoughtless realm of simplicity, calm, and a quiet, surprising joy. And it was nothing special. Completely ordinary, and simply present. Such a moment is only a peak experience in contrast with the inner chaos that usually passes for ordinary mind.

When that state came to an end, I noticed that in some strange way, it was actually me voluntarily choosing to rev up the familiar sludge of daily "worry-mind," as if I could tolerate hanging out in the emptiness of a non-active mind for just so long, and then it was time to fill it again . . . with *me!*

For "me" is the story that fills the empty space of being. I am the noise in my head. And I am also the silence that surrounds it, which is not to be confused with a state of mind, even a pleasant one. It is more the context or space in which all mind states arise and pass away. To rest there, Christopher has said, is to "abide in the unshakeable." Or more accurately, perhaps, to "abide *as* the unshakeable." Who we are is the experienc*er*, not an experience of any kind.

That event with Christopher was a potent reminder of my original spiritual impulse, a long-buried passion to awaken that had been unwittingly replaced by a rather grim determination to merely survive. That momentary glimpse of ordinary, quiet freedom and possibility inspired me to sign on for Christopher's yearly retreat in Bodh Gaya, India. It had been seven years since my first trip to India, and I thought that this time it would be less intense.

India is never *not* intense.

Christopher had surprised me one day, calling me from his home in England to say he had booked a train ticket for me to Bodh Gaya, and that I should meet him and several others at the YWCA in Delhi to travel together to the retreat. That is simply unheard of on the spiritual scene, to receive that kind of unsolicited personal care from a teacher who didn't really know me apart from my having been one of hundreds of people who had taken a retreat with him in the States. I was both moved and impressed by his graciousness. After arriving in Delhi and showering at the YWCA, I went for a walk and immediately fell prey to the old "fake bird shit trick." A man approached me and pointed out that my left shoe had a big brown, messy bird turd on it, and he offered to clean and polish my shoes right then and there. He told me, "In Nepal, we consider it lucky when this happens, because it could have landed on your head." In the midst of this congenial exchange, a well-dressed Indian merchant began screaming at the man and kicking him until he ran away, and then explained to me that he had watched the whole thing. Apparently the Nepalese shoe-shiner carried a bag of brown mush with him at all times, and had slathered it onto my shoe just before greeting me. I thanked the man, moved on, and was confronted soon after by the birdman, demanding payment. I gave him a few rupees to reward his ingenuity.

Getting on a train in India was a mad dash through impossible chaos, hundreds of people pushing and shoving and toting enormous amounts of luggage. There were no English numbers or words on the cars, and Christopher informed us that the only way to find one's seat was to trust a porter with your ticket and your luggage and to just follow him and hope for the best. It actually worked. There were six of us, and we found each other in adjoining berths. The berths were tiny, just slightly smaller than our bodies, and they were sandwiched tightly together, up and down and across the aisle.

On my very first solo overnight train ride in India, seven years previous, a heavyset man in a business suit had politely asked if he could just sit on the edge of my berth, near my feet—naturally I agreed. Gradually, he inched his backside more and more onto the seat, slowly moving up at the same time, and before I fully grasped the situation, I found myself sharing the narrow berth with him, lying side by side and closer to an Indian businessman in a suit and shoes than I would have been with a naked lover.

Bodh Gaya is famous for being the site of Buddha's enlight-

enment. Pilgrims come from all over to prostrate themselves before
the Bodhi Tree, the very tree where Buddha's illumination occurred.
Naturally I did the same, just in case. And naturally, for me, it was
just a tree. But it also occurred to me that the key to the story of the
Buddha getting enlightened while sitting under the Bodhi Tree was
the *sitting* part, not the tree. Had he opted to sit under a streetlight,
you would find people prostrating before the streetlight today.

Due to all the people who are drawn to Bodh Gaya, it has become Beggar's Central. Local merchants actually sell bags of coins
for visitors to distribute to the beggars. A single rupee is worth
about three cents: a hundred of these vendor's coins equals one rupee. One had to endure the horror of stepping over the lame, the
leprous, the deformed, the hopeless, and the ragged, offering what
amounted to .03 cents, and then purchasing, say, a blanket for 50
rupees, or $1.50. And then walking back, passing men and women
crouched on the side of the road, shitting or peeing. Many of the
people walking along the road were wearing face masks, to avoid
inhaling the dust and the smells.

Our retreat was held within the compound of a Thai temple.
The men were housed in the basement of the main temple. We had
to enter through a crawl space and descend into a dark, dank cement
room, where about 50 of us slept on straw mats. Since the nearest
toilets were across the compound, a pee bucket was set up just outside the door, and there was a steady parade there every night, all
night. I couldn't handle the bucket and peed in the bushes. I was already sick when I got to India, and before long, my condition wors-
ened, and I was not alone. The temple basement became a den of
coughing, wheezing, farting, and snoring men. I lay there feeling I
was in a malaria ward and since we were in silence, I realized that
nobody would notice if I died—they would just assume I was resting
beneath my mosquito net.

But after 10 days of echinacea, goldenseal, colloidal silver, nutribiotic grapefruit extract, vitamins, and aspirin, I recovered. I took a shower, which consisted of throwing ice cold water over my head in one of the toilet stalls, which were holes in the ground. Every few days, it was a local Indian's job to bail out the waste system—usually a woman with little children, all standing barefoot in the smelly mess. In the midst of all this, our job as retreatants was to breathe in and breathe out. It's amazing how the meditative practice can gradually and subtly bring one's inner life to a place of equanimity even in the most miserable of conditions. Then again, I wasn't the one standing knee-deep in sewage.

While sitting in silence with Christopher is always a rich and stimulating experience, the retreat was somewhat disappointing in that the glimpse of liberation that had brought me there did not recur. The first 10 days were largely about recovering my health, and the second 10 days were what I have come to generally expect: calming, centering, and joyful, but not particularly profound or liberating in any significant way.

When it was over, I checked into one of the only "expensive" hotels in town—$25 a night, with a flush toilet! And that night I found myself in the town square with a guitar, performing a rousing rendition of "Can't Buy Me Love," fellow retreatants singing along and local townspeople gaping in wonder.

I wound my way up to Rishikesh, getting escorted most of the way by two kindly swamis in orange robes who basically delivered me to my destination, negotiating all the trains and buses and rickshaw rides, me tagging along, extremely grateful and feeling like someone was watching over me. Rishikesh is a wonderful place. It is where the Beatles and Mia Farrow hung out with Maharishi Mahesh Yogi way back when. It is considered a holy city, and is nearly entirely filled

with ashrams and temples and yoga centers, and wandering, or-
ange-clad, barefoot sadhus. There is a sign at the city limits declaring onions and garlic to be illegal there, considered to be foods that
stir up passion. Narrow cobbled streets border the glorious Ganga
river, which divides Rishikesh down the middle—here much closer
to its source than Varanasi, and very clear.

There is a huge suspension bridge for walking across the
river, and in the middle there was always the same one-legged beggar, but in Rishikesh even the beggars seemed happy, at times radiant. (Which reminded me of the time I was accosted in Dharamsala
by an angry worker after I gave a legless beggar a 10-rupee note. "Do
you know how much we make working in the hot sun on that construction site all day long? Ten rupees. That beggar is putting his
children through college on your charity." No wonder some of the
beggars looked radiant. It was a beggar's market in the spots popular
with Westerners. Sadly, some mothers were known to dismember
their children merely to increase their begging potential.)

I found a room that came with three meals, for 50 rupees
a night—$1.50. The room was literally a square, cement, cell-like
structure with a metal bed in it and nothing else whatsoever apart
from a single bare light bulb. But it was clean, animal-free, and
featured a wonderful balcony overlooking the Ganga, and hot water
in the clean showers down the hall. Rishikesh had several spiritual
bookstores, and I spent a few weeks reading on my balcony—particularly the works of Andrew Cohen, the American teacher who had
been enlightened after meeting Poonjaji, and was due to arrive in
Rishikesh shortly to conduct a two-week retreat. I quickly read all
of his books to try to ascertain whether I ought to sign on for his
retreat. I did.

"Most of the spiritual seekers of our generation," said the
42-year-old Cohen at the start of the retreat, echoing what I had
read in one of his books, "may have had a genuine experience of

realization at some point, but usually it was about 20 years ago. Over time, their passion for the real possibility of true spiritual freedom has ebbed, and they've settled instead for a comfortable, alternative, semi-bohemian lifestyle—often in Santa Fe!—with a few spiritual practices thrown in to make themselves feel a little better. But they actually remain fundamentally unchanged, as much a slave to their egos and desires as anyone else in the world. Only it's worse, because at least everyone else isn't pretending to be spiritual."

I couldn't dismiss this indictment lightly, and while in the end I would reject Andrew's path for myself, finding his methods harsh and his community too cultish, my two weeks in his company nevertheless shook me to the core.

On the first day of the retreat, I introduced myself to Andrew as "one of the central characters in your book." That is, I *was* a middle-aged spiritual hippie who *did* in fact have an extraordinary experience of awakening some 20 or more years earlier—in *est*—and who *had* more or less given up on the real possibility of true spiritual freedom and liberation in this lifetime and who *did* have a comfortable, alternative, semi-bohemian lifestyle with a few spiritual practices thrown in, albeit not in Santa Fe. And, most horrible of all, I *was* someone who had, despite countless retreats, workshops, therapists, psychedelic journeys, body work, meetings with teachers and shamans and gurus, remained fundamentally unchanged, as enslaved to my ego and desires as the next guy.

Hence, it was impossible for someone like me to simply write Andrew off too hastily, for it was extremely alluring to consider the possibility that I might not be all washed up, a '60s casualty, a hopeless and cynical spiritual wannabe, but rather, that I might still have a shot at spirituality's Grand Prize! This was essentially the product that Andrew purported to be selling, and it was the same product, presumably, for which spiritual seekers are shopping, namely, "Absolute liberation in this lifetime."

Andrew, who was not at all without humor and laughter, nevertheless insisted that unless one was "deadly serious" about truly wanting to be free more than anything else, there wasn't a chance in hell for genuine spiritual freedom and "liberation in this very life."

My experience with Andrew was spiritually traumatic because on the one hand, I agreed with his premise, confessing on the first day that I *did* fit his profile of the average, quasi-bohemian, contemporary spiritual seeker. Under his piercing gaze and confrontational methods, I saw through the sham that had passed for my "spiritual path" for many years. But on the other hand, because I was not drawn to him as the person to guide me forward, and nor could I honestly proclaim that I was "deadly serious" about wanting to be free more than anything else, I found myself spiritually stranded, and virtually staggered out of Rishikesh, reeling in no-man's land, my previous identity teetering, with nothing to replace it.

In a way, I'm still waiting.

In one of our public conversations, I raised the idea with Andrew of measuring the level of one's enlightenment in light of the quality of one's relationship with one's parents, a notion he scorned as absurd and nonsensical. I had no idea at the time that he and his mom were no longer on speaking terms and that I might have been touching a nerve. When I returned to the States, I published a review of a book that Andrew's mother (Luna Tarlo) wrote about him, called *The Mother of God,* in which she described her own ordeal of progressing from being simply Andrew's mother to becoming his full-fledged devotee and wondering if her son was in fact a living Christ or Buddha, to parting ways with him and being booted out of his community. She was clearly using her book as a way to publicly denounce Andrew, calling her own son "dangerous" and inviting comparisons to Jim Jones and even Hitler. (And I thought *I* sometimes had difficulties with my mother! As I wrote in the review, "It takes *two* fruitcakes to have a relationship *this* dysfunctional.")

I also published an article alongside the review that was very critical of Andrew's scene and I had to endure the wrath of his followers, who then published a letter to the editor in the same publication, basically "trashing me back," and Andrew himself responded soon after by publishing a small volume entitled, *In Defense of the Guru Principle.*

(Methinks the guru doth protest too much.)

The upshot of our differences was this: Whereas I still adhered to Stewart Emery's advice to evaluate a teacher by how you feel in their presence, Andrew and his devotees asserted that when one is truly in the presence of the Real Thing, one's ego is bound to feel threatened by the prospect of its potentially impending annihilation, and therefore cannot and should not be trusted to make an accurate assessment of the teacher. So what I thought was my intuitive sense of things about Andrew, based on how I felt when I was with him, they attributed to my paranoia and my ego teetering on the edge of a spiritual abyss. And they may very well have been right, and I may never know. But teacher aside, the *teaching* got through and hit me where it hurt: after Andrew, I could no longer pretend I was truly on a spiritual path, for my inauthenticity about all these matters had been utterly nailed. And like it or not, that was a real gift. A real, painful gift.

An interesting afterword to this story occurred recently, nearly 10 years later. An advertisement that I submitted to Andrew's magazine, *What is Enlightenment?*, was turned down. I have been a loyal subscriber for many years, and if nothing else, Andrew is a very talented and creative magazine publisher and editor. When I asked why my ad was rejected, they wrote, "Your views have been in direct opposition to the mission of the magazine. Has that changed?" I had a hard time reconciling the idea of Andrew's liberated status with holding a grudge and blacklisting me after a decade, but to give him the benefit of the doubt, perhaps it was akin to the Zen master's stick, smacking me for being an asshole, which is always a real possibility. Or perhaps enlightened people have feelings too, and I had hurt Andrew's feelings.

From Rishikesh I went north to Dharmasala where the Dalai Lama was offering public teachings to a gathering of thousands. Tibetan teachings tend to be rather Talmudic and tedious, especially when they are transmitted via a translator. And so ever since my wonderful meeting with the Dalai Lama in 1990, I decided I didn't need to listen to any of the teachings apart from his most fundamental statement that "my religion is kindness." Therefore, I showed up at the teachings each morning to stand at a special spot I found, just long enough to have him walk by and smile, and then I left to go shopping, buying up these cool drawstring pants for three bucks a pop.

I hooked up with David and Shoshana there and the three of us traveled together for a while, and wound up in Udaipur, Rajasthan. Udaipur's claim to fame is that the James Bond film *Octopussy* was filmed there, about 20 years earlier. Every night, every restaurant in Udaipur advertises continuous showings of *Octopussy*. It's a one-movie town—two decades, every restaurant, every night: *Octopussy*. Think about it.

I left the Coopers and went to Pushkar, famous for camel fairs and *bhang lassis,* a yogurt drink laced with a form of marijuana called bhang—looks like a little ball of mud. They also serve it in tea, which is how I took it. You had to tell the waiter "strong, medium or light." A friend I met there tried a "strong" and wound up weeping and speaking in tongues. I stuck to medium. From what I could gather, nearly every human being in Pushkar, foreigners and natives, were completely stoned on bhang all day long every day. It made for a somewhat laid-back atmosphere.

My last stop before flying home was Vrindaban, just south

of Delhi, and home of Krishna devotees. What I didn't know was that it was the time of Holi, a yearly festival, the main feature of which seemed to be that it was perfectly acceptable for children to walk up to you and spray you head to foot with pink paint. This happened to me.

News that Ram Dass had suffered a stroke reached me, of all places, at his guru's ashram in Vrindaban. His condition was critical, I was told, and my heart sunk as I considered the possibility that I might never see or speak to him again, feeling more sorry for myself, at first, than compassion for him. Because in this mad, frenzied world of 10,000 sorrows and unbearable suffering, Ram Dass had consistently been a source of spiritual comfort, wisdom, and humor that had lightened my burden and that of thousands of other seekers over the years, and many of us had grown to count on him. I even used to fantasize that if push ever came to shove and I was on my deathbed, I would turn to Ram Dass to help me across the threshold, for his experience with people in the dying process is well known. It simply never occurred to me that he might go first, even though he is about 22 years my senior. The idea that he might never be available to me as teacher again was like pulling the spiritual rug out from beneath my very soul: "I guess we're on our own out here," I lamented. "First we lost Lennon, then Ginsberg, and now this—my heroes are dropping like flies." I returned to the States on that lonely note, having utterly failed to get enlightened in India for the second time.

I was thrilled to learn, one and a half years later, that Ram Dass, still recovering, would be present at *bhandara,* the yearly festival held in September at the Neem Karoli Baba ashram in Taos, New Mexico, commemorating his guru's *mahasamadhi* (death) in 1973. About 800 people come to camp on the grounds each year, chanting in the temple from four in the morning until noon, then feasting on traditional Indian foods.

I arrived late, wondering if there would be an opportunity for personal contact with Ram Dass. I knew that he had a personal relationship with nearly everyone there, for that has always been his style: what other teacher could be found at the door of an auditorium, alongside the ticket-takers, greeting and hugging each person as they arrived to hear him speak? I tried to let go of my need for personal contact this time, knowing that it could be overwhelming if everyone demanded this of him. It was enough that he was back in our midst, albeit, I soon discovered, in a wheelchair, without the use of his right side, and with very limited speech.

I decided to enter a small, private meditation room in the back of the ashram, to sit quietly, away from the main temple chamber and all the hubbub. To my surprise and delight, Ram Dass himself was inside as well, sitting in meditation with only two or three others. I entered quietly and joined them, closing my eyes, feeling deeply grateful to share the intimacy of his presence once again, nearly 23 years after our initial meeting. After a time I opened my eyes and found myself sharing a timeless moment of joyful recognition with my old friend and teacher. He looked at me, smiling, for several moments and then made a comment aloud to his escort, who began wheeling him out of the room.

Ram Dass was always known for his sharp intellect and great stories, able to speak extemporaneously to audiences for hours on end. Now, with limited speech, it was as if he had to be a poet, and condense a three-hour teaching into just one, meaning-filled line:

"Every individual," he said simply, after meeting my eyes,

"like a flower," and then was wheeled out of the room.

I found myself suddenly sobbing, my heart weeping with a poignant joy. And it was nothing personal. I realized that as a result of his physical ordeal, Ram Dass was now looking at the world through eyes of such love and clarity that each person he gazed upon appeared to him in all their unique splendor and beauty. I cried, feeling not special, but recognizing, for a moment, through the mirror and gift of Ram Dass's clear seeing, that in God's infinite garden, we are each a perfect flower, even me.

And in a way, my journey had come full circle from that day in 1975, when I sat across from Ram Dass, looked into his eyes and shared my deepest secrets with him. And he told me then that I had been "hooked" and over time would slowly be reeled in by the Guru, by God, by my own true nature. Some 25 years later, *he* looked into *my* eyes and shared *his* deepest secret, the same one he shared with me a quarter of a century earlier: unconditional love. There truly was nowhere else to go.

Epilogue

Each morning our chaplaincy group would meet together to hear the previous evening's litany of disasters: "The lady in 4-West had an aneurysm and is back on a respirator, they'll be withdrawing support after lunch; the man whose furnace blew up has severe burning on every inch of his body and is expected to die this afternoon; the girl with cystic fibrosis has lost consciousness and her father was screaming at the nurses last night and we had to call security," and so forth. And then the head of the department would conclude the meeting cheerfully by saying, "Go forth and serve."

It was a nice way to frame the day ahead, and I did my best to fulfill the injunction. But when I described my chaplaincy work to Christopher Titmuss, I told him that, truthfully, I felt as if I was helping people on a sinking ship.

"The patients might be in worse shape than the helpers at this moment in time," I explained, "but eventually we're all going down."

He said I needed to balance such "Titanic mentality" by keeping in mind that, "just as it is true that all things pass away, it is also true that all things are constantly arising and coming into being." I think he meant flowers and children.

In his novel, *Meetings with the Archangel*, Stephen Mitchell says, "Stories are like the mountains in a Chinese painting: a few lines surrounded by the immensity of empty space. That is true of even the most dramatic human lives, so vast and subtle is the hidden self, so deep are the roots of event. What is most important happens outside the stories."

Including this one.

Yet the story does and can only go on and on and on. Shari and I got married in '99, each for the first time, and I immediately purchased an isolation tank for our living room. Since we would be sharing a one-room, open barn space, I needed a place to get away. I had read John C. Lilly's astounding accounts of the altered realities he entered as a result of spending many hours floating in what were once called "sensory deprivation chambers." (Of course, Lilly *did* help things along by injecting himself with ketamine every few hours. Ken Russell's film *Altered States* was based on Lilly's work.) While I loved lying in the utter silence and darkness, in warm water containing 800 pounds of Epsom salts that enabled one to float effortlessly, as the 99th Monkey, I naturally experienced nothing more profound or life-altering than one might from a relaxing bath in a dark room. However, it *was* useful to our new marriage; if I was acting grumpy or unpleasant, Shari would order me to "Get in the tank!"

For our honeymoon, three months before the wedding, we went swimming with dolphins in the Bermuda Triangle. Three days into our trip we learned that the captain of our boat was actually the *assistant* captain, and that the real captain had disappeared the previous week and was never found.

People often speak of ecstatic, mind-blowing, heart-opening, spiritually powerful connections with the dolphins—direct eye contact, some touching, little swimming dances. But the dolphins completely ignored me, swam right by like I didn't exist. I was thinking: these creatures are supposed to be conscious, intelligent, and telepathic beings; how can they come upon me in the middle of the ocean in the Bermuda Triangle and not even nod in my direction? Or maybe they're so advanced that they identified me as someone to avoid, and figured they'd be better off looking for a more receptive human to hang out with.

Shortly after our trip, the newspapers began reporting that certain dolphins had been discovered behaving like serial killers, battering and munching on their own young, as well as other creatures.

My seeking life seems to be neverending. I took a weekend workshop with Saniel Bonder, an ex-devotee of Adi Da who has established himself in his own right as a teacher, only instead of helping people "wake up," he prefers to assist people to "wake down"; I wasn't any better at waking down than I had been at waking up.

And I went to an enlightenment intensive in Toronto where we sat opposite partners from 6:00 A.M. until 11:00 P.M. every day responding to a single question: "Who are you?" over and over again until everyone became utter raving lunatics.

Then I went to see a psychic who told me I should watch out for meeting a certain "Mr. Knapps." If on the off chance there is a Mr. Knapps reading this book, please contact me ASAP.

I also flew to Atlanta to meet the Brazilian healer, John of God, whose personal message to me was, "YOU I want to see in Brazil." But I didn't go, because I was afraid if I went to Brazil, he'd say to me, "YOU I want to see in Atlanta."

And so forth. The bottom line? I am *really* tired.

But I think I'm almost ready to live. On my new business card, it lists my job title as:

Human Being

When I gave someone my card, recently, I explained, "That's what I do." She replied, "But are you any *good* at what you do?" And then Shari added, "He actually only does it part-time." Feels like overtime to me.

When Aldous Huxley was asked to sum up his learning after a life-time of spiritual and philosophical explorations, he replied: "I think we should just try to be kinder to one another."

Similarly, the Dalai Lama has frequently made this simple declaration: "My religion is kindness."

It's all pretty simple in the end; basically, when all is said and done, it's preferable that we all be nice to one another. Shari and I figured that out after only one therapy session with an oddball couples counselor who sat with his bare feet up on the table, munching continuously on pretzel sticks, with a giant dog at his feet. He wanted to see us regularly, at $150 a pop. We left his office and in an epiphany, we both recognized that we could save $600 a month if we just tried to be nicer to one another. It definitely works.

Ramana Maharshi, the great Indian sage of the 20th century, lay down on the floor of his uncle's house one day at the age of 17 and had an ego-death experience. He arose a while later completely enlightened and became one of last century's greatest saints. I, on the other hand, lie down on the floor all the time, and get nothing, although it occurs to me that I never actually tried it at my uncle's house.

Ramana Maharshi never took *est*, never did Primal.

His simplest teaching, to those who were still looking for God, was to ask them a single question:

"Who's looking?"

Kabir says: When one is longing for the Guest,
it is the intensity of the longing
that does all the work.
Look at me,
and you will see,
a slave of that intensity.

Acknowledgments

Several people were kind enough to read this manuscript and offer feedback at a time when I was having serious doubts. Their enthusiastic and thoughtful responses gave me the confidence to go forward, for which I am very grateful: Perry Goldstein, Reb David Cooper, Bob Reiss, Michael Karp, and my brother, Harry Sobel.

I'm very appreciative of the people quoted on the back cover for agreeing to blurb me. One desperately needs blurbers in this life. I asked Tom Robbins for a quote, and he informed me that due to long-standing eye problems, he was virtually blind and could no longer read or write. "Which is unfortunate," he said, "because I found the Table of Contents very compelling." I wanted to put that on the back cover "Tom Robbins found my table of contents very compelling"—does it get any better than that?

Despite being a lousy student, I am nevertheless indebted to the many teachers I have been privileged to meet and work with over the years, particularly Ram Dass, Hilda Charlton, Werner Erhard, Stewart Emery, Gabrielle Roth, Asha Greer, and David and Shoshana Cooper.

Many thanks also to:

Jeffrey Goldman of Santa Monica Press for choosing to go with this project and being so supportive, available, and the perfect publisher for a guy like me.

My wonderful in-laws, Ann and Marty Cordon, for being so kind and generous, and the extended Cordon family for providing me with such a fun second family.

My ever-faithful aunt, Gerda Kassner, and my beloved

uncle, Norbert Lerner, and both their families.

As always, I'm deeply grateful for the boundless love of my dear mother and father, Manya and Max Sobel, and the undying support of Shari, my intoxicating *basherte*, for actually living with the 99th Monkey, which, amazing as this may sound, is not always a nonstop picnic.

Finally, since I got myself into trouble by failing to personally acknowledge various people in my last book, I would like to basically thank every person alive or dead that I've ever known.

May all Beings be free of suffering

(Especially me.)

In loving memory of my long-lost aunt,
Gertrude Sobel
(1910–1911)

Books Available from Santa Monica Press

The Bad Driver's Handbook
*Hundreds of Simple
Maneuvers to Frustrate,
Annoy, and Endanger
Those Around You*
by Zack Arnstein and
Larry Arnstein
192 pages $12.95

Calculated Risk
*The Extraordinary Life
of Jimmy Doolittle*
by Jonna Doolittle Hoppes
360 pages $24.95

Captured!
*Inside the World of
Celebrity Trials*
by Mona Shafer Edwards
176 pages $24.95

**Educating the
Net Generation**
*How to Engage Students
in the 21st Century*
by Bob Pletka, Ed.D.
192 pages $16.95

**The Encyclopedia of
Sixties Cool**
*A Celebration of the
Grooviest People, Events,
and Artifacts of the 1960s*
by Chris Strodder
336 pages $24.95

**Exotic Travel Destinations
for Families**
by Jennifer M. Nichols
and Bill Nichols
360 pages $16.95

Footsteps in the Fog
*Alfred Hitchcock's
San Francisco*
by Jeff Kraft and
Aaron Leventhal
240 pages $24.95

French for Le Snob
*Adding Panache to Your
Everyday Conversations*
by Yvette Reche
400 pages $16.95

Haunted Hikes
*Spine-Tingling Tales and
Trails from North America's
National Parks*
by Andrea Lankford
376 pages $16.95

How to Speak Shakespeare
by Cal Pritner and
Louis Colaianni
144 pages $16.95

**How to Win Lotteries,
Sweepstakes, and Contests
in the 21st Century**
by Steve Ledoux
240 pages $14.95

James Dean Died Here
*The Locations of America's
Pop Culture Landmarks*
by Chris Epting
312 pages $16.95

L.A. Noir
The City as Character
by Alain Silver and
James Ursini
176 pages $19.95

Led Zeppelin Crashed Here
*The Rock and Roll
Landmarks of North America*
by Chris Epting
336 pages $16.95

Letter Writing Made Easy!
*Featuring Sample Letters
for Hundreds of Common
Occasions*
by Margaret McCarthy
208 pages $12.95

The 99th Monkey
*A Spiritual Journalist's
Misadventures with Gurus,
Messiahs, Sex, Psychedelics,
and Other Consciousness-
Raising Experiments*
by Eliezer Sobel
312 pages $16.95

Redneck Haiku
Double-Wide Edition
by Mary K. Witte
240 pages $11.95

**Route 66 Adventure
Handbook**
by Drew Knowles
312 pages $16.95

**The Ruby Slippers,
Madonna's Bra, and
Einstein's Brain**
*The Locations of America's
Pop Culture Artifacts*
by Chris Epting
312 pages $16.95

**Rudolph, Frosty, and
Captain Kangaroo**
*The Musical Life of
Hecky Krasnow—Producer
of the World's Most
Beloved Children's Songs*
by Judy Gail Krasnow
424 pages $24.95

The Shakespeare Diaries
A Fictional Autobiography
by J.P. Wearing
456 pages $27.95

Silent Traces
*Discovering Early Hollywood
Through the Films of
Charlie Chaplin*
by John Bengtson
304 pages $24.95

The Sixties
Photographs by
Robert Altman
192 pages $39.95

Tiki Road Trip, 2nd Edition
*A Guide to Tiki Culture
in North America*
by James Teitelbaum
336 pages $16.95

Tower Stories
An Oral History of 9/11
by Damon DiMarco
528 pages $27.95

**The Ultimate
Counterterrorist
Home Companion**
by Zack Arnstein and
Larry Arnstein
168 pages $12.95